CW01496737

The New Frontier Playbook

The Political Economic Plan to Win the Frontier of Space

Scott Phillips

ISBN: 9798328932486

Cover photos courtesy of NASA Ames Research Center.

Also by Scott Phillips

Fiction

Phantom Beach
The Climate Fixer
The Prague Deception

Nonfiction

University of America:
A Non-Linear Blueprint for Higher Education in
the 21st Century

The Moral Case on Outsourcing:
How Good, Bad, or Ugly is it for America and
the World?

Strategic Futures Scenarios

No. 1: TSMC: China's Golden Goose or Poison Pill?

The New Frontier Playbook

The Political Economic Plan to Win the Frontier of Space

Scott Phillips

Portland

Table of Contents

Introduction

The visions we offer our children shape the future.
It *matters* what those visions are.
Often they become self-fulfilling prophecies.
Dreams are maps.
Carl Sagan, *Pale Blue Dot*, 1994

This book is a political economic plan for building a large-scale future in space and a discussion of what that future could mean for America and the rest of the world back on Earth.

There are two questions you should ask right away: What do I mean by scale and why do we need such a plan?

First: What do I mean by scale?

Elon Musk, founder of SpaceX (among other things), speaks of making humanity a multi-planet species which means that one day a million people will live on Mars. Jeff Bezos, founder of Blue Origin (among other things), speaks of millions of people living and working in space in self-sustaining colonies.

By scale, I mean what they mean: Millions of people living and working in space or on planets like Mars one day in the future.

Second: Why do we need a plan for this? Why should *you* care? Is there any good reason to support the kind of science fiction future a couple of billionaires want to have in space?

The answer is, yes. We need a plan because the simple truth is that a frontier in space may offer a vast payoff in public value for our economy and country as a whole and for your children individually and specifically back here on Earth in the not-too-distant future. This is what it could mean:

- Minimum wage jobs in space that pay $250/hour or more, come with a 5-year contract, and end with $1M in personal savings.
- An economy in space that operates at a higher level of prices and wages (an **Economic Conjugate**) than our current economy on Earth, which RESULTS in:
- A massive public return on investment (**ROI**) on public money invested in space collected via taxes and fees on that space economy, which then DELIVERS:
- A **Trifecta Economy** on Earth of low taxes, high benefits, and no public debt, which then also DRIVES:
- A high growth economy that is more equal, creates prosperity for all, and FINANCES:
- The cost of a full transition to a carbon-free, net-zero economy, the elimination of all poverty, and the creation of modern institutions and services from higher education to healthcare that are accessible to everyone and the pride of all.

This is a pretty good future if you can get it. And for the record, I think we can get it.

To win this future, however, we are going to have to start by educating the public that this future is even possible while simultaneously overcoming a mainstream cultural bias that money spent on space is a waste of scarce resources given more urgent and compelling needs here on Earth.

Consider Misters Musk and Bezos. On op-ed pages across the country essays have been published suggesting that billionaires with dreams of space are acting out infantile male dreams that are a shameless misuse of resources. *Saturday Night Live* has lampooned the space billionaires to great comedic effect. After Misters Bezos and Branson reached the edge of space in 2021, a broad cultural and media consensus quickly emerged that these flights were the self-indulgent joy rides of tone deaf, out-of-touch billionaires.

The ultra-rich are not always worthy of our sympathy, but in this case the cultural narrative might not just be wrong, but fundamentally self-defeating for us as a nation and for the quest to achieve a more prosperous future in which we are able to solve all of those urgent needs.

To understand why, you have to start with a more modest sounding problem: The questions polling organizations ask when it comes to a future in space. These questions highlight the challenge of mainstream thinking about space.

For decades, pollsters have asked variations on whether we are spending too much on space or too little and whether space is a priority compared to a long list of more earthly needs from climate to healthcare. In response to these questions, most Americans show modest support for more spending on space but prioritize space exploration well below more immediate needs like childcare and housing.

These questions have a bias. They assume a budgetary win-lose tradeoff and they require a choice between one program over another. They assume money spent on space has no direct impact to our challenges on Earth. These are questions based on the Apollo era experience. Given such a framing, who would prioritize any program over their own children or more immediate needs like healthcare? I know I wouldn't. I'm pretty sure most readers wouldn't either.

If, however, you ask different questions based on different assumptions, you get different answers.

For this book, I ran a poll through Survey Monkey that asked a small sample of Americans if they would support large public investments in space IF it resulted in a direct return (payback) of all public dollars spent AND it created high paying jobs at home on Earth. A near majority of Americans were willing to bet big on space if it led to economic growth, high paying jobs, and a return on public investment. The positive response cut across political affiliations and gender differences. How many issues do you know that do that these days?

Traditional polling on space reflects the historical experience in which space exploration was always a cost and there was no direct payback or return from astronauts walking on the moon. That historical view may not represent what is possible in the future. When given a choice in which funding is framed as an investment with a direct link to solving Earthly problems through jobs and economic growth with a potential for payback on funds invested, even a modest attempt at polling suggests a significant share of the public is willing to bet big on space. But that space program must be about more than space exploration. It must come with an economic return that includes direct payback.

The question is then whether or not economic growth, high paying jobs, and a return on a public investment are possible from a future in space at large scale? If it is, then we have been asking the wrong questions and coming to the wrong conclusions about what the public is willing to fund.

In the chapters of this book, I explore a conceptual model of what 'millions of people living and working in space' could mean economically. It starts with the recognition that the cost of living in space is and will always be exponentially higher than living on Earth (ex. water rains from the sky on Earth for free, you have to pay to get it from somewhere in space). The traditional view is that this higher cost is a prohibitive barrier to development. But you can turn this logic on its head by posing a different question. What if the high cost of living in space is a feature, not a bug?

That line of thinking led to the idea of an **Economic Conjugate**. Any future space-based market economy is one that will necessarily be a plural tense with much higher costs to its singular tense, Terrestrial twin. In a market economy, wages must follow costs. The implication is that a living wage in space will be dramatically higher than one on Earth. That's where the idea of a minimum wage job that pays $250 per hour or more comes from.

That space-based economy will be a self-contained entity with very high prices and wages (and costs). With exponentially higher income, a space-based economy also has the potential to return a large sum in tax dollars to the public coffers.

Is it possible to create such a high-cost market economy in space that is economically self-sustaining? We will need a broader public discussion to find out. The stakes, however, are large.

What if an Economic Conjugate in space could help us create a **Trifecta Economy** at home on Earth – one with low taxes, high benefits, and zero debt? By contrast, the future barreling down the tracks in our direction right now will likely be characterized by high debt, stagnant growth, domestic and global instability, and fierce fights over competing priorities for public spending. Personally, if it is even remotely possible, I would be willing to do a lot to get that Trifecta.

Today, the public discussion is only about small-scale space exploration. Outside of the private musings of Misters Musk and Bezos, the public domain is not thinking big about space. The real debate has not even begun. (One wonders how the public response might evolve were Misters Musk and Bezos constantly pitching a vision of jobs that pay $250/hour, come with a 5-year contract, and end with $1 million in savings.)

Is it even possible to think big?

Perhaps not in America, but China is. In 2021, China issued a Request for Information (RFI) on how to build a spaceship (a 'colony' ship) a kilometer long. Experts in America cited by the press were politely skeptical. They noted the cost of building the International Space Station, which is much smaller, took a decade, cost $100B, and still costs $3B a year to support. They suggested China's research project was cost prohibitive and a non-starter.

Skepticism based on historical cost, however, is problematic. Elon Musk's SpaceX already has a rocket, the Falcon Heavy, that could lift today's space station in just 4-5 launches for a total cost of less than $500 million dollars, give or take. SpaceX has brought the cost of launching into space down 95% in just a decade. To build the ISS in space today would be a fraction of the $100B cited from decades ago. And Mr. Musk's SpaceX is building a bigger rocket, Starship, that will bring the cost to launch down even further if he is successful.

The real mystery is this: Why couldn't our media journalists find someone, anyone, to give that newer context? To offer an alternative point of view? Why aren't we reassessing the art of the possible when the cost of something (anything) has dropped by as much as 95% in a few short years?

The inconvenient truth may be that America has acculturated a fear of thinking big, a groupthink belief that space is a waste of resources or that space is only the provenance of a few elite astronauts or the uber-wealthy.

This failure of public imagination is breathtaking. People may reminisce about making America great again, but it's not enough to look backwards. It's about the future and what you do with it. Great nations do great things. While China has the *gravitas* to dream big, America is falling terribly short on any such public vision.

The question begs: Have we become a nation walking backward into the future, eyes staring only at the past at our failures, our mistakes, our sins, and our fears?

Our politics has become very short-sighted on both sides of the political aisle. We once had leaders that were willing to make big bets on our future. The Louisiana Purchase. The Homestead Act. The Alaska Purchase. The G.I. Bill. The Interstate Highway System. The Moon landings. We were once a country of bold dreamers and thinkers (albeit with flaws). If we want our children to prosper, we are going to have to find a way to be a country that makes a few big bets on its own future once again. We are going to need what I think of as a New Frontier Future.

The goal of this book is to articulate a roadmap and framework to get to that New Frontier Future. It is not meant to be a dreamy-eyed appeal to a science fiction future or a philosophical pitch to our better natures on the virtues of human space exploration. It is intentionally focused on the practical political and economic building blocks that must align to create a far simpler and more powerful case for betting big on our own future: Growth, jobs, and economic prosperity along with the direct economic payback of public funds as a sweetener.

This future is one that captures public value for public benefits rather than cedes the future to a small number of the ultra-rich or to corporate entities. Those people will still get rich(er). The private sector will still be involved. But we need to have a discussion to find a formula in which the public will invest.

With public investment, the public can then be a primary beneficiary and receive the massive returns in public value from a space frontier that could help build that Trifecta Economy of the future: one that can afford the transition to a net zero carbon economy, create modern institutions, and end social and economic inequality.

For you as a reader, this is a shot, no matter how long, at a future where America is coming together, not racing apart, and families everywhere can be confident that their children will have a future that is bolder and more prosperous than our own. Ours is a country that desperately needs a national project built on a shared narrative that everyone can benefit from and be proud of.

If the working concepts and ideas in this book hold together and are valid, then we can have this future. But we are going to have to work for it, vote for it, and build it.

A bolder American future is possible. Our children deserve it.

Chapter 1: Problem Statement

Just over fifty years ago, the United States landed 12 men on the moon in a series of historic missions that are still seen as a national triumph and have become deeply embedded as a cultural reference point in America's DNA. Those landings have become synonymous with how we see ourselves as a people: Bold, adventuresome, heroic. The Apollo landings were the very embodiment of the American Dream, symbolic of a nation that can dare to do great, even impossible, things – and succeed.

In the aftermath of those glory days, there were heady dreams of exploring other planets, building space colonies and solar power satellites, and expanding humanity onto the High Frontier.

It didn't happen.

We must try to understand why not.

Today, more than a generation since the heady Apollo era, we can support at best half a dozen human beings at any one time in low earth orbit (barely a hundred miles above the surface of our planet), until recently we lacked the capability to even launch our own astronauts that far (for a decade, we paid the Russians to carry them into space for us), and the budget to return to the moon fifty years later is tenuous at best.

While private space companies like SpaceX and Blue Origin are building the rockets to put people in space (SpaceX has successfully launched astronauts to the International Space Station since 2020), NASA's capability to go into deep space is not yet proven, uses old 80s technology, is not reusable, and, therefore, it is too expensive to grow to any kind of scale more significant than a few launches per year.

The current plan is to put boots on the Moon in a few short years, build a base, and then go onward to Mars. But unless this time is different, delays are probable on the most ambitious and expensive of these schemes. It has happened before. America has a track record of delay and redesign driven by cost overruns and budgetary shortfalls.

Consider the recent past.

In 2009, a blue-ribbon commission of luminaries chartered by the Obama Administration reviewed the American space program and found deep flaws in our approach to human spaceflight. That commission argued that the space program was underfunded and falling behind. They said that to 'advance humanity into space', we needed a flexible approach that matched our means to our goals and would deliver a capability to launch astronauts into space to provide "inspiring moments" for the American public: The first visit to an asteroid, the first landing on Mars by humans, the first nation to return to the moon.

The Obama Administration promptly endorsed the recommendations of the 2009 Augustine Commission by announcing the goals of having astronauts visit an asteroid in the mid-2020s and putting Americans on Mars by the mid-2030s (and perhaps unintentionally delaying NASA's dreams of returning to the moon with an ad-lib comment to the effect that it was little more than 'been there, done that').

Five years farther down the path, another commission of luminaries brought together by the National Research Council reported in 2014 that, once again, we were not funding our goals adequately and that on the current pathway to human exploration, we cannot afford to send missions off into space frequently enough to be able to meet our goals of landing men on Mars safely. That report admitted there was no single compelling reason to fund exploration (a stunning admission), that a mix of pragmatic and aspirational rationales was a worthy enough reason to justify funding, and suggested that a modest 2.5% annual increase in NASA's budget would be enough to meet the most important goals for exploration over the next 50 years including landing a few astronauts on Mars.

In 2018, the Trump Administration re-focused NASA on returning American astronauts to the moon with what they dubbed the Artemis program and they even set an ambitious goal of landing the first crew by 2024. With this plan, the moon would be a steppingstone to Mars.

Today, as of this writing, an American rocket, the SLS, has made just a single test flight in November 2022 and its next run with live astronauts in a crewed lunar flyby is not until 2025. That mission will certainly happen. The ambition of returning to the moon is getting tantalizingly closer. But it doesn't solve the real problem.

The real problem is that we are focused on the wrong thing.

We are focusing on the paradigm of space exploration – sending astronauts to explore other worlds, which is inherently a small-scale, very expensive business. I will argue with this essay that as a vision and strategy, space exploration is deeply flawed and potentially self-limiting.

At best, it gets us back to a future before we cancelled Apollo and scuttled the massive Saturn V rockets that once lofted our astronauts into the heavens, but does not resolve the reasons why we abandoned them in the first place. A similar fate may await the SLS and NASA's boldest plans in a few short years if we are not careful.

What then makes for a stronger vision and strategy that is truly sustainable for the long-term?

A more fundamental test of strategy and vision is whether a proposed effort can gain the financial support required to make it sustainable. In the context of the space program, this translates into a question of political support and public funding. The answer for 50 years has been 'No' or 'barely enough' when it comes to space exploration and returning humans to the Moon and beyond as illustrated with a few specific numbers from the National Research Council's report:

- Percentage of people 'very' interested in space exploration: **21%**
- Percentage of people 'well informed' about space exploration: **5-6%**
- Percentage of people 'attentive' to space exploration: **5%**

- Percentage of Americans that believe we spend too little on space exploration: **22%**
- Percentage of Americans that believe we spend too much on space exploration: **33%**
- Rank of Space Exploration on a list of US national priorities: **16th** (out of 18)
- Percentage of Americans that view NASA 'very' or 'mostly' favorably: **73%** (1)

These numbers don't necessarily rule out a modest increase in funding for space exploration, but nor do they suggest space exploration is something that Americans are pining for or willing to fund in any significant measure. Within our current means, we have maintained a continual presence in space aboard the International Space Station for 20+ years. Yet, people still aren't engaged. The numbers have barely budged. The budget only modestly so.

If we follow the current strategy of focusing on space exploration with 'inspiring moments', we may get a few more of those 'firsts' under our belt: The first nation to return to the moon, perhaps even a small base over time, maybe even a future visit to Mars. But if the past is any guide, none of these events are likely to be sustained beyond a few historic televised moments, replayed endlessly, and footprints left behind in the dust of other worlds for the same reasons that the moon landings five decades ago did not lead to a sustained presence beyond low earth orbit or permanent bases on the moon.

Worse, while we may get a burst of public enthusiasm after each new milestone, the glory may be a little less fleeting each time, overshadowed by the reality of limited resources, a challenge that is likely to get worse not better based on the forecasted fiscal and demographic trends amplified by the economic aftermath of the global Covid pandemic. If this weren't enough, Earthly priorities are getting more urgent. Our environment continues to deteriorate, the economy is stagnant or struggling with low growth rates, and the world has steadily become an ever more dangerous place than before, requiring more guns and less butter. And that was before Russia's invasion of Ukraine and China's growing menace of Taiwan.

A program of space exploration addresses none of these problems. Our public strategy for space is flawed today because it misreads the significance of our past glories, fails to understand both the limits to and potential aspirations of public opinion and political support, and falls far short of any potential for scale and sustainability, much less a public return on investment. Space exploration is not designed to solve any of the major problems we face on Earth. It is doomed not to failure, but a kind of budgetary anemia that gets us nowhere fast.

The vision we are pursuing in space today represents a paradox: It is simultaneously too expensive to fund and too small to sell.

We need a vision that corresponds to what the public wants and is willing to fund. There are a few tantalizing hints that the American public might be open to a more ambitious alternative.

A Pew Research Center survey in 2010 found that 53% of the public envision ordinary people traveling in space in 50 years. A similar study by Pew in 2014, found 33% of the public expects humans to live in colonies on other worlds in 50 years. And more recently, another survey in 2019 found that 50% of Americans believed travel in space for tourism would be routine in 50 years.

These data points offer a hint that the public may be far more ambitious and optimistic in its view of the future than any policy roadmap that currently exists and that optimism has been steady over time for more than a decade.

Policymakers may scoff, but these numbers represent a mix that is part aspirational desire and part educated guess by the public. And while these numbers don't represent majorities, what's truly impressive is that they exist in such large numbers at all – even before any systematic effort to communicate a vision of an expansive effort in space. These polls hint at the possibility that the public wants more – much more – from our space program.

The space billionaires may be closer to the mark than our public officials and public vision. When Elon Musk talks about colonizing Mars, his message finds a ready audience. When Jeff Bezos speaks about a future where millions of people live and work in space, he is simply saying out loud what many Americans may want to hear, albeit with a few more details on the practical economics and payback.

It is to these aspirations and these dreams that this essay speaks.

The gap we need to bridge is the difference between the current public vision of a handful of astronauts exploring the moon and Mars and the vision of millions of people living and working in space. There is as yet no serious plan, even an outline of one, in the public sphere for what it will take to get to mass scale in space or even a rationale for why we should try.

This book attempts to explain why we need scale, what the benefits are, and how to get there.

Our failure to seize the high frontier this past 50 years is not the result of the perfidy of politicians, the fickleness of voters, or changes in geopolitical fortunes. It comes down to the simple realities of engineering, economics, and a vision Americans will pay to support.

For the record, I truly like NASA. I fully support returning to the moon and going to Mars as explorers and I will continue to do so. I hope to enjoy these "inspiring moments" if and when we get them. However, I firmly believe that a program of human space flight focused on space exploration should be the icing on the cake. The problem is that for the last 50 years we have failed to bake the cake. This essay will attempt a new recipe for doing so.

For many, the private sector is the answer and government just needs to get out of the way. Companies like SpaceX and Blue Origin will open the door to a new frontier in space, breaking the stranglehold of governments and bureaucracies. I disagree. Without taking anything away from the innovations and energy these entrepreneurs and companies are bringing to the scene, I will argue (perhaps undiplomatically) that this point of view mistakes hype for reality and is deeply naive. I will argue that 'advancing humanity' into space is going to require a massive public commitment to create the market and build the infrastructure within which the private sector can then flourish.

The rhetoric about opening up the space frontier for the benefit of private enterprise is, at this point, more rhetoric than reality. We should not confuse Silicon Valley Libertarianism with a realistic plan to seize the high frontier. To be successful, the private sector is going to need government contracts at volume and scale. It's going to require a partnership based on much larger public funding (trillions not millions). Yet the hard work of rallying the public to any such large-scale investment has not even begun and it must start with a vision of public benefits that can be realized as a result.

I do believe it is possible to get to scale in space. This may seem wildly naïve given the record that I have just articulated in the past few pages. The perennial underfunding of NASA is so bad, it has become a Hollywood cliché. In the film *Interstellar*, denial of the Apollo missions is portrayed as so widespread that NASA becomes (literally) an underground organization. But it isn't just Hollywood. Writing just before the last flight of the Space Shuttle, *The Economist* magazine, a paragon of rationale economic thought, opined that 'humanity's dreams of a future beyond the final frontier of geostationary orbit had faded.' In their words, outer space was 'history' and the Space Age was 'over.'

They were wrong then and even more so now.

With this essay, I will argue that there is potential to increase funding for our space program in a politically sustainable way. And I don't mean a modest increase of a few percentage points. I believe an increase of several magnitudes of order is possible and I will lay out a case for gaining public support for doing so.

I will argue the paradox that it may be easier to increase NASA's budget by 10x than by 2x. It is true, that the number of Americans truly focused on our space program is modest and support for increased funding is soft, but I believe we have been asking the wrong questions and pitching the wrong vision. I believe it possible that these numbers barely hint at the potential for support and I will put forth a plan in this essay to dramatically increase public engagement and to build the public coalition necessary to fund an American space program at scale.

We don't need to wait for ecological disaster, external help from an 'alien' race, or to solve for gravity to go forward into space. We can do this now. We need no particular magic or help from another dimension. The tools are more mundane by comparison. It comes down to engineering, economics, and – most of all – political will and public support. While not easy, these are problems we can knock down and challenges we can overcome if we have the right vision.

A vision for a future in space that is much more expansive than space exploration must start by understanding the underlying reasons that have held us back for the last 50 years. It must identify what to change and what is changing that will lead us to that bolder future.

Chapter 2: Failure to Launch

I was five years old when we landed on the moon and Neil Armstrong took that giant leap for mankind. I like to think I remember staring at the TV screen in wonder. But I was five. The memory is a little suspect. At 14 or 15, I found a copy of Gerard K. O'Neill's book, *The High Frontier*, on the library shelves. If you haven't been a big reader of space nonfiction of a certain generation, you may not know about O'Neill. He was a Princeton physicist and in the years following Apollo, he crafted a plan to build space colonies and solar power satellites near Earth. His vision got a lot of attention at the time. In those days, a few years after the Moon walks, an incredible future seemed just over the horizon. Big things were possible. Reading O'Neill's book, it really seemed likely there would be Americans living in space colonies in my lifetime. I'm not the only one. Jeff Bezos, founder of Amazon and Blue Origin, was a student of O'Neill's at Princeton and appears to have been equally captivated by the ideas in *The High Frontier* (although from this early common ground, our paths appear to have diverged somewhat).

Nor were visions like these the stuff of academics (and teenage boys and students) alone. In the exuberant days after Apollo, NASA had a grandiose program planned out. Von Braun planned to circle Mars by 1975. In Figure 1 below, NASA planned to have 100 men in Low Earth Orbit by 1990, 40 living on the Moon, and a couple of dozen in a semi-permanent base on Mars.

This was heady stuff.

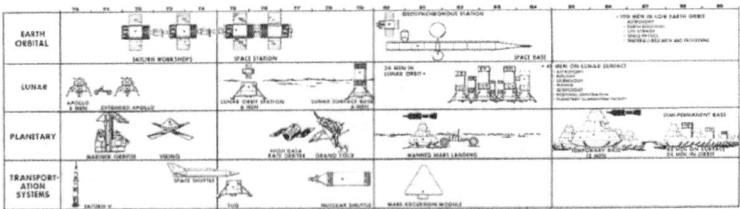

Figure 2.1: Graphic of NASA plan for the US space program from 1970-1990.

Of course, as we know today, it didn't happen.

So where are we now?

Today, space remains the sole province of an elite few astronauts fielded by a small number of governments and a handful of the super wealthy that can afford to pay the price even at full freight. With the exception of the Moon landings 50 years ago, no human has traveled further than Low Earth Orbit, barely a few hundred miles above the surface.

Beyond the hype of billionaires and dreamers, there is no credible plan to seize the high frontier. There is no grand vision to unite around. There is no strategy that is capable of earning public funding for the long-term future of more than a few people in space at a time.

We have a failure to launch.

That's not the way it was supposed to be and there are many that share that opinion.

Jaron Lanier, a technology visionary credited with inventing virtual reality and an author of several books on technology, points out that people of his generation dreamed of moon colonies and flying cars, and he bluntly captures the zeitgeist when he says, 'I miss the future."[1]

A prominent group of Silicon Valley venture capitalists, The Founder's Fund, published a Manifesto some time back that offered a similar sentiment: "The future that people in the 1960s hoped to see is still the future we're waiting for today, half a century later. Instead of Captain Kirk and the USS Enterprise, we got the Priceline Negotiator and a cheap flight to Cabo."[2]

An article in MIT Technology Review, *Why we can't solve big problems,'* lamented that we don't do big things anymore and a moon shot remains, well, out of shot. They summed up the situation thus: "This is not 1961: there is no galvanizing historical context akin to the Cold War, no likely politician who can heroize the difficult and dangerous, no body of engineers who yearn for the productive regimentation they had enjoyed in the military, and no popular faith in a science-fictional mythology such as exploring the solar system."[3]

Then, there is the author of *The Right Stuff*, Tom Wolfe, who wrote in the *New York Times* on the 40th anniversary of the Apollo landing that our space program has been 'killing time' with sub-orbital projects for the last 40 years. Ten years on, he would have to revise his essay in light of NASA's pending return to the moon – but one wonders if he would still call it the 'right stuff'.[4]

Neil DeGrasse Tyson, one of the nation's most prominent astrophysicists, science commentators, and the host of the remade TV series *Cosmos* worries that America is 'fading' and that we have lost the power to dream. He sees NASA as one of those last institutions that inspired big dreams in all of us and has lamented the current shortfall of funding and vision as a sign of deeper problems.[5]

Things clearly didn't turn out the way they were supposed to. The question is why.

Some would blame the fickleness of politicians and the divisiveness and lack of vision in our politics. But politicians are nobody's fools. They are a class of people that know how to sense the wind and cater to what people want. They know how to play on aspirations, dreams, and hopes (and baser motivations as well). They have tried to provide a vision to rally around more than once.

In 1989, on the 20th anniversary of the Moon landings, President George H.W. Bush announced the Space Exploration Initiative (SEI). This was a grand plan that included funding for Space Station Freedom, returning to the moon, and going on to Mars. A follow-up commission projected a moon landing by 2001 and a landing on Mars by 2008. But that same commission also came back with a sticker price of nearly $500 billion over the 20-30 years of the program. With that price tag, the entire program was effectively dead-on arrival at Congress.

The Clinton Administration took the lead to build the International Space Station jointly with the Russians in 1998, a construction process that took over 10 years. That one happened, but it sucked dry the budget for everything else.

In 2004, George W. Bush announced a Vision for Space Exploration (VSE), an initiative to return Americans to the moon by 2020, within 16 years. He inaugurated the Constellation program which included building a large rocket to get us back into space.

Less than five years later, on entering office, the Obama Administration convened a blue-ribbon commission headed by Norman Augustine, former head of Lockheed Martin. That panel came back saying the cost of Constellation was too expensive and behind schedule to boot. They advocated a different, more flexible approach.

President Obama quickly killed Constellation and redirected NASA to implement the Augustin Commission's recommendations which included a new launcher, a new flexible architecture, and a new set of timelines. The new plan called for visiting an asteroid by the mid-2020's and landing on Mars by the mid-2030s. As noted, President Obama also squashed NASA's dreams of returning to the moon as so much 'been there, done that'. But the Obama Administration also began a push to privatize space launches through 'Commercial Crew', a contract program to carry astronauts to the International Space Station on private rockets. Boeing and SpaceX were the primary contractors.

The Trump Administration made a few changes of its own once in office in 2017. First, the President re-established a National Space Council chaired by the Vice President to direct America's activities in space. Second, the Administration captured attention by creating a new, sixth branch of the military when the U.S. Space Force was announced in June 2018. Despite early skepticism, the formal act establishing the Space Force was signed in December 2019.

In addition, the Trump Administration redirected NASA's space effort towards the moon, creating the Artemis program. Initially, NASA's goal was to land a crew on the moon in 2028, but then Vice President Mike Pence suddenly announced a faster schedule in March 2019, targeting a moon landing by 2024, at the close of a notional second term for President Trump. The Artemis moon shot is growing increasingly closer, but there are still doubts on whether Congress will allocate funding for a more ambitious program of space exploration. Much hinges on a successful flight and return to the moon.[6]

Even as the political and budgetary challenges continue, in 2020, SpaceX realized the original goal of the Commercial Crew vision by successfully launching on May 30, 2020, the first two American astronauts to travel to the International Space Station aboard an American rocket since the Space Shuttle stopped flying nearly a decade earlier. Nearly four years later, SpaceX has launched multiple astronaut missions to the ISS, making it routine, and Boeing launched its own first crewed mission to the ISS aboard its Starliner capsule in June 2024.

For its part, as of 2024, the Biden Administration has signed onto the Artemis program that will return us to the moon and the first Artemis test launch using the Space Launch System (SLS) was completed in September 2022. The next launch of the SLS will be a crewed flyby of the moon and return to Earth, currently scheduled for late 2025.

When you read this list of initiatives several themes pop out. For the last 30 years, just about every President has launched a big program in space with great fanfare and a vision that sees us visiting other worlds in 15-20 years – usually after they have left office and with only a little additional funding. And the goal posts keep moving back with every subsequent administration. The Artemis moon launch may finally break this pattern, but it is not a sure thing yet.

Politicians keep announcing new programs. Congress keeps shorting the budget. Commissions keep revisiting the same problem and coming to many of the same conclusions. The public remains mostly ambivalent and seemingly unaware.

The state of the American space program, which is being constantly reinvented without actually ever getting anywhere, has sounded a lot like the marketing slogan for the sci-fi film, *Edge of Tomorrow,* which was: 'Live. Die. Repeat.'

While private sector visionaries like Elon Musk talk about colonizing Mars and Jeff Bezos dreams of millions working and living in space, the truth is both of these visions would currently require massive amounts of public funding and support to realize and, as yet, no political figure has signed on.

At this point, the idea that humans will expand and grow out into the solar system remains solely in the realm of science fiction, continually stuck some 20+ years from now, where it has been since the late 1980s. The NASA plan from the 1970s suggesting we would have 100 people in low earth orbit, 40 on the moon, and two dozen living on Mars within 20 years now looks stunningly ambitious more than a generation later.

Our public vision has become much, much smaller.

Despite this litany of frustrated ambitions, there are hints that the public at large may harbor a more aspirational and ambitious view of the future than its governing classes. Survey questions posed by the Pew Charitable Trust over the last 20 years offer some intriguing insights on what Americans might be thinking.

A 1999 Pew survey found widespread optimism about the future in space with 76% predicting humans would land on Mars and 57% that ordinary people would travel in space.[7]

In 2010, 53% of Americans envisioned ordinary people traveling in space in 50 years and 63% expected humans to land on Mars (slightly fewer for college educated than those without college).[8]

In April 2014, Pew's survey of 'US View of Technology and the Future' found that 33% of American believed there will be colonies on other planets in the next 50 years (64% do not). Younger adults are more likely (43%) to believe this, but among adults with higher income (over 75k) who presumably might have to pay for it, just 20% see this as likely.[9]

Once again in 2018, a Pew survey found that half of all Americans believe space tourism will be routine within 50 years, but that is just an average. Looking at the Millennial population (those under 40) and the same survey found 63% believe it will be routine to travel in space as a tourist.[10]

These public polls hint that Americans might believe something bigger is possible. Mind you, public perception is part aspiration and wishful thinking and part educated opinion and desired outcome. But what Americans have been saying about their expectations of the future is instructive.

Core Constraints

How then can we reconcile what seems like higher expectations and aspirations by the public on one side with the failure to launch to date and the seemingly tepid warmth to any greater funding or prioritization of space exploration which is the flip side of public opinion? There is a standard set of explanations that come up repeatedly to explain why our space program has failed to launch. The roster of culprits includes a failure of political leadership, the fickleness of voters, and the lack of a geopolitical rival. But none of these really seem to suffice. The standard reasoning seems a bit incomplete.

If we want to rouse the public, we need to understand why we have failed to do so already. We need a framework to explain the structural limitations of public support by answering the fundamental question of why public opinion views space exploration as 16th on a list of 18 priorities and is largely lukewarm to more funding for NASA. Finally, if we are going to articulate an alternative vision, we have to do so with the same boundaries and constraints in mind and be able to articulate a strategy to overcome them.

A pragmatic assessment of why we have not been more expansive in space these past 50 years is the key to any ambitious vision, alternative or otherwise. It is my contention that we have not achieved a robust program of space exploration for five core reasons:

- It's (too) Expensive
- Earthly Priorities > Space Exploration
- There's No (Direct) Payback
- There's no Blank Check
- It's an Elite Sport

Reason #1: It's (too) Expensive.

Space exploration is expensive.

Wallace Fowler, a professor of Aerospace Engineering at the University of Texas, calculated the total inflation-adjusted cost of all of NASA's programs since its inception in 1958 through 2014 as over $900 billion, a number that covers Mercury, Gemini, Apollo, Skylab, Space Shuttle, and the Space Station as well as all of NASA's other programs.[11]

Writing in Space.com, Claude Lafleur offered an estimate more specific to space exploration by humans. He calculated the total cost in 2010 dollars for US Piloted space programs (e.g. human spaceflight involving astronauts) as a total of $486 billion from 1959 to 2015.[12] This total differs from the overall NASA budget because NASA also supports and funds multiple aeronautical, science, and engineering programs in addition to programs that put astronauts in space.

Lafleur's own site on 'U.S. Piloted Program Costs', offers specifics and interesting data points about the cost of human spaceflight on a per mission basis.

Some examples in constant 2010 dollars:

- The 11 Apollo piloted flights cost $9.9 billion per flight.
- The Apollo lunar landings (6 in total) effectively cost $18 billion per landing.
- Each Space Shuttle flight cost $1.5 billion per flight.
- The cost to support an astronaut at the International Space Station is $7.5 million per day.

These numbers are subject to debate and interpretation, but they appear at a minimum to be directionally correct.

The incremental cost of each flight might be less. NASA, for instance, has suggested that the cost of each Space Shuttle flight averaged out to a far lower number of $450 million per launch.[13] This is probably true as far as it goes, which is to say the purely incremental cost of each launch. However, most analysts consider the full program cost of research and development as well as all related supporting costs and then amortize that across the total number of missions or flights to arrive at an average total cost per flight.

On these grounds, there appears to be broad consensus that the cost of each Space Shuttle launch was closer to $1.5 billion when you look at the total cost of the program over its entire life, essentially like LaFleur's numbers.[14]

What is beyond debate is that it is incredibly expensive to support a person in space. They also suggest that the cost of space exploration will remain very expensive in the future even taking into account new rockets and reduced launch costs (the subject of the next chapter).

The National Research Council's 2014 investigation of various pathways to a Mars landing, a goal set by the Obama Administration, illustrates how expensive exploration will be in the future. The current funding for human exploration related programs is on the order of ~$8 billion per year, and this has been the long-term trend for many years. Yet, that funding would need to grow in order to achieve a landing before 2050. Based on various scenarios outlined by the NRC, the cumulative cost to land humans on Mars may be in the range of $400 billion and it may take nearly 50 years based on current budgets and/or modest increases to actually achieve the goal of humans on Mars. The Commission notes that there may be unforeseen advances in technology or innovation that could make costs lower and the timeline quicker (re: SpaceX). But there may also be unforeseen failures and delays that offset these gains.

The NRC compares the cost of landing astronauts on Mars as equivalent to 75-150 top line, flagship robotic missions costing $1-$2 billion each to destinations around the solar system or roughly twice the budget of the National Science Foundation during the same period.

It's possible to get there faster if we increase the tempo of operations (and the budget) by a healthy margin, but these costs are not small and belie the long-term funding support Congress appears to have been willing to grant over the decades. Funding has become the natural speed-limit, or threshold, to all plans for operating in space.

What these numbers and the accompanying analysis show is that exploration is very expensive and budgetary support is very soft. The NRC estimated some scenarios that project a landing between 2037 and 2045, but these options would require an increase in funding above the $8 billion per year that has been the long-term trend. Their overall conclusion was thus:

"Examination of the schedule- and budget-driven affordability scenarios for each pathway indicates, independent of the ISS extension, *that the pathways using historical mission rates are not affordable, and affordable pathways based on an HSF budget increasing with inflation are not sustainable.* " [15]

What they are saying, in plain English, is that the current budget won't support launching astronauts often enough to meet the goals we have set and that past history suggests a larger budget for exploration won't be forthcoming.

There is another point to be made, perhaps an obvious one.

The cost of landing astronauts on Mars will be much more expensive than the cost of the Apollo missions when the full program costs are considered (estimated as noted earlier at over $18 billion per Lunar landing). This makes sense because Mars is much further away. The technologies and the hardware needed to get there and get back safely are more elaborate and expensive. You have to send larger vehicles to carry a larger quantity of supplies (food, water, etc.). You have to make sure astronauts are healthy when they return. Instead of a two-week mission to the Lunar surface and a fast return, a roundtrip to Mars will be many months in duration.

Thus, the cost of going further and deeper into space is simply going to be much higher on a per mission and per person basis than it was to go to the Moon when measured in constant dollars.

The lesson here is that exploration is expensive and the further out we go, the deeper into space we explore, the more expensive it is going to be. We've already plucked the low hanging fruit of our own Moon, which is fairly close.

It is worth noting that there exists an alternative debate in some circles on the view that the private sector might be able to deliver space exploration missions at a fraction of the cost and time that NASA can.

We should tread with caution here. A private mission to Mars or the Moon might well be feasible and cheaper. We might well be able to find private sector astronauts or customers who are willing to take on the extraordinary risk. Exploration probably can be done leaner, faster, and cheaper.[16]

But that does not mean that there are no hidden costs to be considered. If there is an accident or a miscalculation, we will have private sector astronauts adrift in space on a countdown to doom. It hardly matters if they are from the private sector or not. If the mission goes wrong and we have a media circus and calls to *do something* matched with a daily litany of progress reports and pleas for help, it will be to government that the public will turn and to which the hard questions will be put. A private sector initiative may be more cost-effective and faster, but the full risk and cost would need to be considered, including the potential political and legal consequences of any failure.

Governments know this and they will not provide the required approvals, approvals no company or billionaire can do without, unless the mission can be confirmed as safe and compliant, necessitating all of the redundancy, testing, and safety that make NASA missions expensive as well.

Overall, space exploration today remains incredibly expensive. It is not cheap to train and field astronauts, to develop the rockets and space hardware necessary to transport them there and back, and to regain the experience we have not had in missions beyond low earth orbit. To-date, despite numerous initiatives announced to great fanfare, the price tag has been deemed too expensive to pursue space exploration with full public support.

Reason #2: Earthly Priorities > Space Exploration

When Nixon cut funding to the Apollo program after the first lunar landing, he pointed out that budgets must be weighed against rigorous national priorities.[17] At the time, the Apollo program consumed nearly 4% of the entire federal budget, or nearly .8% of GDP.[18]

As a result of that budget cut, some people blame Nixon for the state of our space program today. In the larger narrative, he's the villain who cut off funding and kept us from achieving a greater destiny in space. But this is nonsensical. Nixon was merely stating the obvious. The suggestion that budgets must be viewed in the context of national priorities is crushingly obvious. In a democracy, all budgets must pass a test of rigorous national priorities, not once, but year after year after year.

By 1970, when Nixon was assessing national priorities competing for funds, his list would have been rather long and would have included:

- The Vietnam War with nearly 500,000 troops in southeast Asia,
- Desegregating the South where at the start of his term the vast majority of African-American youth were in segregated schools,
- Environmental problems leading to millions rallying for the first Earth Day and subsequently leading to the Clean Air Act, the EPA and a Department of Natural Resources,

- Poverty reduction and income assistance for the poor,
- A troubled economy with increasing inflation and unemployment (Nixon imposed wage and price controls and dismantled the Bretton Woods system of fixed exchange rates in 1971 in what was called the Nixon Shock),
- Civil protest and race riots across the land,
- Rapidly increasing crime throughout the 1960s and 1970s (violent crime more than doubled between 1960 and 1970).

These were the events taking place against the backdrop of the Apollo moon landings at the start of the decade. Overall, the decade of the 70s was exceptionally busy with a long list of national priorities and conflicting demands for time, attention, and resources.

Globally the Cold War was in full swing, there was a war in the Middle East (Yom Kippur, 1973), OPEC imposed embargoes several times, terrorists struck at the Munich Olympics in 1972, and there was a Cold War move to open up of China by Nixon and Kissinger.

Against that list and with Americans dying on far shores, economic hard times and the looming shadow of Watergate, astronaut's driving moon buggies and playing golf on the moon must have looked incredibly wasteful.

Without a compelling strategic or political rationale, it is not hard to understand Nixon's point of view. The pressures and priorities he would have been trying to balance and the resources he had at hand to allocate were finite. The decision to cut funding for NASA in the face of all these competing priorities does not seem particularly surprising.

Several events closed out the 1970s. The Russians invaded Afghanistan, American hostages were seized in Iran, and Skylab, the American space station, fell out of the sky in 1979 because we didn't have the technology (read: rocket) to deliver fuel to lift it into a more stable orbit.

Then came the 1980s.

Reagan and the Republican revolution dominated that decade. When Reagan took office, it was against a backdrop of a festering Cold War and deteriorating domestic economy haunted by stagflation. Like them or not, Reagan's priorities reflected his desire to confront the Soviet Union, reboot the American economy, and establish a different ideological vision for America.

Reagan faced a major economic crisis and recession in 1982 with a period of crushingly high interest rates (the decade started with interest rates over 20%) and high unemployment. He promoted 'Supply-side economics', a contentious theory that putting more money back into people's pockets would inspire economic growth and would trickle down as jobs and income to poorer people. He fundamentally changed the tax structure, significantly reducing rates at all income levels. He faced off against unions, most visibly with the Air Traffic Controller strike of 1981 in which he fired over 11,000 air traffic controllers for going on strike illegally. He won tax cuts from Congress, but comprised on budgets and adjustments to his rates.

During his watch, AIDs broke-out as a major new disease in America and an epidemic of crime and addiction fueled by crack cocaine began to take off in America's cities. The stock market crashed in 1987 and then recovered. He faced a scandal and crisis over arms for hostages that became known as Contragate, or the Iran-Contra affair.

Around the world Great Britain and Argentina went to war over the Falklands. The Soviets were waging proxy wars all around the third world and had invaded Afghanistan in 1979. The Marines were bombed in Beirut. The Iran-Iraq war raged in the Middle East. The US was, itself, pursuing a proxy war in Nicaragua and Afghanistan. There were vociferous debates about basing U.S. nuclear weapons in Europe, talks of détente with the Russians, and a challenge to Gorbachev to tear down the Berlin Wall.

And then, of course, mid-decade, there was the Challenger disaster that put the space program in a tailspin. The decade ended with the fall of the Berlin Wall in November, 1989.

A lot happened in the 1980s and there were many competing priorities for resources.

The 1990s were also interesting. It started with Iraq invading Kuwait and a war led by the United States to remove them. The Bosnian War erupted in the heart of Europe as Yugoslavia broke up. The Soviet Union broke up. A dynamic, young Democrat Governor named Bill Clinton won the White House. A congressman named Newt Gingrich created a Contract with America. The second Republican revolution witnessed partisan polarization, a government shutdown, and the first time in decades that the government balanced its budget by paring back on Defense spending and cutting welfare rolls.

Then came the first decade of the new millennium, from 2000-2009, also a period of momentous events.

That decade opened with a disputed election (Bush vs. Gore) and rapidly proceeded to the 9/11 terror assaults on the World Trade Center and Pentagon in which four airplanes were hijacked and 3,000 Americans killed. That in turn led to war in Afghanistan and a war in Iraq and more broadly a Global War on Terror that ran throughout the decade and into the next. In the middle of the decade, the Space Shuttle Columbia exploded over Texas, killing seven astronauts. Hurricane Katrina inundated New Orleans and much of the Gulf Coast. The decade ended with the election of the first African-American President (Barack Obama), the biggest economic crisis since the Great Depression, a global pandemic (Swine Flu), albeit with modest impact, and the rise of a domestic Tea Party movement that would greatly heighten partisanship and political gridlock.

The years from 2010-2016 included a halting recovery from economic crisis, the passage of national health care in a contentious political environment, a change of hands of the House of Representatives to Republicans, wars in the Middle East, brinkmanship over government debt and threats of a shutdown and default. Globally, we have seen the collapse of Syria, the rise of ISIS, terror attacks around the world. Our politics looks broken across the Western world. Political elites are being rejected by their publics from Brexit to the rise of extremist parties and outsider candidates at home and abroad to the electoral victory of Donald Trump in the US General Election of 2016.

From 2016-2020, there were four tumultuous years of increasing domestic tensions and polarization, driven by the upending of norms and customs and the spread of misinformation and conspiracy theories. Donald Trump may get an outsize treatment in the history books, but the underlying trends were well established before he entered office. In office, he embarked on trade wars with both allies and China and conducted an assault on the institutions created by the United States to manage the free world from the UN to the World Trade Organization. Trump confronted immigration with walls, cages and legal restrictions. He defied the world on the environment and climate change by withdrawing from the Paris Accords, backing coal, and eliminating rules on pollution. He confronted multiple crises in 2020 that simultaneously involved a global pandemic, massive civil unrest and protests for racial justice, and an explosion of wildfires across the western US driven by increasingly challenging drought conditions. And, as we know now, Trump lost his bid for reelection in a very tight and close race whose aftermath has proven to be divisive, to say the least.

In the years since the election of 2020, the Biden Administration has been challenged by the Covid pandemic, spent massively to stimulate the economy and hold off a recession, faced a growing economic crisis as inflation took root driven by everything from Covid supply chain challenges to labor market disruptions. Then, Russia invaded Ukraine causing a massive global crisis in global supply chains for energy and food and putting European politics and security on the front lines. Meanwhile, new elections loom, partisanship is extreme, the Ukraine war drags on, China is menacing Taiwan, and markets are volatile.

With this litany of events across the decades, there is a simple point to be made: Times are *always* interesting and complicated. That is a fundamental reality and it will always be the case. It's time to stop looking backwards through rose-tinted glasses. There will always be compelling national priorities that trump high-minded aspirations, whatever they are and wherever they are focused.

The miracle is that we stuck with the Apollo program in the 1960s and saw it through, but this was influenced by a dramatic sense of urgency and a one-time, single-minded goal of beating the Russians in the midst of a Cold War ideological struggle. It has shown no staying power as a rationale for future spending. The future will not look like the past and the challenges will not stop coming. In fact, they will get worse.

The Congressional Budget Office's Long-term budget outlook for 2022 and beyond shows the impact of two major crises in the last 12 years. The Great Recession caused our Federal debt held by the public to grow from 35% of GDP in 2006 to nearly 76% of GDP by 2016. As a result of the global pandemic in 2020, federal debt has risen steeply and will hit 98% of GDP by the end of 2022. Total Federal debt is forecasted to surpass the highest levels of World War 2 (106% of GDP) by 2031, an improvement over past projections, but rises inexorably to 185% of GDP by 2052, 30 years from now.[19]

The trajectory of debt accumulation is estimated to stabilize in the early 2020s before rising steeply thereafter. The big-ticket items driving higher debt include entitlement spending (Social Security, Medicare, and Medicaid), net interest on the national debt as rates tick up, and the challenge to fund investments from education to infrastructure. These problems looked challenging before the Great Recession. Then, the Pandemic hit. Today, there is more debt and less room to maneuver. The 2020s look set to be a contentious struggle over debt and spending in a hyper-polarized environment and growing external threats.

Meanwhile there is an ongoing debate in which some sides say the forecasts dramatically understate the liabilities we have signed up for even as we face big issues such as inequality, poverty, climate change, and a stagnating middle class all of which will compete for resources, attention, and leadership.[20]

In summary, there are two simple points to be made. The first is that government programs are always facing the gauntlet of criticism and cost, particularly in a democracy. There needs to be an enormously compelling case if there is any hope of a significant expenditure of public funds. The second is that times are going to get dramatically tougher in the coming years as a consequence of two major crises in 12 years that nearly tripled our debt-to-GDP ratio. And that assumes there won't be yet another major economic crisis to contend with in this next decade.

Space exploration, in this context, continually comes up short because earthly priorities are so compelling, urgent, and endless. There is simply not enough funding to go around, a challenge that will be even more difficult in the future.

Reason #3: There's No (Direct) Payback

To my mind, perhaps the most shocking surprise in the NRC Pathways Report of 2014 was the admission that there was no compelling single rationale for human spaceflight. Here it is in their words: "No single rationale alone seems to justify the value of pursuing human spaceflight." That is as blunt as it comes in an official report.

This is a big concession to make and it could not have come easily.

The Commission compared a variety of rationales which they broke down into a set of five common categories including economic, security, national stature and international relations, education and inspiration, scientific discovery and human survival. Having subjected these various categories of rationales to extensive expert analysis, they determined that no one by itself was able to justify and provide an overwhelming rationale for human spaceflight.

The second most shocking point was this: "There exists no widely accepted, robust quantitative methodology to support comparative assessments of the returns to federal

R&D programs in different economic sectors and areas of research, it is clear that the NASA human spaceflight program, like other government research and development programs, has stimulated economic activity and has advanced development of new products and technologies that have had or may in the future generate significant economic impacts. **It is impossible, however, to develop a reliable comparison of the returns from spaceflight versus other government R&D investments.**" (Emphasis added.)

Mind you, this report comes from a broad group of space policy experts that represent some of the best thinking in the country on the future of America in space. Their conclusions are backed by years of collective experience.

What they are saying with these two statements is that there is no business case or value proposition that can be used to justify the expense of space exploration and human spaceflight. In addition, while claims that there have been valuable economic spin-offs from the space program are undoubtedly true, what is also true is that it might well have been possible to achieve similar technology breakthroughs without human spaceflight programs and their high cost. In other words, we could get similar breakthroughs from engineers and scientists focused on similar problems without the expense of sending astronauts into space.

This is a contention that has been made by the scientific community many times and goes to the comparison made earlier with the expense of sending astronauts to Mars. For the cost of a few boot prints in space, we could easily send 75-150 robotic missions mounted with an array of the best sensors and scientific tools available at the time. A human mission to Mars is inspirational for sure. It isn't necessarily the best way to do science or develop technology.

Launching astronauts to the Moon or Mars is always a cost. There is no offsetting revenue. There may well be indirect benefits of science, technology, and new products to the larger economy, but these are not realized by government. They don't reduce the debt that is incurred by taxpayers and left for future generations to pay.

There is no straight line that can be drawn between spending money on human spaceflight and achieving any form of government tax revenue in return. Therefore, the total cost of space exploration cannot be reduced or amortized over time. It is always an expense. Put a person on the Moon and, in economic terms, that is the return you get for the billions in cost you have incurred. (You also get a lot of science out of it, but that does not create a measurable economic return.)

By contrast, invest tens of billions in the NIH and you have the prospect of curing diseases that plague humanity and to which we are all at risk. You can draw a straight line to specific medicines that have saved the lives of people of all incomes and ages. You have met an immediate need that is tangible and that all can appreciate and support. After all, we all know we are going to die and we would all like to push the date back and not succumb to one of the dreaded diseases of our time. Funding the NIH is an easy case to make. We may not necessarily get a direct gain share or direct taxpayer cost recovery out of the vast research establishment the NIH is funding and that the private sector in the form of pharmaceutical firms of all sizes attempts to commercialize. But we do see a net benefit in the drugs that our health insurance provides and we can all support the reason for spending this money. We do get tax income back from pharmaceutical sales and we can often quantify savings to the economy from better health. A payback can be measured even if it takes years to materialize or is indirect.

The space program is different. While we can make the case that the science and engineering expenditures that are made create a return on investment, the truth is there are cheaper ways to fund that same science than sending humans into space. In fact, if we stopped funding human exploration, we could immediately divert many billions to a more focused effort, do more science, more missions using robots, and potentially transfer more technology to the economy, a point the scientific community calls out repeatedly.

This is the core dilemma. Space exploration is expensive and it does not produce anything tangible other than inspiration. It is valuable in that respect, but the case for inspiration versus feeding the hungry, curing a disease, or protecting the American homeland from foreign aggressors – all of which are more immediate, tangible, and compelling – comes up wanting.

Without any tangible, direct payback, space exploration has played a weak hand in the annual budgetary wars.

Reason #4: There's No Blank Check

The three preceding reasons all flow down to the simple truth that the public is not willing to cut a check for a more expensive investment in space exploration. It's too expensive, there are too many competing priorities for scarce resources, and there's no direct, tangible economic payback. The American public is not willing to spend large sums on space exploration and it hasn't been from the start.

That may well fly in the face of the conventional wisdom about the Apollo program. In fact, a common lament is that we don't have the kind of commitment that we used to have during the Apollo days. But this is a shallow argument, a crutch that we have to stop leaning on because public support was never that high in the first place.

The NRC report points out that before the program began, polling in 1961 found only a third of the public was supportive of making the kind of large investment necessary to land a man on the moon, then estimated as the equivalent of $40 billion dollars. In 1967, well along the way and only two years from the first Moon landing, only a third of the American public felt Apollo was worth spending $4 billion a year for a decade. Yet, another poll found only a third of people thought it was important to land a man on the Moon before the Russians.[20]

Roger Launius of the Smithsonian has done the most to debunk the myth that public support was overwhelmingly on the side of the Apollo program in the 1960s. His research shows that public support of the idea that Apollo was worth the cost only crossed above 50% at one point in the 1960s – when Apollo 11 landed and Neil Armstrong walked on the

Moon – and shortly thereafter declined back to an average of just 40% afterwards.[21]

What this tells us is that with Apollo, America's politicians overrode American public opinion and sentiment to carry through with the Apollo commitment until the goal was achieved. They did so in the context of the Cold War stand-off with the Soviet Union in which strength could be equated with a threat of conflict and even survival.

Not only was there no overwhelming public support for landing men on the Moon, there was a strong counter-movement that labelled the Moon Landings a 'Moon-doggle', a story partly recounted by Alexis Madrigal in her 2012 essay in *The Atlantic* magazine.

While we look back in retrospective pride at Apollo, we forget that most Americans were opposed or lukewarm at best, some protestors even marched on Cape Canaveral labeling it a costly diversion of funding against the needs of the poor, and the broader scientific community sniped from the sidelines that it was a poor way to do science (an argument the science community is still making today).[22]

Today, most analysis of polling on where the public stands when it comes to funding space exploration has found a good deal of consistency on two common themes:

- Space exploration is not a big priority if/when compared to other needs, and
- There is not now nor has there been any significant desire on the part of the American public for greater funding of space exploration.

The NRC commission of 2014 found that greater funding for space exploration does not rank very high as a priority for the public today, nor has it for a generation. Over a 40 year span, the percentage of the public that thought we were spending too little on space exploration has varied in the 10-20% range, whereas the percentage of the public that thought were spending too much has been much higher, varying between 30-60%.

The General Social Survey (GSS) conducted in 2012 asked the public to rank 18 spending priorities and whether the government was spending too little or too much. Space exploration fell near the bottom, 16th on the list, beating out only foreign aid and welfare, as the lowest priorities for more funding. Just over 20% of the public was supportive of more spending, whereas over 30% felt we were spending too much in comparison to other priorities. By 2018, the same percentage of the public (21%) felt we were spending too little, but 45% of the public saw the current budget for space exploration as about right and 23% thought it was too much.

The NRC also cites a study by Pew Charitable Trust in 2004 which found that only 10% of the public rated expanding America's space program as a top priority.[23]

More recently an IPSOS poll in 2019 found just 20% of those polled felt that NASA's budget was too little, whereas 27% thought it was too much.[24]

A 2018 Pew Research survey found that just 13% of Americans view sending astronauts to the moon as a top priority and just 18% believe sending astronauts to Mars is a top priority for NASA.[25]

The inescapable conclusions are that space exploration is not a big priority for the vast majority of the American public, the numbers have been broadly the same for many decades, and only a relatively small portion are willing to consider spending more on it. For those that would like to suggest a bigger effort or a faster path to Mars, this brief survey of public sentiment is a bracing reality check.

Reason #5: It's an Elite Sport

There is one more reason that space exploration fails to drive a larger budget. This one is more subjective and tenuous, but I believe the last reason articulates the previous four in a different way. It is this: Only a very small number of people get to be astronauts when exploration is the governing paradigm of a space program.

With space exploration, you need only a small cadre of highly trained astronauts to run a program, especially when the cadence runs out over decades and the number of missions is very small.

Here's a data point. A few years ago, more than 18,000 people applied for just 12 open positions as NASA astronauts. Such openings only come every few years. I suspect that if the odds were better and the process were known, NASA could easily get 10x that number of applicants.

Of course, NASA works hard to make the small number of astronauts that it does select representative of the larger population, from gender to ethnicity, so that we can identify with them as much as possible. But as long as space exploration remains the goal, there is very little hope that the common citizen will ever directly participate or that we will break out into larger numbers.

New victories, new landings on far away worlds are a good match for a small group of elite astronauts engaged in dangerous and risky activities. We will laud every 'First' and lionize the men and women who dare to go and return. The first time. But as a routine activity, it will become rapidly apparent that a program based on exploration is about the few entertaining the many. Unfortunately, Netflix is cheaper.

If Americans cannot participate themselves, then inspiration only goes so far before the cost-benefit economics, the trade-offs, and the budgetary implications must make their inexorable presence felt.

Building a space program around a tiny elite is a fundamental misread of our public's aspirations, especially those of our young people. Most young people in America would like to travel into space. A 2019 CBS News poll found that 52% of adults under age 30 say they personally would like to go to the Moon.[26] That same year a Pew Research Center poll led with a headline that a majority, 58%, of Americans would NOT be interested in traveling into space. Yet, this result was aggregate number was for all age groups. Dig deeper and you find that 63% of Millennials (born between

1981-1996) would definitely or probably be interested in space tourism and traveling into space.[27]

As long as exploration remains an elite sport, it cannot satisfy the yearnings of the vast number of young Americans that would back a program that gave many more of them that chance.

Exploration is not sustainable because it fulfills the dream for so few at a time when so many aspire to go. For the lucky, elite few that do get to be astronauts, it remains extraordinarily expensive – the bill for which the rest of us have to foot.

The Soundbite Challenge

Astrophysicist Neil deGrasse Tyson summaries the challenge of funding space exploration with a simple illustration. In his speeches, he has told his audiences something like this: Imagine we are on our way to Mars and a recession hits. A newscaster goes down to the unemployment line and interviews a man in line. The guy says he's lost his job, is losing his home, and can't afford food. The newscaster says, 'But we're going to Mars.'

Tyson then shrugs with a pained look and a sigh, leaving his audience with a sense of just how enormous the challenge of funding space exploration truly is from a political perspective.

This anecdote captures neatly and succinctly all of the themes I have articulated. When bad news hits and people are suffering, space exploration looks like a terrible waste of money. Earthly needs will always trump aspirational desires to explore. We will always have an economic cycle with bad times as well as good. And when tough times hit, the budget for exploration will get cut.

The tragic insight of this allegory is that we are well into our second and third great crises in a single generation – a global pandemic and a Russian war of aggression in Europe – both of which have delivered yet increasing financial strains and economic hardship. The problems keep coming at us.

How do you overcome the dilemma of funding for space when there are so many Earthly crises to resolve? The challenge is to find a reason to be in space that can be echoed in a soundbite and whose rationale makes sense even to people who are suffering economic or personal loss for which little or less help may be forthcoming in the near-term because of a priority for a program in space.

We have yet to find that rationale, that soundbite, that program, and that is largely why we have not gone into space at scale.

By the end of this essay, my goal is to meet this challenge and provide you with a succinct set of soundbites that make the case clearly and cleanly for a vastly larger program in space, driven by an overwhelming value proposition of public benefits that result.

Summary

Romanticizing the glory days of Apollo is a misread of history. There was no blank check from voters then, there will be none today. We should be proud of that program for what it was, but should not rely on its achievements as a guide to the future nor attempt to recreate it in any way.

The historical context of Kennedy's mission to the moon was utterly and completely unique. The race to the moon was a one-off inexorably bound up in a great power rivalry where the Russians were competing to win the same prize and ahead at every step, giving us sustained attention, a real sense of threat of not winning the race, and perhaps the tragedy of Kennedy's assassination to collectively make the moon drive an iconic mission.

Any program today has to exist within the competitive reality of politics and budgets and what the public is willing to support. We cannot be cavalier with comments about the lack of commitment of our public when we face a range of overwhelming moral and urgent imperatives from the children we don't feed and educate well enough to the environment we are not saving to the wars and conflicts we must deal with.

Space exploration in this context comes up wanting. It solves none of the major challenges we confront as a body politic or a global civilization. High minded talk of aspiration is overwhelmingly the language of those for whom the basic needs of life are taken care of and who have the time to ponder philosophical questions. It is for the rich, privileged, and prissy to pontificate on. It does not connect with or relate to the day-to-day struggles that most Americans face to put food on the table, pay the mortgage, or get the kids through school. Answering the riddles of the universe and the mysteries of human existence do not help Americans achieve a path to the American Dream at a time when our Middle Class is under enormous pressure and social mobility has fallen to all-time lows.

Advocates for space exploration have proven unwilling to admit these basic facts and have, therefore, been unable to overcome them. The result is that NASA's budget has hit a wall over which it has not been able to climb and that has limited our ability to get to scale in space. It simply remains too expensive and too risky. And politicians and voters know it.

Will we get back to the moon in the coming years? Almost certainly. Will we build a much bolder permanent presence of more than a handful of astronauts? More challenging politically and, therefore, harder to predict.

The enduring questions of America's future in space are not how far can we go and what can we do when we get there. We cannot go blindly forth without a compelling vision backed by a very strong value proposition.

The true enduring questions are these:

- How do we get to scale in space without a Sputnik moment?
- How do we move humanity onto the high frontier without a significant great power rivalry with which to justify the cost? (Unless China will

conveniently land a man on the Moon and lay claim to superior national willpower.)

- How do we deliver a program that is strong enough to win support on both sides of the political aisles in an era that is no less turbulent than any of the other periods in which we have opted not to go forth?
- What does a space program look like in an age of austerity, in the wake of a great financial crisis, the aftermath of a global pandemic, and amidst a Russian war of aggression in Europe that is undermining economies and security around the world, the full combination of which has generated massive fiscal, political, and economic challenges?

To these questions, the answers to date have been unsatisfactory, irrevocably demonstrated by the failure to allocate resources and budget not just once, but many times over the past 50 years.

This is the backdrop for judging the failure of Presidential announcements. There has been no easy answer and no compelling strategic rationale for any significant move onto the high frontier.

And yet. With all of that said. The game is changing.

That a strategic rationale has not been found before does not mean that one isn't possible now or that there are not candidates in the air. Describing what has changed, why it is important, and what it potentially means for a new vision is the subject of the next chapter.

Chapter 3: Game Changers

There has never been a more exciting time to contemplate a bold future in space driven by a massive American-led effort to win the high frontier for all of humanity.

That may seem a ludicrous proposition given the thesis of the previous section which is that Americans are ambivalent about funding space exploration, have been since Apollo, and any proposal for a more expansive space program must overcome a daunting list of core challenges and an increasingly volatile political context.

Given its importance, the extent of the political challenge is worth recapping. As of 2024, we have faced in just the last few years multiple, major crises including a global pandemic, an economic collapse rivaling the Great Recession, a massive protest movement for racial justice, and a Russian war of aggression on the European continent. All of these crises have and will require significant funding to resolve and that will shape the ability to spend in the future.

The forecasts of our long-term fiscal situation are now grim. Our national debt is enormous, nearly 100% of GDP by the end of 2022, and forecasted to get worse over the next 10 years and much worse over the next 30. More broadly, our middle class is under threat and now our economy is working to resolve the most serious attack of inflation in 40 years, requiring the Federal Reserve to pivot from expansive to restrictive economic policies with higher interest rates. Inflation destroys real value, hides the larger problem of stagnation, and risks driving income inequality higher than the already historical levels today.

Since 2020, every region of the world seems to have become more dangerous, requiring more guns over butter. In 2022, this fear found expression in Russia's invasion of Ukraine, a brutal war of conquest that we thought was impossible in the modern era. It was not. The war upended security and diplomacy assumptions across Europe and the world, created massive economic disruptions to supplies of energy and food, and led to profound economic and military adjustments that will play out for decades. Then, in October 2023, Hamas attacked Israeli communities near the Gaza Strip and provoked a war that threatens to engulf the entire Middle East at any time. China is also increasingly a national security concern for the United States. As China rises and its leader has disposed of term limits, potentially anointing himself as a leader for life, a new era of Great Power rivalry has begun. A conflict over Taiwan could erupt at any time and draw in the United States.

Major increases in defense spending are ramping up to rebuild European security, respond to threats in the Middle East, and defend Taiwan from invasion in East Asia.

Meanwhile, we face a warming planet that is already imposing significant costs in the form of heat waves, massive flooding, forest fires, and multi-year droughts. A major effort will be required to save the future from even worse outcomes. These issues are occurring against the backdrop of a polarized and seemingly poisonous partisan political environment. We are an almost exactly equally divided nation on every issue that seems unable to reach consensus on anything, choosing conflict, anger, and insult instead.

The list of calls on our resources both now and in the future is long, urgent, and morally compelling, a list in which high-minded aspiration is easily trumped by practical necessity.

And yet, for all that, the game is changing and this is an exciting time to consider our future in space.

Two fundamental game changers have appeared on the playing field that may rewrite the assumptions about what is possible when we think about our future in space over the next several decades along with the balance between the public and private sectors.

It comes down to rockets and rocks.

We'll discuss both and then we'll talk about what I mean by the game of getting to scale in space and why what I will pitch is bolder in scope and timeline than anything Elon Musk or Jeff Bezos has considered or proposed.

Rockets

As argued earlier, getting into space is expensive and always has been. Yet, new rockets with new capabilities have emerged to fundamentally rewrite the rules of the possible. Elon Musk's company, SpaceX, has created the world's first reusable production rocket. The Falcon 9 and the Falcon Heavy make SpaceX the most powerful space launch company on the planet. Trailing, but working to catch up, is Jeff Bezos' company, Blue Origin, with its current New Shephard and planned New Glenn rockets still in development and not yet fully operational, but with similar potential for reusable flight as SpaceX. Last, NASA is inching closer to completing the Space Launch System (SLS) heavy lift rocket. These are all significant developments.

To understand why these developments are important, you need to start with the historical record of what it costs to launch material into space. In Table 3.1 below, an illustrative cost curve shows the actual historical cost of launching a kilogram into space to Low Earth Orbit compared to the original premise and forecast made for the Space Shuttle.

The Shuttle was supposed to give us the dashed line that was going to bring launch costs to Low Earth Orbit down under $250 per kilogram by the 1980s. In the 1970s, with the Shuttle under development and optimism high for a breakthrough reduction in launch costs, big dreams were considered and discussed. As we know now, none of it happened. With the Shuttle, costs remained in the range of more than $20,000/kg and so the budget realities of doing anything at scale were simply too expensive to contemplate. The momentum for and dreams about a big future in space that had blossomed in the 1970s slowly faded from mainstream sight.

The arrival of innovative new firms (SpaceX, etc.) on the scene in the last decade are now bringing launch costs down dramatically and account for the steep decline which is illustrated in Table 3.1.

While Table 3.1 is illustrative (e.g. not exact), the key point here is that actual costs are beginning to converge with the original premise of the 1970s. Ideas once seriously discussed and considered in the 1970s – when the Shuttle was theoretically going to deliver reduced launch costs and then seemed outlandish for decades because those costs remained so high – may no longer be quite so crazy. It may be possible to put them back on the table for public discussion.

But first, let's review how and why the Shuttle fell short and what these new innovations are and what they mean for launch costs.

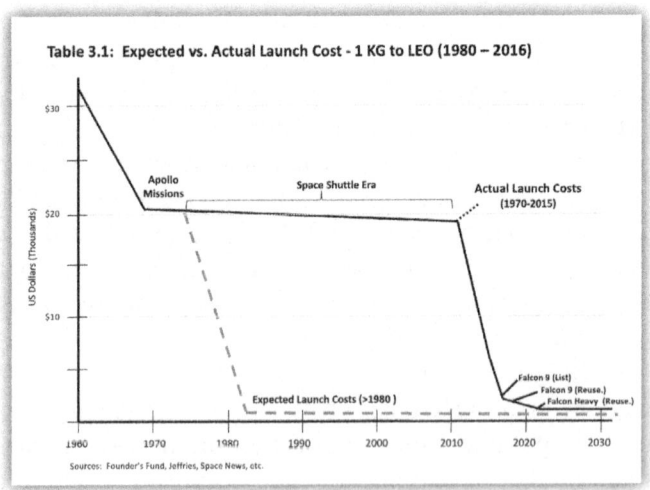

The Shuttle: Promise & Disappointment

The Space Shuttle was a technological marvel and a source of national pride. Designed and built in the 1970s and launched in 1981, the fleet of five production shuttles had a 30-year run as the mainstay of America's space program with a cumulative total of 135 launches. It was also so complex and expensive that the cost of the Shuttle program crowded out all other human exploration missions beyond Low Earth Orbit and its sheer complexity and its significant design flaws led to the loss of two shuttles (Challenger, Columbia) and their crews. The Shuttle failed to meet the primary goal of achieving low cost access to space at scale. This latter point is crucial.

While the Space Shuttle was originally envisioned as being able to reduce the cost of getting to Low Earth Orbit to a few hundred dollars per pound, (Example: $118/lb. in 1973 dollars or $650-$750/lb. in 2013 terms[1]), the truth is the vehicle turned out far more complex than envisioned.

The Shuttle was so complicated it required a massive and time-consuming effort to prepare it for re-launch. It required thousands of hours to refurbish both the shuttle and its booster engines in between each flight, an effort done by a small army of engineers and technicians. The workforce supporting the Shuttle program was nearly 25,000 strong, making the labor bill very expensive. The main engines had to be completely removed, disassembled, and refurbished. Its 35,000 individual heat shield tiles had to be each manually inspected to confirm they were undamaged and remained in place. The fastest turnaround time from landing to re-launch given this near total refurbishment was reportedly two months. In addition, the shuttle fleet never achieved the operational tempo necessary to drive down costs with volume. Instead of a launch every few weeks, the quickest tempo reached just nine launches in a single year (for a fleet of less than six Shuttles) and more often was much less throughout the life of the program. This meant that the standing cost of the infrastructure and workforce could not be amortized through greater volume and frequency of launches.

Given these challenges, the cost of each flight was estimated by NASA as $450 million, implying a cost per lb. to Low Earth Orbit of roughly $8,000 ($18,000/kg). Yet, when all of the development and support costs are added in, the cost per flight as calculated by a number of third parties estimates each launch was closer to $1.5 billion, or $27,000/lb to LEO ($60,000/kg).

The Space Shuttle was only technically re-usable. It flunked the real test with dramatic consequences for cost. The real test of reusability is often described as more akin to a 737. Can you fly it, land it, and take off again with a very short turnaround window. Think Southwest Airlines. But if you had to take apart a 737 plane after each flight, inspect and polish every part, and reassemble it, we would have today precisely five of them flying around the United States with flights only every few months and not the hundreds of aircraft completing several thousand flights a day, moving millions a year (at least during a non-pandemic 'normal' year).

Gaining access to space has faced this fundamental conundrum when it comes to cost. Before SpaceX, we either discarded the rocket completely or we had to rebuild it from scratch.

The 737 analogy (e.g. that launching into space is expensive because we effectively have to build a 737 and then throw it away after each flight) is only partly accurate. A better description would point out that most of what that notional 737 carries would be fuel with passengers and cargo limited to just what you can stuff into the pilot's cabin.

Getting into space used to be enormously expensive with very little chance of getting to scale. That is why the accomplishments of the last few years have been so important and the potential milestones on the near-term horizon may well be revolutionary.

We'll start with SpaceX which has generated enormous enthusiasm and hype for its rapid progress and incredible vision and Blue Origin which was the first to hit the milestone of landing a rocket back on the ground after reaching space.

SpaceX

SpaceX, founded by Elon Musk, has combined bold vision with innovative engineering since it was founded in 2002. Initially supported by NASA re-supply contracts for the International Space Station, the company has steadily innovated and made enormous strides in a very short time to become the world's leading space launch company with a major share of the global launch market.

Prior to 2015, SpaceX already offered the lowest cost access by a production rocket to space of any company in the world. Their list price for a Falcon 9 rocket was $62M and in 2015, it could deliver a pound of cargo to Low Earth Orbit for $2,110. This was an order of magnitude cheaper than the Shuttle, yet SpaceX was just getting started. They also had a heavy lift launch vehicle on the drawing board, the Falcon Heavy, that would have three first stage rockets bundled together which was envisioned to lift nearly 60 tons to Low Earth Orbit at a cost of below $800/lb. Many in the aerospace industry suggested the Falcon Heavy wouldn't work, was too complicated, or would take longer and be more expensive than planned.

But the differentiation that made SpaceX successful was its relentless focus on reusability. As it developed the Falcon 9, SpaceX focused on reusability from the start. They attacked the problem iteratively with each launch, first making the rockets themselves reliable, then adding extendable legs so that they could attempt to safely land a launcher after each flight.

At first progress was slow and launch after launch finished with a rocket falling in the ocean or collapsing and exploding on one of its floating recovery drone ships. But the company learned with each failure and continued to improve.

Then, on December 22, 2015, a SpaceX Falcon 9 launched from Cape Canaveral with a payload bound for space. At an altitude of 124 miles, the first stage of the rocket separated from its cargo, executed a series of maneuvers to turn around, and then returned to Earth – and successfully landed back at its launching pad in Cape Canaveral. This was the first time a production rocket had returned and landed itself and it marked an historic milestone. Science fiction had become science fact.

SpaceX then began to regularly recover its first stage launchers in a variety of conditions including at Cape Canaveral and on its ocean-going drone landing ships, *Just*

Read the Instructions and *Of Course I Still Love You.* As SpaceX made returning the first stage launchers routine, it was also working on learning how to refurbish and re-fly them.

In March, 2017, SpaceX re-used a launcher on a second mission successfully and it has continued to reuse launchers and get better over time.

Meanwhile, the Falcon Heavy was under development and made its maiden test launch from Florida in February, 2018, launching a test cargo of a Tesla roadster with a dummy astronaut in the driver's seat.

By the end of 2020, SpaceX had completed over 100 production flights with its Falcon rockets (Falcon 9 and Falcon Heavy) of which 60+ first stage launchers have been recovered and 45 boosters have been successfully re-flown into space. In 2020, two launchers completed their sixth roundtrip into space, an extraordinary record in just five years from the first successful landing of a launch stage.[2]

To cap it all off, in May, 2020, SpaceX lofted two astronauts to the International Space Station, marking the return of American astronauts flying on an American rocket for the first time since 2011. NASA formally certified SpaceX to carry astronauts in November, 2020, ahead of its second mission, ending America's reliance on Russia to carry American astronauts into space.

As SpaceX continues traveling up the learning curve, they have continued to chip away at the cost of lifting cargo into space. In 2020, the Falcon 9 could lift a little over 25 tons (50,265 lbs) to Low Earth Orbit (LEO) for a list price of $62 million which works out to $1,233/lb. The cost to a higher orbit (Geosynchronous Transfer Orbit, or GTO) is $3,400/lb. The Falcon Heavy offers even better economics. It can lift 70 tons to LEO at a cost, based on a list price of $90M, of just under $640/lb. To the higher GTO orbit, it can lift just shy of 30 tons at a cost of just over $1,500/lb.[3]

What these numbers mean is that the cost of lifting cargo into space has come down dramatically from the Space Shuttle days and it may go lower still.

Just how low costs can go will depend on how successful SpaceX is at reducing turnaround time and continuing to get reuse out of its launchers and all other components. Some commentators have speculated that SpaceX could yet drive down costs by another 50% over current list. After all, these same commentators continually point out that the Falcon 9 rocket costs $60 million to build, but only $200,000 to fuel.

An independent analysis published on a Czech fan site of all things Elon Musk has a speculative but well researched analysis of current Falcon 9 launch costs based on reusability. Citing tweets from Mr. Musk that the marginal cost of relaunching a Falcon 9 was just $15 million, the author (SCR00CHY) calculated the estimated cost of 10 Falcon 9 launches as $209 million. There are some big assumptions built into the analysis (fairing reusability, ten launches, etc.), but they are grounded in information that Musk, himself, has shared. If these numbers are anything close to real, it implies that the cost to lift 10 flights of cargo on a Falcon 9 to LEO, or 25 tons per flight, 250 tons in total, could be potentially delivered for just under $420/lb. While the source may not be an academic journal, it's a well thought out analysis and provides a directional view of what might actually be happening. Kudos to SCR00CHY for putting in the work.[4]

Now ask yourself, what if the Falcon Heavy has similar economics? They won't be the same because the Falcon Heavy uses three launch engines instead of one. If we assume reusability is able to cut the cost of the Falcon Heavy by 50% on the list price (to $45M), then 10 flights at 70 tons per flight (700 tons total) could theoretically be delivered for around $320/lb to LEO.

As a reference point, the International Space Station is less than 500 tons. It took 10 years and 30 flights to assemble. At $450 million a flight at Shuttle prices in the 90s and early 2000s, that's a cost of nearly $15 billion just for the launches. It's stunning to realize that 10 flights of a Falcon Heavy can potentially be done for the cost of one of the original crewed Shuttle missions, but that is where we are at today.

These are revolutionary numbers but that's not where it stops. There are even more indications that costs could go lower still.

First, SpaceX is developing the Starship, a Super Heavy rocket able to lift 100 tons into space and be fully reusable. This greater reusability and still larger lift capacity could continue driving down costs further. As of June 2024, Starship has completed four test flights, each progressing a little further and achieving a little more. The fourth flight on June 6, 2024, witnessed the massive first stage make a controlled slow splashdown at sea as a test run for a recoverable landing in the future. Starship is making great strides and if development is successful, it will be the largest production rocket ever created and operated. Total cost to develop is said to be in the range of $5 billion, but it could eventually also be the cheapest to operate with rumors that the cost of a launch could be as little as $1 million per flight in the future.

Second, SpaceX has applied for the permits to run much greater launch volumes in the next several years, an estimated 70 launches per year (vs. at most 15 in the recent past). This greater launch tempo will greatly help the economics of reusability and continue to drive down costs.[5]

The inescapable conclusion is that SpaceX is delivering a revolutionary breakthrough in access to space and increasingly making it seem routine.

Meanwhile, SpaceX is not the only private launch company working to compete in this market.

Blue Origin

Blue Origin is a company owned by Amazon founder Jeff Bezos and is another private sector contender to create a fully re-usable Vertical Takeoff, Vertical Landing (VTVL) vehicle.

Its current rocket, the New Shephard, is designed to carry six tourists into space to experience weightlessness and a view of Earth through large windows.

Both the capsule and the booster rocket are intended to return safely to be re-used for future flights.

The firm was notorious for being secretive about its progress, but suddenly on November 24, 2015, Blue Origin achieved a major milestone by launching a New Shephard rocket to an altitude of 307,000 feet (at the Kamen Line which defines the very edge of space) – and returning it. The booster rocket returned to land back at the launching pad, settling gracefully down onto its four extendable legs at a speed of less than 5 mph.

In effect, Blue Origin 'scooped' the prize for achieving the world's first reusable launcher returned from space out from underneath SpaceX's nose. However, the comparison was not entirely fair given the New Shepard carried no cargo, was not a full production rocket, and just touched the edge of space.

Nevertheless, it was a powerful demonstration.

Blue Origin went on to launch and return the same rocket multiple times, demonstrating that they, too, had a candidate for a reusable rocket.

Currently Blue Origin is working to scale up on two tracks. First, they are producing a rocket engine, the BE-4, that will be used not only in future Blue Origin rockets, but will also be purchased and used in a new rocket by United Launch Alliance, the Vulcan launch vehicle.

The second track is building up a massive new rocket designated the New Glenn. The plan is for a launch vehicle that is nearly 100 meters high, nearly as tall as the old Saturn V rockets from Apollo. These vehicles will have a 7-meter diameter and be able to lift 45 metric tons to Low Earth Orbit and 13 metrics tons to the higher Geosynchronous Transfer Orbit (GTO). After several delays, Blue Origin is currently scheduled to launch New Glenn for the first time at the end of 2024.

While industry sources note that important progress has been made on the BE-4 engines and building out manufacturing facilities for the large New Glenn, there has as yet been no test flights of a full rocket and the speculation that the first launch would slip beyond 2022 proved accurate.[6]

It's never unwise to write-off one of the most successful entrepreneurs in the world, Jeff Bezos, so Blue Origin will be a company to watch in the coming years to see if they can catch up with SpaceX and deliver a heavy lift launch vehicle.

The Old Guard

The idea of a reusable production rocket that is capable of multiple launches into space is no longer a novelty or merely just theoretical. SpaceX has proven it works with production launchers and the cost advantage has given them a large share of the global launch market already. Blue Origin is trailing, but intent on catching up with the New Glenn in the next few years.

The bigger mystery is what the large, established aerospace and defense firms in America are doing. United Launch Alliance is building a new Vulcan launch vehicle. But it will be only partially reusable at best. The company is looking at trying to recover the engines post-launch, not by having them land on their own, but by snatching them from the air with a helicopter as they parachute back to Earth.

Northrup Grumman is building the Omega rocket to compete for defense contracts, but, again, it is not reusable. Boeing is the prime contractor for NASA's Space Launch System – which is also not reusable. At least one smaller company, Rocket Labs, is working on a reusable rocket for the small launcher segment.

The traditional launch industry in America is being rapidly displaced by SpaceX, but seems to be ceding the market in favor of retaining specific niches in areas like national security launches or cost plus contracting for NASA where cost is less of an issue. In fact, some of the traditional vendors are even skeptical about whether reusability has a business case.

This could be incredibly short sighted. If you believe there is a tiny, modest market for space launches in the coming decades and you cannot compete on cost with SpaceX, then the smart play is to target a niche. You go for a smaller segment that is higher cost, but requires higher quality. But that only makes sense if the future market size is small and if the competition can't also demonstrate its own high quality and then displace you from your niche with lower cost. However, if the market scales greatly, the traditional aerospace companies will have handed over the future to more entrepreneurial upstarts.

These questions are a puzzle. Here's another. Choosing not to innovate and invest in a competing reusable rocket is not for a lack of money or resources. Just three of those US-based aerospace and defense firms spent $50 billion dollars in dividends and share buybacks between them in just one five-year period from 2010-2015. In effect, the big firms appear to be choosing to return money to their shareholders rather than invest in R&D and build new products for the future.

If we have entered a new Space Race to achieve reusability, history will look back and wonder why the big established firms abdicated the future without a response, why they gave back money instead of investing it in a new frontier. The historians may draw analogies with Apple's rise to market dominance with the iPhone, completely marginalizing the market leaders of their time – Nokia, Blackberry, and Motorola. They may mine the internet for the statements and CEO letters that called reusability impractical and compare them to the infamous Steve Balmer rant that the iPhone was impractical when it debuted because it didn't have a physical keyboard. We know how that turned out.

It does not have to be this way. In auto manufacturing, Tesla has been the dominant electric car company for more than a decade. Tesla has paved the way. But the majors are no longer standing still. From General Motors to Ford, Volkswagen to Toyota, the big established players are making big bets on electric cars and working hard to invest in the future. Tesla proved the market. The others are now racing to catch up with dozens of new electric cars launching in the next few years. General Motors has now committed to going all electric by 2035. These are enormous changes. The big automakers are not ceding the market to Tesla now that it is obvious where future growth will be.

If you believe the future market for launch services is much, much bigger as costs come down, then failing to invest in that future looks short-sighted. It is also a loss for

America. We need a vibrant launch market with vigorous competition to drive innovation and reduce costs. If there is good news, perhaps it is that it is never too late to catch up, especially if that future market is massive and runs for many decades. History will not be kind in its judgement of American aerospace leadership if they simply cede the market in favor of short-term stock options.

NASA

Concurrently, NASA's Space Launch System (SLS) rocket is nearing full production use after its first test launch was a success in 2022.

Building the SLS has been a slower, more torturous process metered by budgetary constraints and a trickle of funding complicated by changing designs and dueling directions from Congress and successive Administrations. The rocket was supposed to be ready in 2016. It is more than eight years overdue.

The SLS in its initial configuration will be capable of launching payloads of 70 tons into orbit and can scale in later versions up to 130 tons. The cost, however, is enormous and criticism has dogged the SLS for years.

An analysis by John Strickland, writing in Space.com in 2013, estimated that the true cost of the SLS assuming one launch per year could be as high as $5 billion per launch when you include the Orion capsule, the SLS launch rocket, the cost of operating the supporting workforce for a year, and a share of the amortized development cost. However, Strickland also pointed out that recent news has suggested that the rocket might only be used once every four years and, if that is true, the cost per launch including all of the development costs and the cost of the standing workforce would mean each rocket launch would be closer to a $14 billion price tag, making it a phenomenally expensive rocket to say the least.[7]

That $14 billion price tag seems wildly unrealistic, but according to NASA's own Inspector General, the SLS will have spent $18.3 billion by the time it launches in 2022. If, as is widely expected, the first Artemis mission to the moon is delayed beyond 2023 (it is now 2025 at best), then the total cost will have reached $22.8 billion. The cost to build the SLS is running close to $2 billion per year.[8]

In December 2019, the NASA Director, Jim Bridenstine, said the cost of launching the SLS would be $900 million per launch, but this assumes some kind of volume with these launches.[9]

Numbers like these put the Space Launch System's future in grave doubt. As Boeing and its subcontractors continue to generate cost overruns and delays, SpaceX has steadily developed its Falcon series rockets that can deliver large cargoes to space at much lower costs. If cost is the only issue, SpaceX is a better deal.

However, there are several arguments for keeping the SLS for deep space missions and for larger size missions. Both are important.

The case for deep space rests on reliability and quality, a niche market for lifting astronauts in a large capsule (Orion, built by Lockheed Martin) that is meant for long duration missions to the Moon, asteroids, and even Mars. These longer missions require a bigger crew capsule which requires a larger rocket. The Orion capsule can carry four astronauts, weighs nearly 40 tons, and has over 300 cubic feet of living space. The overall SLS system is designed to fit these requirements.

The SLS can not only lift a large payload for deep space, but that payload can be as much as 10 meters (nearly 33 feet) in diameter which means the rocket can lift very large modules.

As a point of comparison, the International Space Station is a structure that is the size of a football field, composed of multiple modules weighing in at a total of roughly 925,000 lbs, or less than 500 tons. It took over ten years to assemble via more than 30 Space Shuttle flights (and a handful of Russian launches). In its largest variant, the SLS could effectively do the job in just four launches.

Nor are the SLS and SpaceX's Falcon rockets necessarily direct competitors in the same way that a 737 does not compete with a 787 which does not compete with an Airbus 380. They have different purposes for different market segments. There are just over 250 Airbus 380s compared to nearly 1,000 Boeing 787 aircraft as of the end of 2020. Prior to Covid, there were thousands of 737 flights every day. Each of these three aircraft has different niche markets they serve.

That said, it is worth pointing out that the Airbus 380 has become an albatross for Airbus. The 380 was designed to move large numbers of passengers between major airports in a hub-and-spoke type system. However, the airline market moved to a point-to-point system that Boeing anticipated better with its 787 Dreamliner. As a result, Airbus is closing production of its 380 in 2021 after just 251 aircraft and will have failed to recoup any of its $25 billion in development costs.

A similar fate could befall the SLS if it proves to be a rocket that was designed for a different era and is outmatched by a new competitor with a different vision. It will be very hard to continue funding the SLS if SpaceX is able to create its next generation Starship rocket which will be nearly as big (9-meter diameter) as the SLS and also be fully reusable and able to lift cargo at a small percentage of the cost (10% or less of the cost per flight of the SLS).

Nevertheless, the maiden test flight of the SLS was a success in 2022 and the first crewed lunar flyby is on the books for September 2024.

Summary

NASA's SLS is a system trying to outrun a rapidly changing market for its service. SpaceX and Blue Origin are energetic firms in search of a larger market even as some of the traditional aerospace firms continue to doubt the business case for re-usability.

What's clear is that a new era has started, a new space race to achieve reusability at scale and volume that would deliver a dramatic decrease in costs. At the end of the day, SpaceX and/or Blue Origin are likely to capture the lion share of launches with their lower cost. We still may need the SLS, but its future is beginning to get murky.

Rocks

In 1996, John Lewis, a professor at the University of Arizona, authored a book, *Mining the Sky*, describing the enormous wealth of resources that resides in our solar system in the form of asteroids. Lewis wasn't the first to consider this possibility (Konstantin Tsiolkovsky proposed mining the resources of space as early as 1903), but Lewis provided a compelling vision and backed it with details. He posited the potential to mine these resources and outlined the processes for extracting the resources in them. It makes for interesting reading, but while it suggested potentially vast sums that could be gained in space, it seemed very much on the far horizon of our future and well out of reach.

Then something changed.

In April 2012, a study group of nearly three dozen experts led by John Brophy, Fred Culick, and Louis Freedman and funded by the Keck Institute for Space Studies (KISS) issued a report with the relatively dry title of *Asteroid Retrieval Feasibility Study*. What they proposed was revolutionary. Their study detailed out the mechanics and cost of sending a robotic probe to rendezvous with a small asteroid, capture or ensnare it, de-spin it, and then transport it back to a point closer to earth where it could be studied by astronauts.

Whether the approach catalyzed a lot activity or the idea of asteroid mining was already in the air, a lot of announcements soon followed.

On the NASA front, the Keck approach quickly became a candidate for fulfilling President Obama's goal of sending astronauts to rendezvous with an asteroid. After all, if we can get the asteroid a lot closer, then the mission of visiting with astronauts is also a lot easier. The paper inspired the proposal of a formal mission by NASA called the Asteroid Redirect Mission (ARM) that was intended to capture and return an asteroid to near Earth.

Within a few weeks after the study was issued, there were several private sector announcements about mining asteroids that followed in rapid sequence. Two companies caught the most press. They were Planetary Resources and Deep Space Industries. Both were publicly launched with much fanfare shortly after the Keck study was issued.

Planetary Resources was co-founded by Eric Anderson, founder of Space Adventures, and Peter Diamandis of X Prize Foundation fame. The group was backed by some of the most successful entrepreneurs in the world including Larry Page and Eric Schmidt of Google, Richard Branson of Virgin, and James Cameron of *Titanic* and *Avatar* movie fame. Planetary Resources pursued an approach that involved launching small satellites called Arkyds. The first of them, the Arkyd 100, would essentially be a small telescope used to find more asteroid candidates. That would be followed by the Arkyd 300 series that would be sent out in small groups to rendezvous with an asteroid and survey its size and composition.

Planetary Resources attempted to leverage a crowdfunding approach to finance its first small satellite. In June 2013, it launched a Kickstarter campaign that raised over $1.5 million from 17,500 donors in less than 33 days. Backers received a space 'selfie' and a T-shirt for their efforts to create the 'world's first privately owned space telescope.'

Deep Space Industries, for its part, was also active and took a similar approach to exploring first, mining second. Its satellites were called Fireflies and Dragonflies. Deep Space Industries' plan was to start by sending out relatively inexpensive Fireflies on one-way missions to survey Near-Earth Asteroids followed by a Dragonfly to survey and return a sample back to Earth. Once a suitable target asteroid was identified, a 'harvester' would be sent out to pull the candidate asteroid back to a location closer to Earth for mining and processing.

The Keck study appeared to serve as a catalyst for both a NASA mission and two companies that generated a lot of buzz and excitement in the press.

Why the excitement?

It comes down to money. A lot of money.

In February 2013, a 150-foot wide Near-Earth Asteroid, 2012 DA14, came within 17,200 miles of Earth and inspired a huge amount of speculation on what it was worth. Deep Space Industries publicly suggested it had a value of nearly $200 billion in materials, estimating that the asteroid held $65 billion worth of recoverable water and $130 billion worth of valuable metals.

Scientists and economists disputed the composition and the calculation, but the incident served to illustrate that there was a potentially vast amounts of resources in asteroids that may be recoverable. To understand the potential, a basic primer on asteroids is worth reviewing.

A good deal is known about asteroids from samples of meteorites that have fallen from Earth and from surveys of their spectral reflections which tells a lot about their composition. This allows some educated guesswork, although it is still guesswork. The truth is no one knows exactly what any one asteroid contains or is worth until someone begins mining them. What we do know is very intriguing.

We know there are millions of asteroids out there in the main asteroid belt between Mars and Saturn. We also know that there are a large number of what are termed Near Earth Asteroids that are closer or have an orbit that comes close to Earth and may make them easier to access, capture, or mine. There is a good bit of scientific speculation that the bulk of Earth's water originally came from asteroids.

There are three main types of asteroids.

- C-Type Asteroids are called Carbonaceous Asteroids. They make up an estimated 70% of asteroids and are composed of water, clay, and organic materials. The water content is believed to be in the range of 10-20% for any given asteroid and 6% is made of organic material according to recent surveys. These asteroids don't have a lot of metals, but water is important. The hydrogen and oxygen contained in an asteroid's suspended water content can also be used to create rocket fuel.

- S-Type Asteroids. The S-type asteroids make up an estimated 17% of asteroids and are considered 'stony.' They are comprised of silicates (chondrites) that contain 30-100% oxidized iron and achondrites which are made up of silicates and oxides. These asteroids can be mined for oxygen, oxides, and metals. The metals likely include valuable commodities such as gold, platinum and rare earth metals such as rhodium. It's been speculated that a 10-meter sized S-type asteroid contains as much as 110 lb. of rare metals like gold and platinum.
- M-Type asteroids are much rarer but contain a lot more metal content.

What can be made from an asteroid's materials? The short answer is a lot. The products that can be produced from these asteroids are endless, but the basic ones are critical. They are: Fuel, water, oxygen, and metals. The organic compounds found in asteroids can also be used to create fertilizers and industrial chemicals, the basic building blocks of most supply chains and production processes. Water, for instance is critically important. It can be used to make fuel, which effectively establishes a space-based transportation system. Water also supports life and allows for crews in space to operate with fewer supplies (e.g. water, food, etc.) lifted at enormous cost from Earth.

In short, asteroids may hold the key to creating an economic rate of return in space and reducing the cost of operating in space by orders of magnitude. The current cost of lifting a kilogram of material, any material, to a point in space such as Earth-Moon Lagrange 1 is in the range of $100,000. That makes doing virtually anything in space exorbitantly expensive. If, however, we can utilize raw material in space from asteroids, then it potentially makes doing everything in space much cheaper.

(Note: Lagrange 1 is a location between the Moon and the Earth in which gravity cancels out and where it is theoretically possible to build large structures without using costly fuel to maintain their position. It is used throughout this book as literary tool to illustrate a possible destination in near earth space where future activity may occur, but it does not attempt to suggest that this is the final or best location for such activity.)

In addition to the 2012 DA14 flyby and the media speculation in 2013 of what it was worth, there are more estimates of the value of metals and resources in asteroids. These numbers get quite large. According to Asterank, which billed itself as a scientific and economic database of over 600,000 asteroids (and was acquired by Planetary Resources in 2013), here are some examples:

- Asteroid 1991 DB is a C-type asteroid that is .6 km in diameter and is estimated to contain recoverable quantities of nickel, iron, cobalt, water, nitrogen, hydrogen and ammonia. Asterank calculates the value of this asteroid as $168 billion, with a potential profit of $26.6 billion.

- Asteroid Nereus is an Xe type asteroid that is .33 km in diameter and is estimated to contain recoverable quantities of nickel, iron, and cobalt. Asterank calculates the value of this asteroid as $4.7 billion with potential profit of $1.4 billion.

- Asteroid Anteros is an L type asteroid that is 2.3 km in diameter. It is believed to contain magnesium silicate, aluminum, and iron silicate. Asterank calculates the value of this asteroid as an astonishing $5.57 Trillion, with a potential profit margin of $1.25 Trillion.[10]

Given that no asteroid has actually been recovered and its composition verified, some of these estimates might be more illustrative than perfect. But with numbers like these being bandied about, it should be clear why there is some buzz in the air among the private space community about the potential for asteroid mining.

On the other side of the hype, however, there have been several attempts to dispute the value being placed on asteroids and their recoverable material.

When 2012 DA14 did its flyby, economists pointed out that the value of resources in the asteroid were potentially wildly optimistic. You can't recover those resources by magic. You have to have an infrastructure in place to process what is effectively a big rock into the elements that are valuable, whether water, gold, or anything else. That infrastructure is enormously expensive. It would have to be lifted from the Earth's surface and would likely cost a $100 billion or more according to some sources.

After all, it's not like you can just land those asteroids on Earth to recover the materials they contain – that's an approach that didn't turn out so well for the dinosaurs.

Summary

Rockets and Rocks. New tools and new opportunities are coming to bear that might change the game of getting to scale in space. Yet to understand the size of the challenge, it is important to know what I mean by scale in space. That is where we turn next. It's time to talk about what the game really is and why these new developments have the potential to change that game – as well as how much further we have to go.

The Game of Scale

What do I mean by scale? The early NASA plan shared in the previous chapter envisioned several hundred astronauts in space by the early 1990s. Gerard O'Neil, writing in the 1970s envisioned a future in which thousands of space colonies existed around the solar system and we had a true civilization in space. Neither of these visions came to fruition and both are beyond reach today and the reason mostly comes down to a matter of cost. If we want to understand why these visions have not been achieved, we need to understand what they really mean in terms of the cost of getting to scale in space.

Here is a simple exercise to illustrate the size of the problem. The modest numbers and ambitions associated with space exploration tend to hide the true extent of the cost problem that constrains any attempt to break-out into near earth space at scale. To understand the issue, start by positing a future presence in space at a notional location like Earth-Moon Lagrange 1 (as noted earlier, this is a location between the Moon and the Earth in which gravity cancels out and where it is theoretically possible to build large structures without using costly fuel to maintain their position. It is used throughout this book as literary tool to illustrate a possible destination in near earth space where future activity may occur but not to advocate that as the only or best location for such activity).

To then get an illustrative understanding of what it would cost to sustain a group of astronauts or workers at that location, you can break down the cost of transporting and sustaining that astronaut or person into the following constituent parts:

- Passenger transport to Low Earth Orbit (roundtrip)
- Passenger transport from LEO to a Lagrange 1 or suitable point (roundtrip)
- Annual support cost for a person living at a Lagrange point.

This framework is very simplistic and does not account for the cost of building a suitable place for said astronaut to live and work, but as a simple baseline, it can be a useful starting point. The reason O'Neill's original vision of self-sustaining colonies at a Lagrange point never materialized can best be illustrated by a cost table for each of these components. I will attempt to illustrate just two of them – the cost of getting to LEO and the cost of supporting a person living at a Lagrange point. Both scenarios assume no shortcuts and no living off the land or utilizing resources other than those brought from Earth. This is the upper boundary limit on cost, the most extreme example, yet it is a good tool for understanding the cost of getting to scale and where we are today.

Table 3.2, below, is an estimate of the cost of transporting astronauts to Low Earth Orbit to a station like the International Space Station at various price points and at various levels of scale. Until 2020, the flight to the ISS was provided by the Russians and it cost over $70 million for each astronaut and covered the roundtrip. (SpaceX successfully launched astronauts on an American rocket to the ISS in May 2020). There is widespread belief that SpaceX can bring the cost of transport to LEO down to as low as $20 million per passenger (a number that Elon Musk has promised), although the current price is reportedly $55 million per passenger.

Such a cost reduction is certainly moving in the right direction. However, if you attempt to apply these costs at scale, you begin to see just how enormously expensive it would be to move large numbers of people into space.

Table 3.2: Annual Cost of Travel to Low Earth Orbit (*Illustrative*)

People Per Year	Trip to LEO - Annual Cost (Cost per Person)				
	$70,000,000	$20,000,000	$10,000,000	$1,000,000	$250,000
10	$700,000,000	$200,000,000	$100,000,000	$10,000,000	$2,500,000
50	$3,500,000,000	$1,000,000,000	$500,000,000	$50,000,000	$12,500,000
100	$7,000,000,000	$2,000,000,000	$1,000,000,000	$100,000,000	$25,000,000
250	$17,500,000,000	$5,000,000,000	$2,500,000,000	$250,000,000	$62,500,000
500	$35,000,000,000	$10,000,000,000	$5,000,000,000	$500,000,000	$125,000,000
1,000	$70,000,000,000	$20,000,000,000	$10,000,000,000	$1,000,000,000	$250,000,000
2,500	$175,000,000,000	$50,000,000,000	$25,000,000,000	$2,500,000,000	$625,000,000
10,000	$700,000,000,000	$200,000,000,000	$100,000,000,000	$10,000,000,000	$2,500,000,000
Cost Reduction		$500,000,000,000	$600,000,000,000	$690,000,000,000	$697,500,000,000
Reduction Percentage		-71.4%	-85.7%	-98.6%	-99.6%

Transporting ten astronauts a year to Low Earth Orbit would cost $700 million at the old list price charged by the Russians. But the cost of transporting 100 astronauts is $7 billion (virtually all of NASA's current budget for human spaceflight). If we were to get so ambitious as to consider putting 1,000 astronauts in space at the current list price, the total cost to just get them to the International Space Station would hit $70 billion and then jumps to $700 billion if we attempted another order of magnitude jump to a total of 10,000 per year. The Russians won't be carrying our astronauts in the future, so this is the upper boundary for travel cost to LEO.

As noted, SpaceX successfully launched two astronauts to the ISS in 2020 and Elon Musk has promised to get the cost down to $20 million per person from $55 million per person today. Yet, $20M is a cost that is still prohibitively expensive to put more than a few dozen astronauts in space. For example, launching 500 astronauts to LEO at SpaceX's breakthrough price point of $20 million per person is still going to cost $10 billion. Going big and launching 10,000 astronauts to LEO at $20 million per person would cost $200 billion, a vast sum, even though it would generate savings of over $500 billion when compared to what the Russians would have charged.

To make advancing humanity into space at anything resembling scale a real possibility, you would need to reduce the cost from the old baseline Russian price of $70 million by a factor greater than 99%. The cost of transport to LEO probably needs to be in the range of $250k for any kind of scale to be feasible. At that price, the cost of lifting 10,000 per year is less than $2.5 billion. Expensive, yes, but given what you would get (10,000 people in space), such numbers would fundamentally alter the dialogue of what is possible and politically and economically feasible.

It is worth pointing out that, while SpaceX has succeeded in launching astronauts to the ISS and may get the cost closer to the $20 million per person, we still need to reduce cost by a massive amount to operate at a price point of $250,000 per person.

Much the same dynamic plays out when you look at what it would take to support a large group of astronauts and workers at that notional Lagrange 1 point on an annual basis.

Table 2 lays out a simplified scenario for what it would cost to support various populations of astronaut at a Lagrange point in space. It is based on a budget of just over 5kg/day currently needed to support an astronaut at the International

Space Station (e.g. the weight of water, food, oxygen, etc). Table 2 below assumes all supplies are lifted from the earth's surface and transported by rocket at an estimated cost of $11,500/kg (an estimate for illustrative purposes only). This cost is much, much lower than what it actually costs today, but it's a useful starting point for illustration purposes.

The results are both eye-catching and show-stopping.

Table 3.3 shows that once again the costs of getting to scale in space are enormous if we are using the current tools available. Supporting just 10 astronauts in space would cost $235 million a year, and this is likely a gross underestimate as noted. But supporting 1,000 would cost $23.5 billion and supporting 10,000 astronauts at L1 would be an unimaginably expensive cost of $234 billion per annum. And this cost is just for supporting the astronauts at L1. It does not include the cost of building a station for them to live on which seems unimaginably more expensive still.

These numbers – using simple baseline assumptions of the cost of supplying all needs from earth-based launches – are probably on the low side, possibly very low side. But they highlight a fundamental dilemma: We cannot afford a presence in space at anything approaching any definition of scale with these costs as they currently stand. We have to dramatically reduce them to get to scale in space.

Table 3.3: Annual Support Cost – L1 Astronaut Workforce

L1 Workforce - Annual Support Cost								
People	kg/day	Days	KG/pers.	Extra	Total / Yr	Cost/Kg	Total Kg/yr	Total Cost
10	5.03	365	1835.95	200	2035.95	$11,500	20,360	$234,134,250
50	5.03	365	1835.95	200	2035.95	$11,500	101,798	$1,170,671,250
100	5.03	365	1835.95	200	2035.95	$11,500	203,595	$2,341,342,500
250	5.03	365	1835.95	200	2035.95	$11,500	508,988	$5,853,356,250
500	5.03	365	1835.95	200	2035.95	$11,500	1,017,975	$11,706,712,500
1,000	5.03	365	1835.95	200	2035.95	$11,500	2,035,950	$23,413,425,000
2,500	5.03	365	1835.95	200	2035.95	$11,500	5,089,875	$58,533,562,500
5,000	5.03	365	1835.95	200	2035.95	$11,500	10,179,750	$117,067,125,000
10,000	5.03	365	1835.95	200	2035.95	$11,500	20,359,500	$234,134,250,000

By contrast, Table 3.4 sketches out a set of illustrative cost reduction scenarios that show the benefit of greatly reducing the cost of supporting an astronaut at a Lagrange point in space. This illustration, like the ones before, is simplistic and does not presuppose how these reductions are to be made. If the cost of supplies can be reduced from the baseline estimate by a factor of 99%, then getting to scale in space begins to look more promising. For example, supporting 10,000 astronauts at a Lagrange point in space would then cost just a few billion, a pittance given the advantage and productive capability such a large workforce in space could potentially bring to bear if it existed.

Table 3.4: L1 Support – Cost Reduction Scenarios

L1 Support Cost - Reduction Cost Scenarios						
	$5,750	$2,875	$1,150	$575	$115	$11.50
People	50%	75%	90%	95%	99%	99.9%
10	$117,067,125	$58,533,563	$23,413,425	$11,706,713	$2,341,343	$234,134
50	$585,335,625	$292,667,813	$117,067,125	$58,533,563	$11,706,713	$1,170,671
100	$1,170,671,250	$585,335,625	$234,134,250	$117,067,125	$23,413,425	$2,341,343
250	$2,926,678,125	$1,463,339,063	$585,335,625	$292,667,813	$58,533,563	$5,853,356
500	$5,853,356,250	$2,926,678,125	$1,170,671,250	$585,335,625	$117,067,125	$11,706,713
1,000	$11,706,712,500	$5,853,356,250	$2,341,342,500	$1,170,671,250	$234,134,250	$23,413,425
2,500	$29,266,781,250	$14,633,390,625	$5,853,356,250	$2,926,678,125	$585,335,625	$58,533,563
5,000	$58,533,562,500	$29,266,781,250	$11,706,712,500	$5,853,356,250	$1,170,671,250	$117,067,125
10,000	$117,067,125,000	$58,533,562,500	$23,413,425,000	$11,706,712,500	$2,341,342,500	$234,134,250

The purpose of these tables and illustrations is not to offer a detailed specification of the costs of launching and sustaining a large-scale human presence in space. Real engineers and economists can do a much better job of that. The point is to tangibly highlight the obvious – getting to scale in space with current technology and with the current cost structure is virtually impossible for us to afford.

What's also true is that no serious scenario for building on the space frontier has ever been assumed on the idea that we launch and support a large population in space entirely from Earth. Any serious plan tries to use resources in space for water, fuel, etc. The point of these simple models is to show why these strategies are so critical and how challenging the cost issue is without them.

There are great hopes that the private sector may offer a breakthrough in cost on a number of fronts. Musk's SpaceX is already bringing down launch costs in large chunks and is billed as a hero for doing so. Blue Origin may do the same. There is potential to harness the resources of the asteroids to produce water and materials in space that don't have to then be lifted from the Earth's surface (e.g. live off the land in space).

There are enormously creative minds working to solve some of these problems. But the simple illustrations above highlight the Achilles heel that high cost has been to every vision of advancing humanity into space in anything beyond small numbers.

So where does that leave us today?

Effectively without a plan to leverage a wealth of resources that remains tantalizingly just out of reach and that could re-write what is possible for humanity in space (and in general). And that brings us to a discussion about the role of the private sector and the public sector, a debate that may be crucial to truly changing the game in space and potentially getting to scale in the future.

The Private Sector Analogy

We are seeing a surge in private sector activity on the space frontier, a few examples of which were highlighted earlier. The heavy weights getting the most press are companies bringing down launch costs (SpaceX, Blue Origin), proposing colonies on other planets (Mars One), launching micro-satellites at a fraction of the cost of established companies and governments (PlanetApp), or proposing to capture and return asteroids. Nor is this a comprehensive list.

The future feels like it is being defined by free enterprise.

Meanwhile NASA appears to face a quandary despite the near-term potential for a crewed flight of the SLS around the moon. It has built a rocket that uses old technology, is enormously expensive, and it makes every launch high stakes and risky. *The Economist* magazine has called it "A flying turkey....yesterday's rocket using yesterday's technology and brought about by yesterday's thinking."[11]

Congress is tight-fisted with funding and likely to get more so given the rapidly increasing national debt. Commission after commission expounds that our goals in space are being underfunded and plead for just a bit more funding, mostly to no avail.

With this as a backdrop, it's no wonder that a growing chorus is talking up the role of the private sector in leading the space revolution and going where governments have failed to take us. This refrain goes on to suggest that if only government would get out of the way and let the private sector work its innovative, breakthrough magic, then costs will drop dramatically and we'll have a big future in space in a remarkably short time. The conventional wisdom has given up on government leadership or funding at scale.

The analogy that gets brought up in serious works by more serious and credentialed authors is the analogy of the Internet. As the story goes, the government helped establish the very basic infrastructure and standards in the 1970s and 1980s with pioneering work by DARPA and others to fund the research.

Government then opened up access and allowed the private sector to take the lead, in effect getting out of the way. At that point, economic activity and growth exploded and one of the most vibrant sectors of our economy emerged spontaneously and at enormous speed, producing thousands of companies including behemoths like Google, eBay, Facebook, and more. The Internet analogy suggests we are moving in a similar direction when it comes to space.

We should pause at this point to consider the role of analogies.

Analogies matter. They provide a construct around which to organize support and a language with which to define the direction we wish to go. They encapsulate and define the strategies we pursue. We need to think about them carefully.

When people use the Internet analogy in the space context, they are effectively saying that the private sector is the engine of growth and government needs to both enable and get out of the way, allowing the private sector to do what it does best. If only the government will open up the frontier and allow the private sector and free enterprise to innovate and develop rather than restrain and regulate, we will be able to quickly advance humanity into space.

It sounds great. There's just one problem: It's wrong.

Innovation on the internet could be done with a two-pizza team volunteering their time in the hopes of a hit that would attract eyeballs and funding. Space is a vastly different proposition with a vastly different investment required.

Here's an alternative analogy for your consideration: World War II.

In a World War II analogy, SpaceX is to the space frontier what Boeing was to the war effort in the second great war to end all wars, a maker of critically important weapon systems in the form of the B-17 and other aircraft. Without a huge number of aircraft like the Flying Fortress, America and its allies could not have won the war. That is clear. Our nation's industrial might and ability to scale up and deliver the ships, planes, tanks, and sundry munitions and armaments of all types in the vast quantities needed was critical to the eventual victory. It was the private sector led by people with names like Knudsen, Kaiser, and Higgins that built that 'Arsenal of Democracy'.

But looking back at World War II, it would be hard to confuse the role of the private sector and individual industrial companies of the era that produced so many aircraft, ships, tanks, or guns with the overarching role that the government played in mobilizing the public will and resources of America to fight a major conflict.

It was government that mobilized the nation and the economy and funded that effort through taxation and financial controls. It was government that set up the procurement process, provided contracts to companies, and issued loans to capitalize the factories and the tools necessary to build the arsenal of weapons that would be needed. It was government that recruited, trained, and fielded the vast armies and deployed the armadas of ships and planes. It was government that set the strategy and drove the war effort. It was government that led, fought, and won the war.

When we think of the heroes of that great effort, we think of Roosevelt, Eisenhower, MacArthur, Patton, and others. We think of the President who rallied us and the generals who led the battles and fought the enemy foot-by-foot, mile-by-mile across Europe and the Pacific. Many private sector industrialists contributed enormously to the war effort and their efforts were fundamental to the eventual victory and are well known to historians of the era. (The contemporary example is the war in Ukraine. Everyone knows who Volodymyr Zelensky is. Almost nobody knows the name of the CEO whose company makes the artillery rockets that are changing the course of the war.)

Without the private sector producing and innovating, the war effort would have been vastly more difficult, expensive, bloody, or lost outright. We would not have gotten the best and most efficient weapons in the huge volumes that were critical to winning the war. You cannot minimize the role of the private sector in creating, innovating, and producing all the weapons and systems needed to defeat our enemies.

But truthfully, the effort was so vast in scope and effort, that it would be absurd to think or suggest even retrospectively that the private sector could have won the war faster if government just got out of the way. It was government support and funding via government contracts and loans that enabled the production of the arsenal of democracy in the first place. It was government that fielded the soldiers, sailors, and airmen that used those weapons to fight and win the war.

When it comes to analogies, the space frontier may be more like World War II than the Internet.

Consider this: The private sector may be better optimized for the shallows of Low Earth Orbit, the lowest price of entry for any kind of significant presence in space. The cost of doing anything significant in space is so extraordinarily expensive that even there the space entrepreneurs keep finding their way back to NASA's doorstep in search of contracts that will provide actual revenue. These contracts range from carrying cargo and now passengers to the ISS to proposals to provide a fuel depot in space.

The cost of access to space is getting cheaper and cheaper courtesy of SpaceX (and soon Blue Origin), but it is still enormous. It costs hundreds of billions to do anything at real scale.

Unless you are launching satellites, doing anything involving people in space has been so enormously expensive that NASA and government contracting has been a key enabling source of revenue. SpaceX is changing the cost equation, but the cost dilemma of supporting any sizable activity in space is still an issue. If tens of billions of dollars in investment could be rallied from venture capital, if the investor community were really ready to throw down and invest massive amounts of capital to seize the high frontier, then why did one of the most hyped companies (Planetary Resources) backed by billionaires with vast fortunes use crowdfunding to finance its first satellite telescope with selfies and T-shirts? This at a point when a small company was at the peak of hype about its potential.

The cognitive disconnect seems enormous, but it really isn't.

The truth is simple and understanding this paradigm is fundamental: Any real riches in space remain highly speculative, extremely risky, and extraordinarily expensive. Three key words bear repeating. Speculative. Risky. Expensive.

What the billionaires and venture capitalists of Silicon Valley are saying if you read between the lines is that companies like the former asteroid mining firm, Planetary Resources, cannot count on a blank check. People are willing to back them with their names, and some limited funding, but no one really knows if pay-off will be in five years, 50, or ever. These companies have to find incremental revenue and define a business model that finances their activity until the day comes when a real return is straight forward, easy, and the infrastructure is in place (largely financed by someone else). At that point the VCs and the wealthy will swoop in to provide the bridge financing needed in exchange for a very high return on investment – and a sweeping claim of credit for their farsightedness and risk taking.

Despite the hype and the self-congratulation, the private sector abhors risk. Elon Musk is the exception, not the rule. But even there, Elon Musk has to find revenue to fund his dreams. In the case of SpaceX, he is gobbling up the space launch market, but he has also created a communications network, Starlink, that will let him become a telecom provider and earn terrestrial revenues to support his dream for Mars. This is not the same thing as saying there is a blank check from venture capital to go into space.

It's important to realize that venture capitalists are focused on spreading their bets and reducing their risks as much as possible. When new companies are small, speculative, and risky, the venture capital and angel communities invest very carefully in very small increments, tightly watched, and closely controlled. They serve as a forcing function to push start-ups to find revenue fast. Venture capital's interest is to lose as little money as possible. It rarely backs long-term visionary efforts where revenue is a distant and questionable prospect. This is a formula optimized for Silicon Valley and the digital economy. That is why we saw Planetary Resources managing the hype cycle with such skill and selling crowdfunding and T-shirts, selfies and school projects to get to a Minimum Viable Product that delivers actual revenue immediately.

But when a company becomes a unicorn, valued at a billion or more, with enough momentum to offer 'proof' of a market and a business model, the investors stampede to offer tens of millions more. No one wants to miss the pay-off of a sure thing.

Anyone who doesn't understand this dynamic should read a little less Ayn Rand and a lot more Mariana Mazzucato. The private sector, despite the hype, does not (or at least rarely) invest billions on risky adventures without proven markets and a clear path to payback and exit. Very few of these ventures succeed unless they can find significant revenue. Even

SpaceX would be a bankrupt and derelict company in Chapter 11 without a few timely contracts from NASA in 2008.

When Founder's Fund, a group of venture capitalists, lament that their industry (venture capital) is not taking enough risk to back very long-term ventures with breakthrough potential, my only response when it comes to the space frontier is: *Of course!* When that Fund argues that the semiconductor industry was an example of Venture Capital taking on a risky long-term bet in which the long-term outcome of a mass consumer market was highly uncertain, it must be pointed out that those investments occurred against the backdrop of a Cold War spending surge in which government was a guaranteed market for innovation, purchasing semiconductors for defense purposes and offering long-term contracts. Investments in this industry were far less risky than they are portrayed and came on the back of massive public funding and revenue.

In fact, the much-hyped asteroid mining companies are a perfect example of the limits of venture capital to fund long-term speculative ventures and a reason to question the assumptions that the private sector will lead us into space at scale. Despite a roster of billionaires lending their names to an exciting idea,

Planetary Resources ran out of cash in 2018 and was acquired by a blockchain software company, effectively as a trophy. But by 2020, as times turned tougher for that company, it liquidated what was left of Planetary Resources right down to its Asteroids arcade game. Deep Space Industries met a slightly better fate. It was acquired by Bradford Space, a small aeronautics company that purchased DSI's technology for small propulsion systems.

The dream of mining asteroids is currently defunct, its companies bankrupt and gone.

What happened to these companies is a perfect illustration of the points made here. Venture capital does not have an appetite to back long-term ventures where real revenue is more than a decade away and speculative even then.[12]

The government sector, despite years of being talked down and belittled, is critical to opening up markets on the frontier. Government is the primary enabler of basic science and long-term bets.

The problem is that NASA's budget remains anemic, so both the private sector and the public sector remain frustrated and have lost faith. While there are exciting innovations occurring, the role of public sector leadership and funding at scale is missing from the equation, so we are not making any progress.

It's as if Congress had authorized war after Pearl Harbor, but had limited procurement to 10 planes a year for the foreseeable future. Boeing would have made the B-17 with hopes of selling more (assuming the government provided financing for the factory), but could hardly throttle up the production line and achieve cost savings without a commitment from the War Department to buy in near unlimited quantities. Such a small quantity of B-17s would have meant each one cost an enormous sum and the critics in and outside of government would have leaped on this fact to decry how expensive and irresponsible it is to fight a war using such weapons. On the front lines, the B-17 would have been deployed in limited numbers and would, as a result, have offered no decisive advantage. Each and every loss would have been an expensive disaster creating further restrictions on their use, commission after commission to review what went wrong, and endless criticisms of their viability. The war would have dragged on, ended in stalemate, or been lost to the Axis.

With the space frontier, there is no infrastructure in space and no market in place. To build it will likely require mobilizing investment on the scale of $5-$10 trillion dollars. Trillion. Not billion.

The private sector will benefit enormously from the contracts and procurement effort that will be needed to advance humanity onto the space frontier at anything like scale. Likewise, a government led effort at scale will need a vibrant and innovative private sector to drive progress, find solutions to critical problems, and deliver results that are cost competitive and continually moving down the cost curve. It will have to be a partnership.

The World War II analogy requires a synthesis of government and the private sector working together. It is not a perfect analogy – we are not fighting a war and we do not need to mobilize at anything like that scale and our entrepreneurs will certainly be heroes in this story. I've over-rotated by intent. The best analogy is a hybrid of World War II and the Internet in which both the public and private sector have critical, mutually reinforcing roles to play – and with room for heroism on all sides.

The private sector will create and field the most effective tools and systems possible (think SpaceX, Blue Origin, etc.) which will be procured (as goods and services) in large numbers by the public sector. In turn, the public sector must mobilize the vast resources needed to procure at scale and effectively create a sustainable market in space.

If building out the space frontier is simply a matter of reducing launch costs and letting the private sector take charge and create a market for services, then perhaps the internet analogy will hold. If you believe a few tens of billions in investment will get us the infrastructure in space to establish an economically self-sustaining foothold, then read no further.

But if you believe as I do that building a market in space at scale will require a massive investment from and leadership by the public sector, then that means we need a viable strategy to explain this both within the space community and to the public at large. It means the hype about the private sector, if not completely wrong, threatens to lead us in the wrong direction.

Such a premise forces us to acknowledge a truth – that our politics and policy making have given us no vision around which to rally, no path forward that makes economic and political sense, and are, therefore, incapable of mobilizing resources at scale when it comes to space.

This is what needs to change.

Conclusion

This is truly an exciting time to watch America's space program in motion. There is a dynamic new private sector building rockets led by SpaceX, Blue Origin, and more. We no longer have to rely on the Russians to carry our astronauts into space. A mission to the moon is tantalizingly close.

But there is also a missing ingredient. Government funding at scale is missing and there is no vision to rally around. Space exploration as a governing vision has significant limitations and has not proven effective in rallying and mobilizing resources. It offers only a small-scale future of highly expensive missions that can provide no economic payback. At best, we are limping our way into a future that has led to failure and stagnation in the past rather than seizing the opportunity to lead with a bold new vision.

A vision is built upon multiple interlocking programs and components. With the next chapter, I will propose an example of a program that blends public investment with private sector innovation to advance humanity into space. We will then close this essay with a vision that attempts to set a broader strategic vision and combine it with an action plan for gaining public and political support to break-out into space at scale and achieve the enormous public benefits that are possible.

Chapter 4: L1 Strategic Materials Reserve

In the previous chapter, we saw that the concept of capturing an asteroid is one that NASA was developing and private sector companies were exploring. The engineering challenges of such a mission looked feasible based on the Keck study group findings and the subsequent proposal for a NASA ARM mission. There was both hype and optimism.

So, what happened?

On the public sector side, Congress refused to fund an Asteroid Retrieval Mission (ARM). NASA proposed a cheaper version (grab a small boulder off of an asteroid instead of an entire asteroid). But Congress still balked. NASA was forced to cancel ARM.

What they did fund was the OSIRIS-Rex mission to the asteroid Bennu. This mission was a robotic scientific analysis – chemical composition, mapping, etc. – of Bennu combined with a sample collection. The collection goal was to grab 60 grams (a little over 2 ounces) of material from Bennu. That effort succeeded in October 2020. The sample was returned to Earth in September of 2023 for analysis.

Instead of an asteroid weighing a ton or more, we traded an asteroid retrieval mission for a science mission to retrieve a sample of just 2 ounces.

On the private sector side, the key firms that launched in 2012 were both acquired after the hype receded and they failed to raise enough funds for ongoing operations. One of these firms, Planetary Resources, was eventually liquidated right down to its Asteroids arcade game. The other was purchased for its small propulsion units. Currently there are no serious private sector initiatives to harvest or retrieve asteroids.

The public sector vision for asteroid mining has been neutered. The private sector industry for asteroid mining is effectively still born.

When it comes to mining the heavens, I can sum up the recent history of America's bold can-do spirit in one single word: *Ignominious*.

It's time for a reboot.

My goal is to move beyond a public sector that is divided and can't think at scale and a private sector that talks up vision but lacks the resources to act independently and goes out of business without government contracts. In this respect the ARM mission was a perfect example of the limitations we are imposing on ourselves as a nation and the failure of private sector hype when substantive public sector revenue is lacking. We are all collectively missing out on a bolder future as a result.

Our country, our political leadership, is missing out on an opportunity to achieve a substantial win for the future of America in a way that is fiscally prudent and potentially meets the criteria of a wise investment. But if our political leadership is falling short, so too are our private sector, Silicon Valley visionaries who cannot grasp the singular importance of a public sector vision that can earn funding and support nor envision how to help create and sustain that vision or engage the public in a credible way.

ARM as a mission for exploration, a one-off effort to return a small sample, is good science, but barely resonates beyond the science community. As a program with the potential to catalyze an industry in space and create Earth-based jobs, applying ARM at scale is much more intriguing.

In this chapter, I will attempt to describe what a program to acquire asteroid material at scale would look like and how it can rapidly bring down the cost of this resource, cement American leadership in space, and create the basis for an industrial economy in near Earth space. In addition, the net cost to the American taxpayer may well be positive over the long-term, a possibility that, if true, means this approach could offer policymakers the breakthrough to 'advancing humanity into space' that they have long appeared to be searching for.

The Proposal: An L1 Strategic Materials Reserve

I am proposing that the US Congress authorize and the US Government move forthwith to implement a program of open market acquisition of asteroid material to be purchased upon delivery at Lagrange 1 (L1) *or other suitable delivery point in near Earth space.* The delivery of said material should be contracted with the private sector, primarily, but not necessarily exclusively American entities, which will be responsible for delivering in unprocessed form at a fixed price per unit of measure a specific quantity of materials at a specific location. The fixed price will be based on a payment schedule that will decline over time at an aggressive, but predictable rate that provides suitable financial incentive for the contracted parties to make rapid progress. Upon delivery and payment, said material will become the sole property of the US Government and the American people.

The goal for this strategic material fund would be to acquire in the range of 100,000-250,000 tons of asteroid material over a 30-year period beginning as soon as can be operationally initiated.

I will demonstrate with this proposal that the net economic benefit of the material acquired is greatly in excess of the cost of its acquisition and that moving to purchase at scale will create both an industry of high paying jobs as well as an asset for the American people. In blunt terms, this program will create jobs at home on Earth for Americans, demonstrate American technological leadership, and open up the frontier of near earth space for both development and exploration.

In simple terms, my big idea for getting to scale in space comes down to this: A purchasing agreement. Why this makes sense starts by comparing the cost and effort to do one ARM mission versus the cost of doing many.

ARM 1

At the core of this proposal is a speculative view of the original baseline case for an Asteroid Retrieval Mission (ARM) in its original form (full asteroid retrieval).[1]

In that original study created by a group of researchers funded by the Keck Institute for Space Studies, the cost of a single mission to capture a single asteroid and return it to Lunar orbit was estimated as $2.647 billion in FY12 constant dollars. These estimates were based on a first mission to capture an asteroid of between 6-8 meters in diameter which would have a mass of approximately 500,000 kg, or 1.1 million pounds. (This is significantly more than two ounces.). The original mission profile estimated that it would take 6-10 years to complete the rendezvous, capture, and return of the asteroid depending on the size and location of the asteroid targeted. The cost on a per lb. basis for this very first mission would be in the range of $2,400/lb.

This is not cheap, but it compares favorably for the current delivery cost of a pound of material to L1 from Earth. Today, that cost has been estimated in the range of $40,000-$50,000 per lb (or $100,000/kg).

Of course, such a comparison is not a perfect apples-to-apples view since materials delivered from Earth would be processed and higher value than raw asteroid material, but the initial comparison is important and has some validity and I will explain why that is so more thoroughly later.

To understand why this initial estimate is not the final word, we need to explore what makes up the cost at the line item level. Below in Table 4.1, there is a breakdown provided by the original design team.

Table 4.1: Baseline ARM Mission Budget

Budget Item	FY12 $M	Percent	Description
1. NASA Oversight	$204	7.7%	NASA Overhead and administration. Calculated as a percentage of overall contractor cost. Assume intensive development and coordination with NASA.
2. Phase A	$68	2.6%	Preliminary analysis and a project pan.
3. Spacecraft	$1,359	51.3%	Cost to develop technologies, assemble, and deliver the spacecraft.
4. Launch Vehicle	$288	10.9%	Cost of launching the mission from Earth on Atlas V rocket.
5. Mission Ops	$117	4.4%	Cost of maintaining mission oversight for the 10-year duration.
6. Reserves	$611	23.1%	Contingency reserves estimated at 30% of total cost.
Total	$2,647	100.0%	

These costs are significant, but like anything they represent the cost of creating something from scratch the very first time and then doing it only once. They are not representative of what it might cost to run dozens or hundreds of similar missions over time. It is worth looking at each of these elements and speculating about how low the cost could go to launch the 2nd, 10th, or even 50th vehicle. It is likely that the cost can drop dramatically with operations at scale and we shall illustrate this below.

Let's take them one at a time.

Line 1 – NASA Oversight. Some people skeptical of government costs might take a dim view of this line item, but the truth is that the first attempt at an ARM mission will require heavy government support and oversight. NASA's engagement will be extensive and it will be expensive as it works to develop and integrate all of the technologies in a first mission together to meet the mission goals and increase the odds of success. It represents slightly less than 8% of total mission cost. But once the technology and knowledge are transferred to the private sector, NASA's oversight should become much less intensive or necessary. This line item can and should drop precipitously as NASA involvement shifts to more of a procurement function than a detailed development and oversight effort. It seems plausible that, as operations transition to the private sector and increase in scale, NASA's cost of oversight can drop by more than 95% to a cost of $10M per mission, and possibly much less.

Line 2. The line item called Phase A describes the preliminary analysis phase and the development of a project plan in order to demonstrate proof of concept. This phase details out the specifics of the mission including what is to be done, when, where, and how. It also includes specifications of what can be bought versus what needs to be built.[2] As the technology and experience for creating an ARM mission is transitioned over from NASA to private sector companies, this development cost should decline dramatically, if not zero out completely. Private sector firms will still engage in planning for each mission, but they will not be starting from scratch like the original mission. They will need nothing like the original Phase A budget. This cost should drop to a nominal sum. I've estimated $2m to be conservative, but truthfully this activity may drop below $1m or even zero.

Line 3. Spacecraft. The estimated cost of creating the first ARM mission is $1.4 billion, or 51.3% of total cost of the mission. Yet the study team suggests that development costs account for nearly $1bn of the total cost of the first spacecraft. The recurring cost of the spacecraft hardware itself is estimated in the original study as just $336M. In other words, after you build the first one, the incremental cost of the next one is just $336M, a fraction of the original cost. In the hands of the private sector and if there is a chance to develop multiple copies and move down the cost curve, one can assume that significant efficiencies can be achieved and this cost will drop from over $300m per unit to something much lower over time. It is not unreasonable to assume that an aggressive private sector provided with a standard package of technology will vie intensely to compete and deliver the unit cost of incremental ARM missions over time by a large percentage. It seems reasonable to assume a cost per unit eventually falling below $100M per unit, perhaps even less.

Line 4. Launch Vehicle. The cost of launching an ARM spacecraft on its way is currently very high, but we know from the previous chapter that the cost of launching cargo is dropping fast and that SpaceX is expected to bring it down further. From $288m today, SpaceX has already demonstrated that its Falcon Heavy can deliver a large cargo for a list price of $90M and possibly much less with volume.

Line 5. Mission Ops/GDS. Mission operations entails the monitoring of the spacecraft over the life of its mission outbound to the asteroid belt, through the capture process, and the return. A team of engineers will be heavily involved at each of these steps the first time out. However, when run by the private sector one can assume these costs become more optimized and automated. One can expect to do this at very low percentage of the cost estimated in the original ARM study, especially if operations are done at scale and the cost of fixed operational coverage can be shared or amortized over multiple missions and automation is put in place.

Line 6. 'Reserves' as a cost represents nearly a quarter of the full cost of the first ARM mission and is essentially a contingency estimate to provide a buffer in the event of cost overruns. This makes sense in the context of a path-breaking development effort to create or refine cutting edge new technology and put it together in a new way where surprises can easily arise in the development process. It is not a cost that makes sense in anything like this size when the technologies are more mature and if production runs are repeatedly building units in a competitive environment. It is also not a cost that NASA would budget for if it is purchasing resources at a fixed price. For a private sector firm, contingency can be greatly reduced by comparison to the original ARM mission.

None of the cost reductions explored and speculated about will happen instantly or over the life of the first few units, but if a long-term purchase arrangement is created and firms have a chance to compete and deliver, I would argue that the end-state is likely to reach a very low cost relatively fast.

There are other ways to optimize costs as well. For instance, it may be that we find asteroids closer to Earth which would greatly reduce the cost of capturing and returning them compared to the original baseline study assumptions. This point has been actively speculated on by the current NASA design team.

ARM 1..N

Below, I've extrapolated out some of the cost drivers into a set of scenarios describing how the incremental cost of future missions may change over time and how rapidly the cost of executing a mission and, therefore, the cost of materials delivered, can fall very fast.

Table 4.2: Potential Cost Evolution of Multiple ARM Missions

	Cost Profile 1	Cost Profile 2	Cost Profile 3	Cost Profile 4	Cost Profile 5
NASA Oversight	$204,000,000	$25,000,000	$5,000,000	$5,000,000	$5,000,000
Phase A	$68,000,000	$5,000,000	$2,000,000	$2,000,000	$2,000,000
Spacecraft	$1,359,000,000	$336,000,000	$275,000,000	$150,000,000	$25,000,000
Launch Vehicles	$288,000,000	$120,000,000	$80,000,000	$80,000,000	$50,000,000
Mission Ops/GDS	$117,000,000	$10,000,000	$5,000,000	$3,000,000	$2,000,000
Reserves	$611,000,000	$50,000,000	$10,000,000	$10,000,000	$10,000,000
Total Mission Cost	$2,647,000,000	$546,000,000	$377,000,000	$250,000,000	$94,000,000
$/lb	$2,406	$496	$343	$227	$85
$/kg	$5,294	$1,092	$754	$500	$188

These scenarios show a shift in costs over time and it is worth considering their assumptions and the underlying cost drivers. They are offered not as an expert estimate of exactly how this process will proceed, but as a directional view of what may be possible so that we might reasonably estimate what the value proposition of increasing scale in this sector could look like.

Scenario 1. This is the original baseline cost for the very first ARM mission. As has been noted, subsequent NASA analysis has suggested that the cost of this first mission can be reduced if a suitable asteroid can be found closer to Earth than the original team considered in their baseline study.

Scenario 2. This case is based on a transfer of the mission technologies created by ARM 1 to private sector companies that can deliver faster and more competitively on cost. In addition, this scenario assumes little or no additional technology development (new technologies are covered in the original ARM mission) and a significant drop in NASA overhead, mission operations, and contingency reserves. Further, Scenario 2 assumes a competitive decrease in launch costs as SpaceX and/or other launch firms bring down the cost of launches. In Scenario 2, the mission cost declines to $546M per ARM and the cost per pound of material delivered to L1 is estimated as falling below $500/lb.

Scenario 3. Scenario 3 assumes incremental cost reductions in all categories as the private sector accumulates experience and drives cost lower. This scenario assumes as many as 10 launches per year. In Scenario 3, the cost of each launch falls to $377 million per ARM and the material delivered to L1 is further reduced to below $350/lb.

Scenario 4. Scenario 4 assumes further cost decreases as more units are launched and the private sector continues to launch new ARM missions at a rate of 10 per year. The cost of each mission declines to $250 million and the material delivered to L1 is further reduced to around $225/lb.

Scenario 5. In the final scenario, a new mission assumption is considered. In this case, the population of ARM vehicles that have delivered material to L1 has reached over 100 and a significant number of them have arrived at L1. These vehicles should be designed for refueling and reuse. Scenario 5 assumes that launch costs drop further and that what is launched is not full-sized spacecraft, but fuel modules for refueling one or more ARM vehicles. This scenario assumes that ARMs are re-used and re-launched from L1 at a cost below $100 million. This serves to drive the cost of one pound of asteroid material delivered to L1 down to ~$85/lb.

These scenarios are illustrative at best. They may not reflect how low costs can actually go or how fast. What they do show is that if we consider operations at scale, the cost of contracting with the private sector to deliver large quantities of materials to L1 will likely witness a dramatic reduction in cost compared to a single ARM mission conceived and run centrally by NASA today.

A one-off is incredibly expensive. The first time you do anything, it is always the hardest and the most expensive. Get into a pattern, produce at scale, deliver dozens or hundreds of the same thing and this is what happens: The learning curve begins to deliver efficiencies and the marginal cost of each incremental unit drops rapidly and significantly. Think of the Liberty Ships and Flying Fortresses of World War II.

Conceptually, what I am proposing is not a single ARM mission, but a Near Earth Asteroid ARM Conveyor comprising dozens and eventually hundreds of vehicles capturing Near Earth Asteroids, de-spinning them, and returning them to a reserve location at L1 where they become the property of the American people. Given each mission takes 6-10 years to deliver its cargo, the initial impact of vehicles launched into space will seem small, but very rapidly a decade hence, a store of materials will begin to accumulate at a location that is very advantageous for any nation interested in doing something – anything – substantive in near Earth space. Fifteen to twenty years downstream, and with upwards of a hundred ARM tugs in continuous cycle operations, the reserve of material that accumulates at L1 begins to get very sizable indeed.

We'll explore what this program looks like in more detail.

The Proposal

An L1 Strategic Material Reserve would be a fund authorized by Congress to conduct open market fixed price purchases of asteroid material delivered to L1. In effect, this is a strategic purchasing agreement not unlike the National Petroleum Reserve. It is a program that would rely on the private sector to delivery specific cargo to a specific destination at a specified price. The materials purchased would become the exclusive property of the United States to administer, lease for exploitation, jointly develop, or sell into the market or bilaterally at its discretion.

The fund would be a multi-year framework agreement administered and supported by NASA (or other authorized entity). It would provide a guaranteed purchase price per unit of measure (pound or kilogram) that declines year over year based on the estimated cost it takes to deliver. In other words, NASA would be deeply involved in the program and in understanding the private sector's cost to launch missions and deliver material. It would set an aggressive schedule of declining prices, but one that realistically provides private sector entities with the chance to get a return on investment. We want to catalyze and build an industry, not hamstring it at the start.

The cost of the materials acquired via the program would be in the range of $50 billion over a 30-year period. There may be additional costs to develop and expand the technologies and NASA should have access to the funding necessary to aggressively work with its partners to develop technologies that can further cut the costs of missions. For instances, rapidly increasing the power of the Solar Electric Propulsion modules might allow the ARM missions to capture and return larger cargoes at a cheaper price point, so it is in our interest to support both private sector innovations as well as rapidly develop advanced technology that can be disseminated to our private sector partners to make them more effective. In addition, there are additional costs associated with a more aggressive survey and mapping effort among the asteroid belt to identify suitable targets for acquisition. These additional costs should be considered in an overall program.

The program should be designed to purchase materials from companies based in the US or that are US incorporated. This should not rule out working with joint ventures or the local affiliates of our EU and Asian allies. However, it seems less prudent to purchase from firms representing countries that are emerging rivals or those that steal our technologies. We should support our friends, not our rivals.

The intent of the program is to catalyze larger investment, innovation, and engagement within our private sector by providing targeted support to limit or share development costs and reduce investment and launch costs. Because of the substantial risk involved, support of the private sector could take additional supportive forms such as providing joint technology development, shared risk (insurance subsidies), and joint ventures.

Once materials are delivered to L1, they become the property of the USG and the American people. They are available to hold, sell, or develop as priorities evolve. The most likely and interesting outcome is that NASA, or suitably chartered public body, is authorized to jointly develop and process materials with investing companies using gain-share agreements both for the delivery company, the processing company (should they be different), and the US Government with initial payback heavily weighted to USG purchase cost recovery before investor payout.

As noted earlier, the goal of the program is to create a NEA ARM Conveyor Belt. A key set of design principals should include modularity, reusability, and networkability. Each ARM Mission launched by one of our private sector contractors should be designed to be reusable once refueled and the cost of doing this should get lower over time. The program should witness the creation of a fleet of robotic asteroid tugs that can work steadily to retrieve and return Near Earth Asteroids.

As the fleet grows and matures, it may be feasible to use multiple tugs in concert to grab much larger asteroid targets.

Benefits

There are several advantages of a program to accumulate asteroid material at L1 and the concept of implementing a Near Earth Asteroid ARM Conveyor at scale.

Payback. The first is Return on Investment (or ROI), the idea of payback. It is very possible that a full-fledged ARM program operating at scale will be capable, over an extended period of time, of collecting and either processing or selling asteroid material for a price that is equal to or of greater value than the cost of the programmatic effort to capture it.

Consider that mere possibility for just one second. Space exploration is always a cost. You land. You plant the flag. Collect some samples. Return. It's inspiring and you may get some science out of it. But when it's done, it is always an entry on the expense side of the ledger without any offsetting revenue. It is a closed ended outcome unless you are then moving onto ever more distant and expensive missions.

A NEA ARM conveyor program, by contrast, offers the potential to achieve revenue. That revenue either defers some of the cost, represents the potential for full program recovery, or even, just possibly, a net profit or return on investment for the taxpayer. Very few other public services can make that claim and so unlike any other space program, an NEA ARM Conveyor cracks open the door to a value proposition that Americans may be willing to support with significantly greater funding.

Leverage. The other intriguing possibility with regards to a NEA ARM Conveyor program is the potential for funding leverage. If an L1 Strategic Material Reserve is structured to make full or final payment on delivery and receipt of materials, there is a possibility that such a program may need less federal funding up front. By this I mean if a viable guarantee can be crafted and faith in that promise is high enough, it may be possible for the private sector to invest significant funds in launching missions. After all, the private sector invested $1 billion in Webvan. They are willing to invest substantial sums and take on a level of risk if there is a strong belief in gaining a return on investment and a market with some certainty exists. Nor does the investing sector mean just venture capital which seeks high rates of return. The world is awash in cash to invest in bond-grade relatively low return investments if the risk is commensurately low and guarantees are in place.

All this means that future asteroid mining companies may not have to rely on Kickstarter, t-shirts, and selfies to raise modest sums. They might actually be able to go directly to the financial markets and raise significant resources. If it's a choice between selling a t-shirt or a bond, a bond may be a better path if you need to raise big money.

Investors will need some assurance or guarantee of payment and the likely upfront cost will be too high at the start for specific firms launching ARM missions without such guarantees. It will require some forms of federal partnering and risk mitigation insurance or other forms of subsidies to nurture and support a fledgling industry and set of companies that wish to launch NEA ARM missions, but will face significant investor loss if they go awry. But what is true is that the full cost of the program may not necessarily have to be funded up front by the taxpayer. Funding will need to steadily pay out some level of expense, but the full outlay may be deferred until delivery.

Leverage is possible if we show will and intent and provide some level of market certainty and sizing.

Asset. The potential of asteroid retrieval at scale to create an asset for the future cannot be understated. The accumulation of material at L1 that can be processed for water, fuel, metal, and leftover slag rock creates the building blocks for something much bigger and more important.

It creates a target for innovation and investment. With resources suddenly within reach, both public and private sector actors will find ways to exploit these resources. This program creates a center of gravity with a powerful catalytic effect that will drive innovation to make use of the materials at hand.

If we cannot fully conceptualize how it will be used 20-30 years from now or how we can afford it, that is of less import than the fact that we have accumulated it and created a pathway for innovation to focus on. Even today, we are accumulating significant breakthroughs in the cost of access to space. What is almost certainly true is that there will be even better technologies available 20 years from now and the cost of everything from getting into space to operating there will almost certainly have declined further. As these breakthroughs occur, an L1 Strategic Materials reserve will offer a chance to work with a ready source of raw material that can be used, processed, and formed into a viable industry in space.

At home, this will translate into new jobs and new companies many of which may not be around or even imagined yet. There is an economic case for an L1 Strategic Materials Reserve and it is to that we turn next.

The Economic Case for an L1 Strategic Materials Reserve

No nation today has access to any significant material in space and the cost of doing anything on the space frontier, whether that is sending a mission to explore another planet or building and manning a space station, is extraordinarily expensive when it is entirely comprised of materials lifted from the surface of our planet. Under these conditions, it is, as we have seen, simply far too expensive to consider any real substantive effort on the space frontier. We are stuck with the Nixon challenge of competing with important national priorities and limited funding.

Cost is at the heart of the challenge of getting to scale in space, so it is worth considering the economic case of an L1 Strategic Materials Reserve, which has been alluded to but not fully detailed out.

A simple model building out scenarios over a 30-year time frame using the scenarios outlined earlier illustrates what is possible in aggregate terms.

In my model, I assume after Scenario 1 (Baseline) that we launch four additional launches over the next two years at an annual cost of slightly more than $1 billion per year. In years 4-6, we scale to 10 launches per year at a cost per mission of

$377 million. In years 7-15, we launch 10 per year at a cost of $250M per launch and an annual cost of $2.5 bn. From year 16-30, we move to re-usability and begin cycling the ARM tugs into continuous operation based on refueling at L1, at a substantial cost reduction.

This is a simple model. A true rocket scientist or reasonably competent economist could do a much better job of modeling out a better set of assumptions with detailed cost scenarios and assumptions. But as an illustrative model for directional purposes it is worth considering how this program shapes up in economic terms.

In Table 3 below, the average expenditure per year for the life of the program is less than $2 billion, although it peaks closer to $4 billion before declining to below $1bn per year after year 15. The total program cost at a declining, fixed price/lb. rate is estimated to total out at $51bn. But this would results in the accumulation of nearly 300 million pounds of asteroid material, or just shy of 150,000 tons.

The cost of lifting this much material today in rough order terms based on using a Falcon Heavy at current list prices and assuming a discount on the cost of going to Mars (let's say 2,000/lb) would cost nearly $600 billion dollars. This is just a rough order estimate. The point is that it is very expensive.

But the more important consideration is what this material is worth.

Table 4.3: Potential Cost Profiles of ARM Missions over Time

Arrival Year	Year 1	Year 2-3	Year 4-6	Year 7-15	Year 16-20	Year 21-30
Cost/Mission	$2,647,000,000	$546,000,000	$377,000,000	$250,000,000	$94,000,000	$94,000,000
Mission Price/lb	$2,406	$496	$343	$227	$85	$85
Pounds/mission (500k avg)	1,100,000	1,100,000	1,100,000	1,100,000	1,100,000	1,100,000
Annual Missions	1	3	10	10	10	10
Annual Cost	$2,647,000,000	$1,638,000,000	$3,770,000,000	$2,500,000,000	$940,000,000	$9,400,000,000
Reserve Cost (cum)	$2,647,000,000	$4,831,000,000	$14,633,000,000	$37,133,000,000	$41,833,000,000	$51,233,000,000
Reserve Total (lb)	1,100,000	5,500,000	34,100,000	133,100,000	188,100,000	298,100,000
Reserve Total (Tons)	550	2,750	17,050	66,550	94,050	149,050
Cost to lift (L1)	$550,000,000	$2,750,000,000	$17,050,000,000	$66,550,000,000	$94,050,000,000	$149,050,000,000
Net value (Notional)	-$2,097,000,000	-$2,081,000,000	$2,417,000,000	$29,417,000,000	$52,217,000,000	$97,817,000,000

If you assume the economic value of a lb. of the basest material at L1 is equivalent to the cost of lifting a pound of equivalent material from the Earth's surface to L1, then the cost of lifting that today is, as noted earlier, in the range of

$40-50,000/lb. But a more aggressive calculation would assume that the cost of launching will decrease dramatically over the next 20-30 years. Let's assume that cost declines dramatically to as little as $500 to launch one pound of material from the surface all the way to Earth-Moon Lagrange 1, within the near vicinity of the Moon.

Assuming such an aggressive cost reduction occurs, the final cost to accumulate the entire reserve is $51 billion, but the cost to lift an equivalent amount of volume at that $500/lb price in the most optimistic scenario is much higher, at nearly $150 billion. In my rough model, the cost of launching upwards of 120 launchers over a 20 period of time and then moving to significant re-use for a further 10 years delivers a large storehouse of reserves at L1 at a value this is much higher than the expected cost of lifting the same amount of material from the Earth's surface. And without a dramatic and optimistic reduction in launch costs, the value of this reserve increases dramatically.

The economic value of this material can be recovered in multiple ways: By processing it and extracting some value for local use and/or returning some of the material to earth if it is rare or precious; selling it to other countries that have a plan for getting to scale in space; or selling it to the private sector to process or use; or by using it in pursuit of projects that could not be otherwise considered.

The key point is this. There is a potential that an L1 Strategic Materials Reserve can create a large storehouse of materials that has an economic value and that represents an asset for future generations in terms of economic growth, new industries and jobs at home.

Issues & Answers

There are several obvious questions about the viability and practicality of an L1 Strategic Materials Reserve and we'll explore a few of them.

1. *As a signatory to the Outer Space Treaty of 1967[3] which prohibits "national appropriation" of celestial bodies "by claim of sovereignty, by means of use or occupation, or by any other means" which is broadly interpreted to limit legal ownership or claims to ownership of space resources, can the United States even consider funding an L1 Strategic Materials Reserve that implies taking ownership of resources in space?*

There have been some arguments made that the Outer Space Treaty of 1967 was a terrible treaty that has limited the economic development of space by restricting incentives in the form of the property rights needed to mobilize private sector resources and entrepreneurial energy in space.

This is absurd.

The extraordinary expense of launching material (or people) into space, much less doing so at scale, is and remains the single, over-riding reason why we have not seized the high frontier. There is no other reason that is material.

The Outer Space Treaty is not the bogeyman prohibiting us from the economic development of the high frontier. It is a reasonable treaty crafted at the close of the decolonization period in which stronger states had a record of seizing by national appropriation large swaths of (inhabited) lands based on the fashion of the day. It prohibits doing so in space. It also prohibits the militarization of space including deploying weapons of mass destruction, a significant concern in the midst of what was then a Cold War arms race and nuclear brinkmanship. It codifies the concept of equal access, of space as a common resource for humanity, and of treating astronauts fairly even if they land in someone else's national space. The Outer Space Treaty contains some high-minded ideals and valuable principles and it may well have headed off some bad outcomes and significant risks in the 60s and 70s.

That said, there are valid questions about the role of the Outer Space Treaty in terms of the establishment of an L1 Strategic Material Reserve at the scale that I have proposed. Does not the Outer Space Treaty preclude such an initiative? I don't think it does and I believe the Treaty provides three viable strategies for addressing such questions. Lawyers will argue the merits of these – that is what they get paid and incented to do – but common sense can also be a guide.

First, Article II prohibits 'national appropriation' of celestial bodies or claiming sovereignty of swaths of space. This is true. I think they meant planting a flag on the Moon and claiming the entire body of it as the exclusive property of one country. Others interpret this more expansively and believe that any claim of ownership is not valid. The interpretation and legal basis have not been fully tested in the context of asteroid mining. Article VIII, however, suggests that the ownership of any objects launched into space "including objects landed or constructed on a celestial body, and of their component parts, is not affected by their presence in outer space or on a celestial body or by their return to the Earth." Ownership in such cases remains that of the sovereign state or firm that launched the vehicle in the first place.

I would argue that an asteroid or asteroid material once captured, de-spun and returned to L1 is no longer a celestial body, but a component of the ARM vehicle and subject to Article VIII. Further, once material from the ARM mission is processed into components and incorporated into any kind of structure or used by any such structure, vehicle, or mission, then it may be argued that their ownership is the same as on Earth and belongs to the nation state or private entity that has created them. Many will argue that this interpretation is wrong and legal action might well be threatened or filed. But there is a process to arbitrate said claims and it may well be worth exploring this interpretation and testing the legal process.

But if that does not hold, then a second step is available.

Article XV allows any state or signatory to propose amendments to the treaty. Amendments come into force when a majority of signatories accept them. There is no reason that we cannot engage in a diplomatic process to amend the treaty with provisions that allow for full economic development of the space frontier. It is in the interest of humanity to expand into space.

What is also true is that any such process will inevitably have to balance the interests of all parties. There are some people that can't imagine a negotiation like this working, yet, we have proven time and again in recent history that the international community is well capable of managing complex multi-lateral negotiations and agreements and arriving at a reasonably satisfying conclusion for a majority of parties, even despite a contentious and prolonged process. There is no reason to expect anything different from a process to amend the Outer Space Treaty. Simply put, we have diplomats who know how to do this and we are capable of acting in a professional manner to achieve much of what we want by finding common ground with the larger international community. Our default course of action should be to try.

The larger community of signatories to the Treaty may, of course, expect some form of economic sharing of the benefits gained from economic development, especially if the vast majority of states that are signatories to the treaty are not economically capable of direct participation. I believe this would be a valuable discussion to have. Some form of gain-share, one that recognizes and prioritizes the substantial up front cost and needs for payback (and profit) of the initiating parties, but that also seeks to create some common benefit from what are otherwise un-utilized assets in space can easily be imagined. I believe that the international community is capable of finding common ground and amending the Outer Space Treaty in a way that preserves the incentives needed for economic development while sharing some of the benefits with all of humanity, which is consistent with the original spirit of the treaty in the first place.

Finally, if all else fails, Article XVI allows any signatory of the treaty to withdraw from the Treaty with one year's notice. There are significant benefits to the treaty and no one should consider withdrawing from it lightly. But some parties have suggested that it is the force of the treaty itself that has precluded bad behaviors such as introducing WMD or militarizing space and that the threat of such consequences would make withdrawing from the Treaty difficult if not impossible to consider. I believe this is an over-reach of the value and weight of the Treaty. Of any treaty, in fact. One need look no further than the weight that existing international law has had on the annexation of Crimea in 2014 or invasion of Ukraine in 2022 by the Russian Republic led by Vladimir Putin, the behavior of China in the South China Seas which has been judged illegal by the World Court, or the reckless testing of anti-missile technology in space leading to the widespread hazard of debris in orbit for all (a test conducted by a signatory nation). Vladimir Putin has threatened to put a nuclear weapon in space regardless of the Outer Space Treaty. These example highlight a simple fact. International agreements only work as long as all parties are committed to their success (both in spirit and law) and feel that there is a mutual benefit worthy of adhering to said principles or legal agreements. Events show time and again that this is not always the case and that states with relatively greater power at any point in time are well capable of acting in their own perceived self-interest regardless of international law, treaties, or convention.

Withdrawing from the Outer Space Treaty will not *ipso facto* immediately condone, encourage, or result in such actions as introducing WMD into outer space. Likewise, we should be honest about the force of the Treaty in preventing similar bad behavior in the future. Simply put, staying in the Treaty does not necessarily mean that these actions will not be taken by a Signatory party *anyway* if that party is not fully committed to the principals of international law and which sees a material advantage in violating the related Articles.

If we have concerns that the Outer Space Treaty limits our ability to develop the high frontier, we should begin the long-term dialogue of finding a solution that is palatable to a majority of the signatories to the Treaty. My personal thought is that an Amendment that creates a mechanism for eventually sharing the wealth of space with all nations while respecting the need of pioneering nations and entities to gain an appropriate payback commensurate with their risk is a good and likely outcome. The alternative of withdrawal after all would mean that the vast majority would get nothing. In principle, something is better than nothing (a point most rationale parties will note) and so I would advocate we begin the hard work of diplomacy early in order to avoid the outcome of withdrawal that is much less desirable for the vast majority of the international community.

2. *What about the recent U.S. law recognizing an asteroid mining company's right to own what they mine? This law is the U.S. Space Launch Competitiveness Act (H.R. 2262)[4].*

On November 25, 2015, President Obama signed H.R. 2262, the U.S. Commercial Space Launch Competitiveness Act, a law that included Section 401, the Space Resource Exploration and Utilization Act of 2015. This law has been described as the 'finders, keepers' law.

This act promoted the right of US citizens to engage in commercial exploration and recovery of space resources in accordance with international obligations. The law specifically says that United States citizens are entitled "to any asteroid resource or space resource obtained, including to possess, own, transport, use, and sell the asteroid resource or space resource obtained in accordance with applicable law, including the international obligations of the United States." (Section 51303)

The bill went on to say that the United States does not "assert sovereignty or sovereign or exclusive rights or jurisdiction over, or the ownership of, any celestial body."

The bill attempts to both secure the right of US citizens and companies to have property rights over asteroid or space resources that they explore, obtain, and mine as well as suggest that these rights are consistent with the international laws that the United States as signed up for, e.g. the Outer Space Treaty.

In effect, this act attempts to put on a legal footing the position stated earlier, that the Outer Space Treaty does not truly inhibit US companies from engaging in commercial operations and owning the asteroids or space resources they obtain and use. The bill puts that position on a more formal footing. It is an important step forward.

However, there is no guarantee that other signatory countries will agree with this position and there may still need to be significant work to address and potentially amend the international treaty to provide additional certainty for future asteroid and space resource commercial operations.

Further, this law does not fully address the ability or right of the United States government to own or procure asteroid or space materials either directly or by purchase from private companies.

The law is a step forward and squarely states U.S. interests, but it is not necessarily a full answer or one that is yet completely accepted by the international community. We are still likely to need to go through a diplomatic process to resolve any concerns with our international agreements and responsibilities, such as the Outer Space Treaty.

3. *How does the previous Trump Administration's and current Biden Administration's Artemis Accords fit into the picture of using resources in space?*

The Artemis Accords were publicly proposed in May 2020, by the Trump Administration ostensibly to update and clarify the Outer Space Treaty. The Accords have multiple clauses, but the most controversial is the one covering extraction and utilization of resources in space (e.g. mining) from the moon, asteroids, etc.

The Accords essentially defines the extraction and use of resources in outer space as consistent with the intent of the Outer Space Treaty and states that mining and recovery do not constitute national appropriation as defined by the Outer Space Treaty. It allows signatories to mine, extract, and use resources as desired as long as these resources are used for safe and sustainable space activities. It allows contracts and legal agreements for space resource extraction and utilization to be interpreted as fully consistent with the Outer Space Treaty.

Rather than go through the full UN negotiation process, the Artemis Accords are being negotiated as a series of bilateral agreements. As of November 2020, countries that have signed on to the Accords include: the U.S., Australia, Canada, Japan, Luxembourg, Italy, the United Kingdom, and the United Arab Emirates. NASA has made signing the Artemis Accords a precondition for participating in future NASA-led Lunar missions.

The Artemis Accords have been criticized globally as highly favoring the United States. Russia has objected to the Accords as one-sided agreement that promotes U.S. interests. The bilateral approach lacks diplomacy and tact. It is true that this new agreement attempts to represent U.S. interests on top of the Outer Space Treaty. The document is barely seven pages long and you can read it yourself.

My interpretation is that some form of similar agreement to recognize and allow for extracting and using resources in space without resorting to a cumbersome international body or process of oversight is both necessary and desirable. The primary objections are less the substance than the form of how it is being pushed that are the most objectionable to the larger international community. The biggest fear is that the U.S. currently leads in many of the technologies and is the likeliest to benefit while other nations may be left out.

For Americans, we should recognize the valid concerns of other nations and attempt any reasonable means of addressing those concerns. We should also apply what I think of as the 'Other Foot' test. We should also ask ourselves how we would feel if China were in the lead, got to the moon first, and/or implemented similar accords in a bilateral fashion that excluded us. If we would feel concern or anxiety about that, then we should recognize the concerns of others about our own approach.

These Accords are relatively new and they bear watching over the next few years to see how they, or a similar framework, are developed and matured. [5, 6]

4. *Doesn't the program misstate the true cost because raw asteroid material delivered at L1 is 'useless' until it is transformed or processed into material that can be used such as water, fuel, or metals and these activities will cost a lot of money?*

The answer to this question is both 'Yes' and 'No'.

Clearly activities to process and transform asteroid material into useful substances such as water, fuel, metals, and shielding material will require future investments, rocket launches, and cost. Nor will it be cheap.

But until such materials exist, the investments are purely speculative. There is no way to estimate what is possible until there is a true focal point of activity in near Earth space and we have a chance to begin planning and experimenting with the material at hand.

It may also be that these operations are much cheaper than we think. For instance, small, autonomous robotic missions can begin initial processing at very low cost relatively speaking. This is the business model for the private initiatives already on the market. The difference is that they would be operating much closer, much cheaper, and the market would be that much more likely to be able to afford the development costs.

The role of the private sector in this process is crucial. Competition among firms will drive innovation up and costs down. If these firms can compete for contracts and revenue, they will create rapid progress that will propel the program forward.

Finally, what is also true is that the cost of launching any material from Earth to L1 is extraordinarily high. And yet, we need material for a variety of purposes including shielding against radiation. Therefore, even unprocessed materials or left over materials, or slag, that have been fully processed of any useful material are still almost literally worth their weight in gold by virtue of the great expense of lifting comparable material off the surface of the Earth.

So, will it cost more to process the materials we accumulate? Yes, of course, but the economic value of these resources may well be much greater than the cost of any viable alternative and technology breakthroughs on the horizon may well significantly reduce the cost of working with them. At this time, we only know it will be an incremental cost to make use of this material, we cannot reliably project how big or small that cost is.

5. *How can we afford this in a time of austerity? Shouldn't we defer this until times are better?*

Many will fall prey to such sentiments, but I would propose two simple counter arguments.

First, times will always be interesting and we will always have competing challenges and priorities for time, resources, and funding. They will come in the form of wars, crises, or just the long-term battle of differing ideologies over the role of government. Future governments, like our own, will always face the challenge of balancing social programs, defense, saving the environment, educating our kids, caring for our sick, injured, and poor, enforcing our laws, and doing so within the proper balance between the role of government and the role of its citizens, a point that has been continually under ideological pressure and struggle since the dawn of the Republic.

There will never be a convenient time when we are flush with cash and there is consensus on spending it in space.

The second point is that the role of political leadership is not only to balance all of the competing priorities for time and resources, but also, very occasionally, to transcend them in the interest of inspiring or catalyzing something greater than short-term considerations. In the 1980s, Reagan jump-started the economy by reducing the role of government and the amount of taxes paid, making it possible, along with an explosion in consumer credit, to create higher levels of spending and a trajectory of economic growth that lifted us out of recession at the time. This change in direction was made feasible by a previous era in which taxes had been high, investments in everything from education to infrastructure had been made and our capital stock as a nation was very mature. The challenge today is to create new markets, new industries, and new jobs. Our nation is capable of jumpstarting a great race onto the high frontier, one that will bring the tangible benefits of jobs today and for future generations. We have plucked the low hanging fruit of economic development. It is time to build taller ladders.

The worst-case scenario is that once we collect the material at L1, we cannot find an economically viable path to processing it and utilizing it. In that case, we would just hold onto it as a true reserve, banked for future generations. It will remain an asset and at some point, a more sophisticated and technologically advanced society will be able to use them. Hopefully this will be an American one.

The final rationale, the bottom line, is that this program creates an asset with a future value. It will create a profit and – at the same time – catalyze an industry.

6. *Wouldn't robotic missions to return processed materials be a better approach than attempting to retrieve entire asteroids?*

For the near term (by which I mean the next 30-50 years) any significant activity done by humans in space will require materials in a variety of forms, whether processed or even unprocessed. Therefore, we need to accumulate as much material as possible in the lowest cost and most efficient way. This argues heavily for asteroid retrieval vs. processing farther away. Even if it is worthless left-over slag, effectively gravel, it can still be used for shielding on any future manned outpost in space.

And so, every single pound of material will have a use and a value – the minimum of which is the cost of bringing it from the surface of the earth.

For the immediate future, it actually makes much greater sense to capture and return raw material to L1 instead of trying to process it remotely. This supposition does not preclude building a better mousetrap to process materials at point of capture, but it simply suggests that this is not the most cost-effective or practical approach at this time (based on what I believe to be true at this point in time).

7. Isn't this a waste of taxpayers' money in collecting asteroids that have no use today?

No. It is not a waste. By retrieving and repositioning asteroids at L1 where they can be collected and processed and useful materials made from them, we have created an asset, even in unprocessed form. An asset cannot be considered a waste. As an asset, the value may only be realized in the future, but it will almost certainly be realized.

Conclusion

Achieving scale and sustainability on any frontier requires living off the land. Yet when it comes to space, the very stuff of life, the materials needed to survive and thrive are not conveniently placed. In fact, they are extraordinarily expensive to lift from the surface of the planet to a location where they are useful in space.

The establishment of an L1 Strategic Material Reserve and the creation of a fleet of space tugs to capture and retrieve asteroids and return them *en masse* would begin to solve this problem. A program to establish an L1 Strategic Material Reserve would result in a massive storehouse of materials that have a strategic value above and beyond their more simple nature.

Long-term it may make sense to return only processed materials. Short-term there is no doubt that accumulating a storehouse of materials at L1 conveys a strategic opportunity and creates a catalytic effect on what is possible in space.

As a game changer paired with decreasing launch costs and increased heavy lift launch capability, it is possible to change the game of what is possible. Technically this is feasible. The engineering is being worked out. The economics look interesting. The politics, however, is not aligned. There are reasons for this, but the big picture is that there is no strategic rationale, no guiding vision, that has been articulated for why we should do this, why anyone should actually bother.

It is time to change that. It is time to stop dreaming small and squandering a bigger more prosperous future. What we should do and why is the subject of the next chapter.

Chapter 5: New Frontier Future

America needs a new vision for space and for the future. The failure of human spaceflight to gain scale and sally forth over the last 50+ years is because space exploration is too expensive to fund given what you get in return (a few footsteps in the dust of other worlds and bragging rights about who got there first) and the public is not willing to foot the bill. This problem will not be bridged by aspirational goals, enduring questions of the human spirit, or calls to rally the public from politicians eager for a bounce in the polls or to rhetorically harness a new Sputnik moment. Nor will it be fully resolved even if the private sector makes a breakthrough in launch costs.

Despite what commission after commission concludes, the answer is not about matching ends to means. The answer is to change the ends – and thereby to change the means. The end goal must be a vision that achieves scale. Without scale, volume is low and costs are high. But scale is not possible without a direct payback or return that delivers tangible benefits on Earth.

Space exploration is an inherently small-scale business involving a few elite astronauts flitting about the solar system, planting flags on other worlds. It is not a business of scale. Therefore, such a program doesn't allow you to travel down the cost curve. If we truly want to 'advance humanity into space', we need a vision for America's future in space that solves this conundrum.

A valid strategic vision must be one that the public believes is worth investing substantial sums into and for which there is a viable and tangible reward that the public values above the cost. Engage the public with the right vision, strategy, and plan and it is possible that a large majority will vote to support a program at scale and, in due course, the politics and funding will follow.

True scale is a budget for NASA on the order of $200-$250 billion per year, upwards of 10x what NASA funding looks like today. This is in the range of 4-5% of the federal budget in any normal year. This is an enormous sum by any measure and will be met with justifiable skepticism. My yet untested thesis is that we are capable of committing large resources if a program can meet foundational tests in engaging the public imagination.

Those foundational criteria are:

- It must embody the American Dream. That dream is not dead, but it has become a distant hope for too many. It is a simple proposition that binds us together: The hope of a better life for our families and a better future for our children;
- It must draw a direct line to pocketbook issues and concerns, namely economic growth, jobs, and wages and offer a viable path to creating a stronger economy for all Americans;
- It must resonate with our history of frontier expansion yet do so without the negative consequences and aggression of that same history. From the Louisiana Purchase to the Homestead Act, America has a frontier narrative and the cultural yearning for space today, right now, has less to do with inspiration, human destiny, jingoism, past sins, or quasi-religious expression than with the historical affinity Americans (regardless of where they come from) have always had for the wide-open spaces and the potential for a better life. The courage to cross the open seas is a virtue and the frontier is, quite literally, in our DNA;
- It must extend beyond the elite. The Frontier cannot be about tourism for a wealthy few, a means to greatly enrich the 1%, or limited to exploration by a tiny cadre of highly trained and exclusively selected astronauts. It must be about the common

person getting a chance to grab a new opportunity as a pioneer. A viable vision for scale in space must articulate a roadmap in which there is a potential for a large number of Americans of all stripes and means to participate;

- It must pass the test of stewardship by being fiscally responsible and offer not just a pathway to payback but a return on the investment of public funds that is large enough in scale to help us resolve some of the long-term financial challenges our nation faces, even if said payback takes time to materialize and largely benefits a future generation; and, finally,
- It must qualify as a top priority for the public in a long list of urgent and contentious issues. We must be able to explain to voters how and why the space program is a true national priority and our explanation must resonate strongly enough to fire up their imagination. Here's a sniff test it must pass: We must be able to explain why funding a larger program in space is more important than an urgent, immediate, and emotionally compelling earthly priority (ex. Lower tuition) if the choice must be one or the other.

Aspirational and practical. Fiscally responsible, yet expensive. A true strategic vision worthy of a great nation must thread a series of seeming contradictions and it must be large enough in scope to meet the test of a 'great' nation. *Great nations do great things.*

Context

Strategy requires a context and to set a context, we'll draw on an historical metaphor of America as a frontier. We'll start by going back to those first early American colonists, the challenges they went through and the advantages they had for a comparison to a frontier in space.

Most grade-schoolers are well versed in early American history. The simple, sanitized version goes like this: Columbus discovered the New World in 1492 thinking he had found a short cut to Asia. In the following years, there were a series of expeditions to map out the new continent by the European powers of the time. The first English colonies in America were established in the early 1600s, starting with Jamestown in 1607. The Pilgrims landed at Plymouth Rock in 1620. Others followed.

Getting there was not easy. People had to brave the North Atlantic in creaky wooden sailing ships for weeks on end depending on the season, the state of the winds, and the quality of the ship. But the winds that propelled these ships were free and the wooden ships people sailed on, while state of the art for their day, were built and operated with relatively basic materials and easily obtainable resources. They were reusable for multiple voyages. The expense of the journey was still very high and the early Pilgrims had to get the latter-day equivalent of a corporate sponsor and effectively indenture themselves for seven years of hard work in return for freedom in a new land.

Once they arrived, the world in which they had landed had free air to breath, free water to drink, land for crops, timber and resources within reach, and the nearby seas were teaming with fish. From a handful of settlements at the start of the 1600s, the American colonies grew rapidly to slightly more than two million people by the time of the American Revolution, roughly 150 years later, and to over 315+ million today some 230 years after that.

(We'll also note, here, that this sanitized version does not attempt to account for the severe negative impacts on the existing indigenous populations from this foundational story of the American colonies and their growth into a nation. This history was tragic and brutal, but it is not the key point for this discussion.)

The space environment is different. Getting there is enormously expensive. Only governments and the very wealthy can afford it and then only as far as LEO which is basically like hugging the shallow bays and shores of the Old World, a modest and rather timid level of adventure.

Assuming you can get into space, you have to build your own destination and bring your own everything (BYOE) including air, water, food, and any material you build with. Step outside your door without the right suit and tools and you die instantly in the vacuum of space.

The economics of working in space are so forbidding that we are forever trying to emulate the early glory days of sending a few astronauts on a short trip back to the moon or onwards to Mars or other destinations. There are, of course, a few entrepreneurs who dream of colonies on Mars or hotels in space, but these are not mainstream visions and they lack significant funding.

Small-scale space travel (e.g. exploration) is enormously expensive, achieves only fleeting, unsustainable glories, and is thus not able to gain significant support as a result. It's always a cost competing against more urgent, earthly priorities. Against this challenge, the most recent panel of experts admitted that there is no good single rationale for a program of exploration and they ultimately fall back on what every other recent panel has as well: human inspiration in the form of inspiring moments and enduring questions.

For the record, it is my belief that their logic is flawed and their conclusions are wrong. It hasn't worked for the last 50 years. It won't for the next 50 either. It's time to consider something different.

New Frontier Future

As an alternative to space exploration as a governing vision for America's space program, I would propose a strategic doctrine of a New Frontier Future in Near-Earth Space as an alternative to human exploration and high-minded aspiration.

I define a New Frontier Future as the creation of a set of basic capabilities in space where human operations in the Near-Earth space environment are economically self-

127

sustaining and, eventually, profitable. Near Earth Space is the immediate vicinity of space extending out to the Moon's orbit and associated Lagrange points, an area the space community refers to as CISLunar space. Achieving a New Frontier Future in this region means reducing the cost of living and working in this space by 99.9% or more.

New Frontier Future as a strategic rationale is about building a destination on the frontier, a fortress on the plains of space, if you will, and providing it with the raw materials of life that we take for granted on Earth all at an economically sustainable price.

The key capabilities of a New Frontier Future are:

- In-Space Production of air and water;
- In-Space Production of fuel;
- In-Space Capability to process raw materials into metals;
- In-Space Capability to machine and fabricate metals;
- In-Space Ability to build structures;
- In-Space Capability to produce food;
- In-Space Capability to produce energy; and, finally, the
- In-Space Capability to produce something of economic use to earth with which to trade.

This is not new. These are not original thoughts. Many more credentialed members of the space community have speculated about these capabilities or made the case for their expansion and seizing a new frontier in space. There are existing organizations dedicated to achieving these ends (ex. National Space Society, Space Frontier Foundation, New Worlds, etc.) and people both in and outside of NASA, industry, and academia that advocate similar points of view. This is not a dazzling, breakthrough insight on my part.

Jeff Bezos regularly talks about millions of people working and living in space with most heavy industry done there. He suggests a future in which Earth might be rezoned for residential and light industry only. I've been in a friendly, space-oriented audience where this has been said and yet it was still treated like a (polite) laugh line. No one believes it is possible.

These organizations and advocates (wealthy or otherwise) are pitching policies and programs that do not make the case to the public for going big and therefore they are likely to achieve very little. What they have not done to my knowledge is articulate a governing vision, strategic rationale, and a political value proposition for getting to scale in space and that vision has not become mainstream policy nor been effectively introduced, much less sold to the public.

But the time has come to start immediately.

Two things have changed to that make it urgent to start this journey.

The tools for lifting large quantities of material into space at a greatly reduced price per kilogram are already at hand. The private sector led by Elon Musk and SpaceX has brought the price of launching cargo to LEO down dramatically, already a 95% reduction with room to reduce further in the near future. Blue Origin is expected to add to this capability in the next several years.

What has also changed is the potential for asteroid retrieval and the ability to bring large quantities of raw material from far away locations to a stable point within the near-earth environment where we can extract usable materials including water, fuel, and metals. The 2012 Keck study for Asteroid Retrieval is a seminal work. Yet, we have stood by and allowed a newborn industry to wither away and die for lack of vision and funding.

In contrast, I have proposed more than a single science mission to study an asteroid and retrieve two ounces of dust and gravel. I have proposed an L1 Strategic Materials Reserve served by an extensible, scalable, and reusable Near-Earth Asteroid ARM conveyor system that delivers an growing quantity of usable material at an appropriate point in near earth space (L1 here as a convenient literary device, but scientists and engineers can determine the actual location). This Near-

Earth ARM conveyor is intended to deliver ever larger quantities of materials at progressively lower cost that can then be mined and processed into the outputs that are the key ingredients in establishing a presence in space that becomes increasingly self-sustaining. A growing reserve of material in near Earth Space will represent a tangible manifestation of the Frontier to all Americans. Along with a dramatic decrease in launch costs, an L1 Strategic Materials Reserve is a second driver of a New Frontier Future.

This is the crucial point.

A governing vision for a New Frontier Future offers a value proposition that can be explained and measured. Can we get an eventual economic ROI out of government led and commissioned activities? That such an ROI will be heavily negative in the early years of such an effort goes without question. But if resources can be mined and processed, there is the potential for rapid cost reduction. And if any high-value materials can be returned to Earth at anything like scale and/or if any other economic activities can be developed that create revenue, then it is possible that, unlike virtually every other public agency or expenditure, a significant effort to build frontier capabilities, may indeed generate a positive ROI over time.

Does a New Frontier Future meet the other tests articulated earlier?

A governing vision for a New Frontier Future connects the narrative of our historical expansion as a nation to the contemporary forces and culture that drive us today. It has the potential to be a broader, more inclusive national effort than any that has gone before. From the Louisiana Purchase to the westward expansion, from the Land Grant movement to the purchase of Alaska, the American narrative has been expansive and ever moving outwards and onwards, exploring the edges of what is possible. This narrative combines with the greater equality and justice that has been slowly evolving since the New Frontier era of Kennedy and Johnson. New Frontier Future offers continuity with our national story and the grand sweep of American historical development, but also implies a more inclusive and fair version of that narrative going forward.

At the close of the 19th Century as the westward frontier came to a close, Frederick Turner proposed his *Frontier Thesis*, the idea that the national culture was formed by the frontier. The thesis, a product of its time, still has resonance today. American culture is uniquely suited to building a new frontier and a new frontier now beckons. The call of this frontier has always been at the heart of America's interest in the space program and there is a deep residual affinity and desire to expand and grow that has simply been waiting for the right tools, economics, and political dialogue. A New Frontier Future has the potential to tap into that core stream of America's cultural (and perhaps physical) DNA. Exploration whets the appetite. Building a frontier is what truly resonates.

A New Frontier Future, if it can be achieved, also creates jobs and economic growth. Growth on a frontier always looks small at the start, but if we can establish a beachhead and grow it, then the potential for growth is vast, with a corresponding payback in government revenues and long-term economic vitality. A New Frontier Future takes the focus off a handful of astronauts and puts it on the prospect that millions may one day move onto the space frontier, precisely what Americans have been telling us they want – if we but chose to ask the right questions and listen.

A New Frontier Future offers a vision for a more prosperous nation and connects directly with the American Dream of a better future. If we open up a frontier and make operations that are economically sustainable, much less prosperous, then we have the chance to create a better future for our children. Driving an expansion into space will require pushing the frontiers of science and engineering at an accelerated pace and that will, in turn, foster economic productivity and prosperity throughout the entire economy. All will benefit. This is about a better, stronger, and more prosperous American future, one where we leave our children better off than present trends currently suggest.

A New Frontier Future as a governing vision also has the potential to meet the fiscal challenges our nation faces not only as a program that earns back its investment over time, but for its potential to break open a new frontier where rapid and aggressive economic growth is possible. It is possible to imagine a scenario where the US economy is uplifted significantly a few generations hence by rapid growth on this frontier and our long-term fiscal situation is greatly improved. There is no immutable law that says our trend growth rates have to remain in the very low single digits – if we can harness a vast new frontier with unlimited resources and exponential possibilities.

A New Frontier Future is not the same as day-dreaming about the big colonies in space envisioned by O'Neill. These are likely to come to pass as an outcome if we are able to achieve that New Frontier Future and if they make economic sense. It's also true that our presence and capabilities may be heavily robotic. But to fairly test what is possible, we need to dramatically reduce the expense of being in space and then we need a vision of what to build and what it should achieve. We have to build the right capabilities and chase the right metrics.

Building these capabilities is more than a national adventure or an inspiring moment. It's about creating entire new industries and the jobs that go with them. If a frontier in space can become economically sustainable and produces even a modest return on investment (or dramatically reduces the level of negative ROI for corresponding economic activity), then it can scale and if it can scale, American ownership of these capabilities becomes a material strategic advantage in every way, including economic.

Therefore, it is my contention that we now have a practical pathway towards a New Frontier Future and it begins with bold, scalable programs like establishing an L1 strategic material reserve and a reusable ARM conveyor that begins moving asteroid material in a continuous loop in progressively larger quantities that results in dramatically reducing the cost of raw material at a point in space that is advantageous for near Earth space operations.

I have not attempted to address the significant cost of what it will take to process asteroid materials or build the critical capabilities. This should become a matter of debate and it should be approached as an effort in which the private sector will be harnessed both for ideas and for implementation. We should look at mechanisms that allow private entities to deliver innovation in a competitive environment and to succeed or fail.

This point is this is just one example of what a New Frontier Future looks like in practice. We need to assemble multiple building blocks like this to craft an overall vision and strategy for space.

The private sector has a huge role to play in this effort. There are visionaries in the private sector e.g. Elon Musk, Jeff Bezos, that are actively promoting bold visions for America's future in space. But we should not make the mistake of underestimating the fundamental role of the public sector in rallying the American public and providing funding at scale. It will take a massive effort to create public support, enlist our political leadership, and fund a large-scale space program through the U.S. Congress in order to succeed. The space frontier will only be cracked by enlisting the public directly in the cause and building a strong enough political coalition to win the votes, pass the bills, and fund at scale. And this can only happen if the public believes there is a public benefit, not just a private one.

This is a critical point illustrated by some simple data points. When asked in a survey, Pew Research found that 65% of Americans want NASA to lead America's program in space, not private space companies. While 44% of Americans believe private space companies will earn a profit in space, just 13% believe strongly that private space companies will minimize debris and pollution in space (a good proxy question for corporate behavior in general).[1]

The take-away is that Americans do not entirely trust space companies and they want NASA to continue to lead America's space program. The optics of ceding activity in space to any one private space company versus a national mission run by NASA is very dangerous. If a small number of wealthy individuals capture most of the economic benefits or are even perceived to be at risk of doing so, then there will be a public backlash, no matter how good the intentions may be. If such individuals espouse politics or demonstrate behaviors that are not a model for the entire nation (an impossible task in divided times), then a very hostile political environment will be created. Promoting a vision for America in space when it is so tightly integrated with private sector gain and individual private personalities, will be that much harder to achieve. Billionaires, above all others, should seek to build public participation and a public agenda and vision. There is plenty of credit, acclaim, and hubris to be earned. Doing so selfishly at the expense of a national sense of mission is dangerously self-indulgent and short-sighted. We must have a public vision and a publicly-led agenda for space

So, are these points merely the rambling of a wild-eyed dreamer (or a crackpot from left field)? Perhaps. The difference between an impractical dream and a vision that can become reality in this context comes down to the practicality of gaining political and public support. At first rub, the natural skeptic will note the heavily partisan environment, the low rates of economic growth, the multiple and overlapping crises from pandemic to economic depression to racial justice, and the deepening strain on our public finances and will conclude that no such political or public support may feasibly be forthcoming for a large new program in space.

I disagree. The deeper irony may be that the relatively more modest aspirations of space exploration are both too expensive to fund and too small to sell, a phrase I have returned to repeatedly in this essay. Conversely, my contention is that a far more ambitious, expansive, and, yes, expensive program could achieve more support and meet the public's true aspirations for leadership from our nation's governing class.

Such a vision must be based on three components:

- Strategy & Doctrine

- Ideology & Economics
- Public Will

We will explore each below.

Strategy & Doctrine – Vision First

I define Strategy and Doctrine as the specific political and technical framework that articulates a vision of a New Frontier Future and describes how to implement it, the language used to describe it, and the specific goals and operational mechanisms used to achieve it. A pathway to scale in space must offer a convincing answer to the cost question and it must lay out a roadmap that demonstrates which technologies will be deployed on what timeframes and in what ways to reduce those costs dramatically.

A roadmap to the future is critical and it must offer a pathway that is politically and strategically possible.

In Chapter 3, I outlined the conundrum of getting to scale in space with a simple illustration of the current economics of transporting an astronaut or passenger to Low Earth Orbit and another table to show what the estimated annual cost would be to support that same astronaut at a Lagrange point.

The costs today are extraordinarily, unimaginably high. Getting to scale is impossible within the current cost profile. But I have also illustrated what the economic costs could look like under various cost reduction scenarios. If we can learn to 'live off the land' in space, to leverage the resources that we can acquire in space to support ourselves, then these cost reduction scenarios may be feasible. These were rough models, but they are enough to make the directional point and illustrate the critical challenge.

A strategy to achieve a New Frontier Future will require a roadmap that articulates the specific technologies and applications that will allow for the dramatic cost reduction (on the order of 99%) needed against today's baseline cost structure in order to achieve a New Frontier Future in the near-earth space environment along with a timeline and a plan for fielding them. It must articulate the cost, the value proposition, and the business case that each specific investment or technology will have on reducing the overall cost of that New Frontier Future. This is much more than simply saying we'll get water from asteroids. A viable strategic plan will need to show exactly what the full lifecycle of water production will look like, what the inputs are and outputs will be, and how low costs can go. The same goes for fuel, metals, and food.

A viable strategy must articulate what such a presence in space would do – and scientific research and human inspiration from enduring questions had better not be the answer. A large presence in space must return economic value to Earth and the American economy in the form of some tangible economic activity, whether that is building solar power satellites (something speculated about for many years), mining high-value resources for Earth, or producing a unique or very high value good that cannot be done on Earth (production requiring zero gravity, for instance). A strategic vision must articulate what these products are and how to build them.

Such a broad strategy must also outline a set of goals for building a New Frontier Future or its equivalent and an action plan leading to a sustainable, vibrant, and growing presence on the frontier of near-Earth space.

Ideology & Economics

In Christopher Nolan's 2014 film, *Interstellar*, the protagonists must solve an equation for gravity in order to lift humanity off the planet to safety and avoid extinction in a dystopian future. In real life, we don't need to solve for gravity, we need to solve for NPV, or Net Present Value.

Net Present Value is the current value of all future discounted cash flows resulting from an investment. In the business world, if an investment results in a positive NPV over its calculated life, then it is worth investing in. (At least in the simple version.)

When I speak of the role of economics in building a New Frontier Future, I refer to the calculation of the aggregate public costs and public revenue returned in the form of taxes and other cash flows. In other words, can a massive investment in advancing humanity into space pay itself back in part or in whole and can we show that in the form of a positive and *public* Net Present Value?

Space exploration has no prospect of direct payback. By contrast, a New Frontier Future will return cash flows to the public purse. We need to model what these returns look like over time. The strategic roadmap is the key input into beginning this modeling effort. It should help us identify what the investments will cost, their corresponding impact on reducing the costs of sustaining a workforce in near Earth space, and the assumptions we need to make. In the near term such cash flows are obviously negative and very large. But over time there are offsetting revenues in the form of taxes, both corporate and individual, and revenue streams from economic activities done directly or jointly with the private sector.

When I think about the challenge of modeling the economics of a New Frontier Future, I think of it in terms of both Microeconomics and Macroeconomics. Microeconomics allows us to explore small interactions and how they impact larger value streams and supply chains. They tell us what the big picture looks like and how it may evolve through extrapolation.

Macroeconomics is the big picture and with it you model not just the public expenditures and revenues, but the impact of private sector investment and activity and how the total mix will add to GDP, tax receipts, and economic growth.

There are intriguing questions at both small and large scale.

Microeconomics

What will a cup of coffee cost in outer space?

Coffee is a great test case for the microeconomic analysis of a future human presence in space and what it implies for our proposed a New Frontier Future. Imagine there is a future colony at a Lagrange Point and it houses 10,000 people. How will those people live? What kind of environment will they have? How long will they work and live there before rotating back to Earth? What will they get paid?

The coffee illustration sets up a test condition that can be used to model and explain the kind of analysis needed, what it will show, and perhaps what those results imply for the technology roadmap and the viability of an economically sustainable human presence in space.

Here, in rough order form, is what I mean.

The cost of a cup of coffee if both the water and the coffee grounds are shipped from Earth can be roughly calculated as $2,500 per cup (rounded). I'm assuming for this example that the cost of cargo launched by rocket from Earth is $10,000/kg (by the time we are serving coffee to workers at L1) and a 'cup' is 8 ounces of water plus one ounce of coffee grounds. This would be enormously expensive – which makes it very interesting.

To achieve a New Frontier Future, we would need to bring the cost of that cup of coffee down to something more 'reasonable' and economically sustainable, although it may never be as cheap as walking into a Starbucks on Earth.

Water is the first component of that cup of coffee that can be produced locally from harvested asteroid material or moon regolith. Water represents the bulk of the expense of that multi-thousand-dollar cup of coffee. You can probably reduce the cost of a single cup of coffee by 80-90% by producing the water locally from materials in space. The analysis, of course, would need to derive the economic cost of mining and processing the water and every gallon will still be very expensive in comparison with Earth costs.

Then there is the matter of the coffee in whatever form it takes. Can it be grown locally? Or must it be shipped from Earth? How much can be grown on-site given the competing needs for other foodstuffs and the mix of labor and machinery available?

The cost of labor must also be added in. If that coffee is grown locally, and no matter how automated the process is, there still must be people that are involved in the production, harvesting, distribution, and ultimately roasting and serving of the coffee. An entire supply chain must be created even if it is a relatively small one and the cost of every input along the way must be accounted for when contemplating virtually any good produced on the space frontier. It may be that an ounce of freeze-dried coffee shipped from Earth is still cheaper than producing coffee locally. The ultimate cost of coffee will tell us a lot about what life will be like on the frontier as humans begin to establish and build scale.

You can ask the same question about olive oil, a pair of pants, an iPad, an electric razor, a big screen television, or a single orange. Will humans living on the frontier of space, even relatively close to Earth, ever have access to these goods and, if so, what is the cost of their production, distribution, and sale?

Each of these goods requires a supply chain and a set of production processes some seemingly simple (an orange) and others more complex (an iPad). These are consumer goods. If we wish to build industrial goods – a rocket engine, for instance – then the end product will in turn require a complex supply chain built up over time. What will it take to build up supply chains for consumer and industrial goods? How can we use new technologies (robotics, 3D additive printing, etc.) to short-cut the production of goods via long, extended supply chains? What will it all cost in terms of investment, the cost of production, and the evolution of marginal unit cost based on expected volumes?

These are the questions that require analysis. To create a long-term sustainable presence in near-Earth space, the economics of some form of presence must ultimately make sense.

My suspicion is that any analysis will tell us that the cost of living will be very high and the quality of life very Spartan. There will be few luxuries and it is hard to imagine an environment of lush abundance or much by way of consumer choice for many generations. Living in a space habitat may involve a paradox of very high-tech accommodations paired with very low tech communal living conditions. The cost of living and the implications of hardship also suggest salaries must be high compared to Earth-based jobs. In aggregate, those high salaries must then translate into some form of economically useful activity that allows for a positive return on investment.

Living on the frontier of space in an economically sustainable way will require resources be used and reused hyper efficiently. I see any kind of significant human presence in space as redefining the very terms environmentally sustainable and serving as a catalyst to drive environmental innovation at scale. Nothing will be wasted, everything recycled and reused.

The high cost of transportation may also imply long-term contracts. These will not be short rotation assignments, but multi-year in duration and potential contract terms in the range of 5-7 years in duration may become the norm. After all, for a long time, perhaps generations, it will still cost a lot to transport a person out to a Lagrange Point (or any destination in space) and so this cost will have to be amortized over as many years as feasible in a productive way that still generates an economic rate of return.

Isolation will be a problem if the community is not large enough and this implies a space station big enough to avoid 'island fever' or long-term physical problems and harmful effects.

A New Frontier Future is going to be harder than it sounds and the implications of even simple microeconomic analysis will likely show that achieving true a New Frontier Future means a working and living environment that is highly automated, extremely Spartan, and highly sustainable.

The microeconomic analysis of a sustainable human presence in space will offer critical insights that can then be aggregated into a projection of what the long-term macroeconomic costs and benefits of a New Frontier Future will be for the sponsoring nation-state(s) at home on Earth. It is there we turn next.

Macroeconomics

Microeconomics tells us that living in space will be very expensive and the high cost of living implies very high salaries. The high cost of transportation implies long-term contracts. Working and living in space will not be easy, the conditions simple (I don't buy the business case for luxury hotels). And yet, people will want these jobs and will want this experience.

Macroeconomics, by contrast, tells us what the aggregate flow of cost and revenue implies for our public finances, national income and future economic growth.

Consider the following graph in Table 5.1:

Table 5.1: Program Expense vs. Tax Revenue

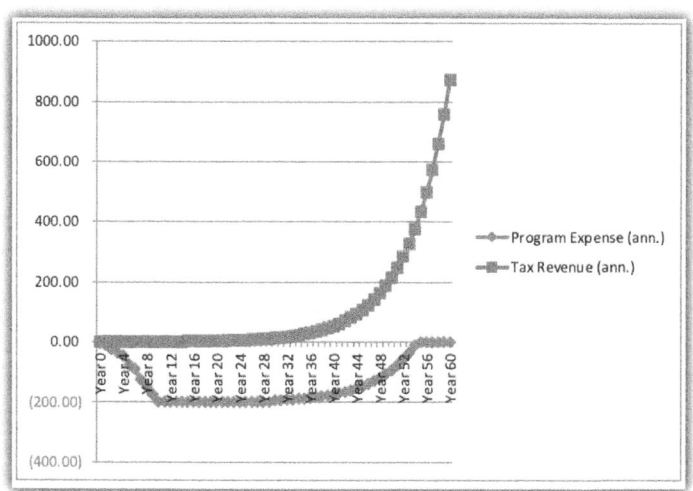

The assumptions behind this graph are very basic and my intent is to sketch out in rough order estimate form what will be needed in the form of qualified analysis. Simply put, I offer this graph as an illustration of what needs to be done and to describe what might be possible.

This graph portrays a point of view comparing the significant outlays and costs of government expenditure over a sustained period of time lasting 60 years. It offers one scenario for what achieving a New Frontier Future could look like. Cost is the blue, or negative, line.

The cost line assumes we as a nation choose to make a very large investment for an extended period of time lasting decades, peaking out at around $200 billion per year. To put this in context, our current Federal budget is nearing $4.5 trillion per year (in a normal year) and we argue over every penny spent.

In my simple model, it takes 10 years to ramp up to that full annual expenditure rate and then the $200 billion per year is maintained for 20 years before it begins to ramp slowly down to zero by Year 54.

The investment of $200 billion per year is the cost of building out according to the Strategic Plan a set of capabilities to make living in space economically sustainable. It suggests an investment over those 60 years on the order of $8-$12 trillion dollars. Mind you, when a price tag for space exploration has been tossed around in the past with much smaller numbers ($500 billion over 30 years), a mere pittance compared to what I am proposing, the answer has always been that such requests are dead on arrival at Congress's door.

But here is why this time is different: The red line.

The red line represents public revenue. Space exploration has no revenue to model and the benefits are indirect at best. A New Frontier Future, in contrast, assumes that we begin to achieve some form of public revenue from a human presence in space. We begin to build a space-based economy with activity that drives taxes. And that is where it gets interesting.

As economic activity increases as a result of a massive investment of public resources and a workforce in space begins producing something of economic value, the government begins to collect revenue in multiple forms (income taxes, corporate taxes, public-private gain share, etc.). At first, these revenues will be very modest and relatively small. But they will grow.

In the simple graph I've created, I've assumed a modest growth rate of 15% per year in public revenue. This model assumes that it takes many decades for the revenue to build enough to begin scaling back the input of public funding. In numbers, my simple model assumes the local space economy is zero at the start and grows at 15% annually. The tax rate is a flat rate of 20% on all income and economic activity. The model assumes after 10 years the size of that space-based economy is barely $4 billion and tax revenue is less than $1 billion. Progress is slow. By Year 20, the space economy is just over $16 billion and tax revenue is $3.25 billion. It takes until Year 50 for the space economy to cross $1 trillion in size and the tax revenue is just over $215 billion. By Year 60, the space economy, continuing to grow at 15% per year, is $4.3 trillion in size and tax revenue is nearly $900 billion.

This model assumes that after a massive cumulative rate of investment over an extended period of time, that a significant, dynamic, and growing presence in space is rapidly building and that an economic 'take-off', a point of self-sustaining ignition, has occurred. At the point, public revenue from the space frontier matches public funds being invested and we have achieved a sustainable and growing economy in space that is creating a rapidly increasing sum in tax revenue.

What's also true is that it probably won't happen like this. I've been as conservative as possible. I've modeled an economy that starts at zero and grows at 15% a year. More likely is that a space-based economy will start bigger and grow in rapid burst or step jumps in the early years that may double or triple the size of the economy in a single year. Eventually, when it gains some size, the rate of growth will slow to something approximating 15%. What that means is the blue line might be shorter and shallower than it looks and the red line may leap higher much faster.

For some this is pure science fiction, but I'm not the only one that has speculated at how fast economic activity may grow on the space frontier. Chris Impey, author of *Beyond: Our Future in Space* and a Distinguished

Professor at the University of Arizona, has written that the space economy could match the terrestrial economy in size within 100 years. His forecast suggests it could be equal by 2115 assuming significant growth takes off on the space frontier in the very near future.

This is not wildly implausible when you consider that to expand into space will require acquiring and processing resources at large scale, building out infrastructure from a starting point of nothing, creating entire supply chains in space for both consumer and industrial goods in order to become self-sustaining, and creating entire cities where none exists today. It will require a massive build out of every kind of economic activity, a huge volume of factor inputs from resources to labor. Growth, if it can be financed at the start in a sustainable way, will be extraordinarily fast. That 15% annual growth rate I use in my very simple model is probably ridiculously modest.

Nor is this entirely new. We've seen this story before on Earth – it's called China over the last three decades. (Or America a century earlier.)

This kind of growth engine has far reaching implications. In aggregate terms, the intriguing possibility is that the most important export back to Earth for the next 100 years in space may simply be: Tax Revenue.

The true importance of this can be seen in my illustration of the red revenue line at the far right of the table. Revenue is growing very fast and begins to drive a Return on Investment (ROI) for the public as a whole. The red line means not only complete payback of all public funds invested over time, but also an increasing contribution to the US Federal Budget in the back half of the century.

Imagine a future where there is twin US economy in Near Earth Space that is just as big and has a flat tax of 20% on all economic activity. If that economy were $17 trillion in current dollar terms (roughly the size of our economy today), the tax revenue would be $3.4 trillion, roughly equivalent to all Federal tax receipts today. Of course, a portion of those public funds will be needed to support public services in the space economy, but given the demographics, education, and high income of that community, it is easy to imagine relatively modest needs, resulting in a large surplus returned to Earth for a very long time.

In addition, that space-based economic twin may be growing at double digits (even triple digits early on), limited only by how many terrestrial-based inputs we can add (re: people, machinery, etc.). Combined, the US economy, terrestrial and space, may begin to achieve accelerated economic growth rising from a low 2-3% forecast to high single or even double digits for an extended period of time.

Table 5.2 is what that future may look like in graphic form:

Table 5.2: Lifetime Revenue (Illustrative)

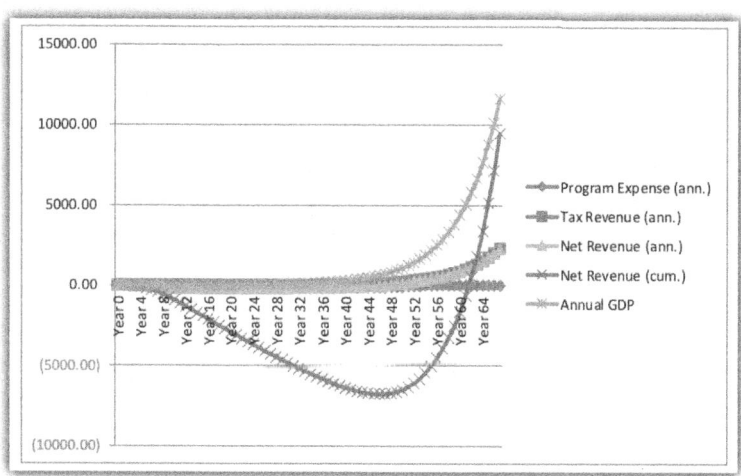

In the graph, the net revenue reflects the cumulative program expense (that $200 billion per year) as well as the impact of the tax revenue over time. It takes a long time for the space-based economy to grow and begin providing significant taxable revenue to offset and eventually drive down the public funding. The cumulative picture shows a deep negative trough that hits nearly $6.7 trillion dollars before significant tax revenue begins to enter the picture. Then as the tax revenue grows rapidly in lock step with a rapidly growing space economy, the cumulative picture changes dramatically. Tax revenue begins to pay back the cumulative expenditure and crosses the line to a net profit in Year 60. After that it grows rapidly each year and the cumulative picture represents a net contribution to the US budget from then on.

It's that net contribution in public funds that is the jackpot we should be playing for. Winning it changes everything. If this scenario is even remotely feasible, it has the potential to reshape our perception of the future and what is possible on all sides of the ideological spectrum. And it does so not just for America, but for humanity as a whole.

In American terms, if scale is possible and a net positive return on investment becomes very large over time, then there is potential to drive lower taxes for Americans on Earth while delivering long-term sustainability to our current fiscal outlook. Republicans dream about this kind of thing, but there are serious challenges in delivering this agenda in an economically and politically sustainable way in the low growth economy we have today. Likewise, Democrats dream about addressing inequality with greater government expenditure and using government to address many economic injustices. There are also challenges in meeting these aspirations and obligations given the economic assumptions today about future growth and revenue. Yet, the scenario outlined above may help square this circle for both sides. It suggests the possibility that currently grim views of our long-term fiscal situation just might be wildly off base. The analysis we need now is to what extent this may be possible and what the funding flows, both positive and negative, look like.

Given that our current annual budget is over $6 trillion per year (in a normal year) on spending and I am proposing we invest $200 billion annually at full run rate, I believe this is a modest proposal for a potentially large payback. Put another way, the total outlays in non-inflation adjusted dollars in my admittedly unsophisticated model are roughly $8.3 trillion and phase out by Year 55. By Year 65, the total cumulative tax revenue is $13.4 trillion and the net 'profit' is over $5 trillion and growing. In Year 65, the space economy adds $1.7 trillion in revenue to the budget and it is expanding rapidly

But my model is very simple and the growth rate is very modest. Its assumptions are debatable. Even so, the implications are profound. Why should we bother to build up a space frontier? Because the right-side of that graph potentially helps us solve many of our Earth-based problems. If we can create a source of rapidly growing taxable income, a fountain of perpetual budgetary surplus, it changes the outlook of our future – and for humanity as a whole. In a world growing towards a population of 9-10 billion, we are going to either have to reallocate the wealth of the global economy that we have on a global scale to meet the ever-growing needs or we are going to have to create a new source of wealth, an economic machine capable of supporting so many mouths to feed.

Here's how to make it practical. I would propose that we put competing teams of true economic experts paired with a technology roadmap to produce a set of credible studies that map out what a forecast of the economics of a New Frontier Future would actually look like if we make significant investments and attempt to achieve scale in space. My model is simple and illustrative. Let's get some real economists on the job building a forecast for what the future could look like.

These teams might also address several other intriguing questions at the macroeconomic level as well.

Purchasing Power Parity (PPP)

Another way to view this macro-economic construct and its potential ramifications is to consider Purchasing Power Parity (PPP). Consider, if you will, the cost differential of a worker that travels from Dhaka, Bangladesh to Los Angeles, California today, right now.

The cost of a meal, housing, basic supplies or services such as a haircut in Dhaka are a tiny fraction of the cost of many of these same goods and services in Los Angeles. The wages workers in Dhaka get are a tiny fraction of the American minimum wage. Despite these differences, workers in both locations may share similar levels of consumption, if not similar environments and similar choices.

Economists use the concept of Purchasing Power Parity (PPP) to compare the relative value of income and spending across very different places. For instance, a seamstress in Dhaka may make as little as $.50 per hour compared to a similar seamstress in LA that makes $10 an hour. But both may be able to buy a bowl of noodles for the same proportion of their hourly wages. In this respect, they have similar levels of Purchasing Power Parity, but the worker in LA will be able to spend and save more in absolute dollars, even if they are spending and saving a similar portion of their income in PPP terms. If the seamstress in LA visits Dhaka, they might marvel that a cup of coffee is 10 cents. However, the seamstress in Dhaka might be appalled on a similar visit to find that a cup of coffee in Los Angeles is $3.00 at the local Starbucks, and prohibitively expensive. When it comes to paying taxes, the worker in LA will pay what looks like a small fortune in taxes to the worker in Dhaka in absolute terms, even if they wind up being relatively similar in PPP terms.

Where these concepts get interesting and need analysis is when it comes to the space frontier. In a near future where there is a significant human presence in space, the question is whether wages, prices, and the supply and demand of goods and services will be controlled and set centrally (the astronaut model we operate under today) or if market mechanisms will be allowed to manage supply and demand. In the centrally controlled astronaut model, the astronaut receives their Earthly pay at Earthly wage rates and all goods and services they consume in space are centrally allocated and rationed, usually free of charge or included as part of their mission. This model does not allow goods and services to find a market clearing price that reflects actual costs and that means it does not encourage innovation and entrepreneurialism. It misses a huge opportunity when you think at scale.

In the market economy example, wages and prices are set by actual costs and are market driven by supply and demand. In space, costs are going to be much higher than they are on Earth. That cup of coffee will never be as cheap to create in space as it is on Earth. If all goods and services find their real value, then wages will also. That means that what a worker makes in space compared to Earth may look very much like the difference between Dhaka and LA. The Earth-based worker is in a fundamentally different environment, one of earthly abundance and relatively low prices. The space-based worker is in a situation of scarcity where all goods and services are extraordinarily expensive.

I can imagine a minimum wage that looks incredibly high in space compared to our Los Angeles example.

For instance, what if a true 'minimum' wage in space is $250 per hour and an average worker makes $450k per year in dollar terms? In PPP terms, they may be able to spend and consume no more than an average worker in LA. But in space, the cup of coffee they drink may cost $100 and the bowl of noodles they eat may cost $200. At a flat rate of 20%, they may also pay $90k per year in taxes and save an equally large sum (while also paying an astronomically high monthly rent expense).

A market-based economy in space that reflects true costs probably implies very high wages matched by an extraordinarily high rate of innovation and productivity growth.

These are very speculative examples, but they highlight the need to begin modeling what a space-based economy looks like, how it will be managed in terms of market economics, the relationship with the terrestrial sponsoring economy, and what it will take to become fully sustainable. What are the implications to our terrestrial economy if workers on long-term contracts in space, having saved upwards of a million dollars each, begin to circulate back home after their tour?

This is merely interesting if the numbers are in the thousands, but the impact is much larger and more far reaching if the number of people participating in this economy begins to climb into the millions by the back half of the century.

Economic Conjugation

Here's yet another conceptual way to think about this.

If you carry out our metaphor a little further, imagine that Bangladesh, a very poor country of 167 million people with a GDP of $225 billion and an average income of less than $1,400 per person, actually owned a slice of Los Angeles today (an economy over three times larger as a metropolitan area). Let's say they owned 50% of today's Los Angeles economy, could claim a flat tax on all individual and corporate income as well as a few joint ventures in the local economy, and a large number of Bangladeshis worked and lived there on 5-7 year contracts before returning home.

The revenue back from the Bangladeshi colony of New LA would not just be in the form of individual remittances to specific families, but in the form of direct tax revenue that could be used to pave roads, build schools, and finance pensions at home. The Bangladeshi government would have a surplus to invest in public services from health care to law and order. Such revenue would significantly change the outlook for the entire population of Bangladesh. They would not need foreign aid or external help. They could build a society that is prosperous entirely on their own. And it would be debt free.

In this illustration, America, of course, is the notional form of Bangladesh. And the 'New LA' metaphor represents a space economy of the future that has scaled and become self-sustaining.

That economy is what I think of as an *economic conjugate*, a copy of our own domestic, Earth-based economy operating at an exponentially higher level of prices and wages – a plural tense to our singular tense. If a twin economy can be created in Near Earth space and it operates at a fundamentally higher level of wages and prices with a vastly higher level of automation and productivity, then it can potentially deliver back a surplus in public and private revenue that may alter debates on everything from inequality to productivity to the potential for economic growth.

This doesn't just have to be an American story either. If we can conjugate our own economy, then we can potentially help every other country in the world do the same with theirs. We can build a template for other nations to replicate. And if that is possible, then the benefits of the space frontier are not exclusively American, but open to every nation on Earth and could potentially rewrite the future for all of humanity.

The bigger point is we have not begun to seriously grapple with or sketch out the potential size, scope, and growth of a near-Earth space economy and its impact on our domestic growth and economic development. Yet this is potentially strategic in every way. We need to start this effort as an urgent priority.

Creating a set of economic baselines of what might be possible is a core requirement for beginning to rally public support. It also tells us a bit about the implications for our political landscape.

Ideology

Many of our greatest political battles are fought over how much government should spend, what its priorities are for spending, and the appropriate balance between the private and public sectors. This is a national argument that has been going on since the founding of the republic and it has lasted this long precisely because both sides have valid points, something both sides frequently forget.

Today, there are significant concerns about the long-term direction of government programs and our nation's long-term liabilities. We are fighting many of these battles against a backdrop of austerity, reduced rates of economic growth, and fears of long-term secular stagnation which are now amplified by the political and economic impacts of a global pandemic. There is even a growing debate over whether the golden age of American economic growth is over, a possibility that very modest economic growth is the best we can hope for in the future.

Yet, an economic analysis of what a sustainable economy in near-earth space looks like as well as what it returns to a sponsoring government may change our assumptions about the future. The macro implications for the American economy, assuming it were the primary sponsor, might potentially look something like the illustration in Table 1 in the preceding section.

The cost at the start is very high, but over time it begins to return cash flows that grow exponentially. When you consider the long-term outlook of our economy with our fiscal and demographic challenges just highlighted, this begins to get interesting.

The implications for both sides of the political spectrum are potentially profound. A vigorous and expansive effort to achieve a New Frontier Future and achieve an expansive and sustainable presence in space could materially recast the long-term trend for our economy. They are:

- Creates the potential for sustained, rapid economic growth at rates well above the long-term trend of 2-3% and potentially in the range of double digits.
- Creates the potential for new and significant flows of public tax receipts.
- Potentially rewrites our understanding of our public finances and their long-term solvency in the second half of this century.

This means the long-term outlook may not be as bad as it currently sounds. It suggests that it makes sense to increase public expenditures significantly now as long as there are offsetting cash flows in the future. It means that unlike any other government program, a vigorous effort to build a New Frontier Future could result in economic payback in large measure to both the public and private sectors.

This does not necessarily change bedrock ideological assumptions on either the right or the left. For Republicans the mission will be to control discretionary and non-discretionary spending in order to channel significant funds to an accelerated space program, but it may imply something anathema to the right as well: higher taxes and bigger government (or empowering a more vigorous IRS to collect the taxes that are actually owed). For Democrats it speaks to a significant role for government and investments that lead to greater economic growth, but it probably cannot be achieved without significant sacrifices and a grand bargain or two across the aisle in constraining costs in areas Democrats have traditionally defended aggressively.

Both sides will have to make some tradeoffs in what are currently rigid ideological stances. For many this will seem impractical, but I would suggest that this is precisely why there is a third component to the strategy: Public will.

Public Will

Public will is the third leg and the most strategic in a New Frontier Future. The other two (strategy, economy & ideology) provide the raw material for the broader public discourse that will be necessary to gain traction and increased public support.

Public will is not set in stone. It is malleable and it changes over time. Al Gore is fond of saying that 'public will is a renewable resource.' His point is right, of course. In the context of space, there have been periods where public perception and support have shifted in small but significant ways and it is important to understand how and why that has occurred.

Roger Launius of the Smithsonian has noted that after the release of *Apollo 13* in 1995, there was a significant and extended increase in public interest in human spaceflight. Between 1989 and 1995, when polls asked the public if they favored robotic missions to explore space compared to human missions, the answer came back consistently favoring robotic missions. In 1995, the public suddenly shifted its point of view to favoring human missions and it has stayed that way since. This profound transformation is thought to be linked to the impact of the movie *Apollo 13* and its depiction of a NASA mission gone awry and the heroic effort to recover it successfully.[2]

What the existing data suggests is that public opinion can change when presented with either new information or new opportunities or with new ideas that have better packaging, the latter being the basis for an entire industry called advertising and marketing. There is another related industry called political campaigning that is also built on the assumption that public interest and desire for change can be shifted and channeled over time.

Shifting public opinion and translating that into public will to fund a political vision for America's role in space and to fund it at scale is the key to success of a vision to advance humanity into space.

I would argue that what the Pew Research Center surveys of what Americans think is possible 50 years hence are rough indicators of a desire on the part of the American public to engage in a more meaningful way and to find a more compelling vision. But the Pew surveys are merely touch points in the dark about what the public may be thinking or willing to consider. They do not really explore deeply or broadly the contour of public interest in the concept of getting to scale in space.

I believe there is potentially a great hunger for a New Frontier in our population and deeply embedded in our culture than we may realize and a possibility that we may have missed it entirely. It is possible we have been asking the wrong questions and have failed to capture a full sense of what the American public is willing to support. It is possible that the Pew questions are not simply capturing an idle interest in science and technology or a common view of what may be possible, but rather instead a sense of what people want and are potentially willing to fund. At the very least, we need to ask some different questions. In the grand scheme of things, this is not terribly expensive and would offer a first proof or test point of my thesis of a New Frontier Future.

Here are a few examples of the kind of questions we need to ask:

- Would you support a large increase in NASA's budget if it meant we could sustainably station thousands of people in space doing something that would pay for itself over time?
- Would you be willing to invest $10 trillion dollars over 50 years in a NASA program to build a large presence in space engaged in asteroid mining if, over the course of that 50 years, the program would become profitable and pay back the entire investment several times over for future generations?
- Would you be willing to make a massive investment in a NASA program to open a new frontier in space if it meant normal people might one day work and live in space profitably?
- Would you be willing to increase NASA's budget today from $20 billion to $200 billion per year for 30 years if it meant that NASA could create a self-sustaining human presence in space that creates high paying jobs both at home on Earth and in space and that returns most if not all of the investment to the taxpayer over time.
- Would you be willing to invest in a transportation system for humans into space that lowered the cost of a ticket from $70m to $250,000 and made it possible for normal Americans to travel into space for either work or tourism?
- Would you invest $10 trillion in taxpayer funds over a period of 50 years if that investment would return $30 trillion in taxpayer revenue over that same period of time?

Professionals can craft better questions than I can and these are overly redundant. But some form or variation of these questions is necessary to begin establishing a baseline of what Americans really believe is possible and to explore the full scope of their willingness to make a major strategic investment in the high frontier. (Here's a spoiler alert. I've tested this hypothesis and I believe my thesis is correct and the polling industry has missed it. As the elections of 2016 and 2020 abundantly demonstrated, it wouldn't be the first time.)

With this information as a starting point, we then need to convince a hundred million or so of our fellow Americans that it is possible and desirable to achieve scale in space and that doing so is a critical necessity for future generations and a worthy cause of a great nation. This effort will take time, but it is the basis, the critical foundation, for getting to scale in space. It cannot be a fringe movement of a few thousand people. It must be an effort and message that resonates with tens of millions which then translates into votes.

Is that possible? Can we make developing the frontier of space a mass movement?

There are two contemporary examples of mass movements in today's politics that are worth considering for context: The Environmental movement and the Conservative movement. Both have been reshaping domestic US politics dramatically over the course of a generation even as they come from polar opposite sides of the political spectrum.

Both movements offer lessons on how to establish a narrative, build a movement, and achieve a desired result. Both are valid examples no matter what side of the political spectrum you come from or are currently on. Both have weaknesses and lessons to learn from. Both are traveling towards the political center and both have hard opposition that may be intractable. Both are supported by a network of grassroots organizations and an historical narrative or narrative story that is powerful and has resonance with a large number of people.

Building a similar movement for space is going to be hard, come with its own challenges, and may take a generation. But it also has a couple of advantages that neither Environmentalists or Conservatives started with or have today.

First – It starts from the political center.

There is an enormous residual pride on our heritage in space and the fact that we, as Americans, were the first and so far only country to land astronauts on the moon. That pride is why no politician would consider shuttering NASA today. Starve it for funds and constrain its growth for a lack of a governing vision and strategic vision, yes. But cut it back drastically and close out the American story of venturing into space? Not a chance. Our space program is on par with Mom and Apple Pie. It is closely intertwined with the American Dream and there is a reasonable narrative that can be created that a bigger future in space is also our best shot at a more prosperous, high growth future that benefits all rather than a winner-take-all economy that rewards a relative few.

Second – It is less ambitious.

As ambitious as a massive increase in funding for space is, the scope of it pales to insignificance when compared to the much larger financial implications of either the Environmental movement or the Conservative movement.

Environmentalists want to reshape the entire energy industry by converting to renewables (solar, wind, etc.) and ramping down massive legacy investments worth many trillions of dollars, making an entire industry obsolete in the process. They want to achieve a culture change with quasi-religious and spiritual implications to current behaviors. They seek to shift the common psychology of voters at a fundamental level. Mind you, I am personally sympathetic to the scope, scale, and ambition of the Environmental movement and, fair disclosure, support it in most every respect. Saving the planet is a personal value for me as well. But I offer this description as comparative context at just how ambitious the Environmental movement really is from a political and social scope, how far it has come in a generation in achieving these ends, and how far it has yet to go. The Green New Deal is just the latest narrative theme and it is instructive to see how challenging it is to implement it.

Conservatives are equally ambitious. They wish to have an impact on our national politics and fundamentally reshape the public safety net, how much government spends, and the size and scope of what the federal government does on a daily basis. Conservatives seek to reshape, reduce, or eliminate spending programs that total several trillion dollars each year. They also seek to achieve very large philosophical, cultural and behavioral changes in how citizens behave and engage socially and economically. There are some virtues in this agenda and some of the ideas are worthy and worth considering regardless of where you sit on the political spectrum. But the bigger point is that as a movement, it is hugely ambitious.

I'll simply repeat the obvious. Even a massive effort to create a new frontier in space is not as ambitious as either the Environmental movement or the Conservative movement.

Third – It will have less opposition.

Opposition is likely to be much less limited and hostile to an enhanced space program. In many respects, a vastly larger effort in space comes at less political cost and provokes fewer established industries and interests than the much larger and more ambitious examples of Environmentalism and Conservatism. Of course spending more in one place threatens expenditures elsewhere, but a ramp-up in funding for space does not create an existential threat to entire industries or bedrock values. The opposition, therefore, will not be as impassioned, intense, or organized. It will have opponents, but some of them are relatively small or do not clearly realize their own self-interest.

In fact, we might be able to enlist many larger movements and interest groups. I'll offer some examples.

Business community. Companies across many industries today are sitting on cash or paying out to shareholders rather than investing in future products. There is a great uncertainty over demand and no compelling reason, no great need, to build or invest. A new frontier that promises unlimited scale for growth also opens up growth opportunities and expectations. Growth trumps everything. A credible business case for a massive expansion that creates greater demand within the American economy has the potential to enlist broad support from the business community.

Science community. The science lobby has traditionally seen human engagement in space as a win-lose proposition that reduces spending on science. Astronauts are expensive. If you are a scientist, your self-interest is in fewer astronauts and more robotic science missions. A much greater scale program in space, however, would mean a massive infusion of funding for science. Once a credible political vision that includes more science is articulated, the scientific community can be enlisted.

Environmentalists. The space frontier offers the potential to get our Earth-based ecosystem to 100% renewable energy, the potential to move 50% or more of industrial activity off planet, and to reduce the human footprint on Earth through migration rather than apocalyptic catastrophe. Such possibilities may take centuries to realize if we start now, but if we move at scale over the next 50 years, it opens up another, complementary path to long-term sustainability and creates a laboratory for innovation at scale that will return new technologies and processes to Earth. Our best pathway to saving the planet and returning it to a much more natural state is to divert the drive to grow off planet. Such possibilities create the potential for enlisting environmentalists to support an expansion of the space frontier.

Ironically, this is the exact line Jeff Bezos of Amazon fame has been saying. He suggests we move heavy industry off Earth and rezone the planet for residential and light industry. He gets a polite laugh when he says this, but this is coming from one of the most successful entrepreneurs America has ever seen. And he is serious. We should be listening.

Conservatives. We are divided nation split between two great traditions – Hamilton and Jefferson – on the role of government. This has been the case since the republic was founded and will last as long as the republic exists. Space offers the intriguing possibility of creating like-minded colonies that can experiment with a purer form of conservatism in smaller self-sustaining communities. This might imply I'm suggesting we send conservatives into deep space, but I mean this quite seriously (although the humor is not lost on me). Political utopia may be best achieved when people can sort themselves out and live and experiment with a variety of political forms. Political sorting in a democracy is not a virtue. Doing so in space may well be so and offer a chance for freedom and liberty that is defined by the people that choose to associate in more self-sustaining communities of like-minded citizens bound together in a looser confederation with ties to the home world. Today's Pilgrims may need the outlet of space.

The point of this quick review of potential sources of support is that there is likely to be less opposition from major movements in American political life and potentially many allies.

Fourth – It has a powerful narrative story with broad reach.

Most efforts to create a supporting narrative story for America's space program focus on the themes of exploration, human inspiration, and enduring questions of existential existence. These are the least powerful narrative themes that can possibly be deployed with the least power to change behaviors and rally support to spend actual money that I can possibly imagine. Their failure to rally political support has already been described and has been proven across the decades over and over and over again.

A narrative story focused on jobs, growth, and creating a bigger, bolder future for our children and their children on a frontier that will lift our entire nation to a higher level of growth and prosperity over the next 100 years is a powerful story that has yet to be communicated at scale. The mere possibility that we could potentially banish the economic cycle and win prosperity for a 100-year run of sustained, rapid economic growth, making America a beacon of hope for the entire free world is powerful. That's the narrative we must offer. It directly responds to the voters today who are rejecting the status quo in the search for a better future. They are telling us what they want. It's time to finally listen.

This narrative already has an established foundational interest, a bedrock instinctive baseline, and it can be built upon at scale to establish political support and deliver votes. We need to align the narrative story of American's journey in space with our historical story of American expansion and the common aspirations for better jobs, higher wages, and the desire to achieve the American Dream individually and for our children and future generations.

There are contemporary examples in American politics of large movements reshaping the political agenda. Two have been highlighted: Environmentalism and Conservatism. While each is able to connect with people at a visceral level with a powerful narrative story, the two highlighted above also come with powerful baggage and implacable opposition.

By contrast a vastly large effort in space has the potential to start from the middle and capture people's attention in a bigger and bolder fashion and with less resistance than current efforts suggest.

There is one more example worth highlighting.

The Scottish National Party won a resounding election victory in 2015, effectively wiping out the traditional majority Labor Party in Scotland.

Here is what happened: In 2013, the Scottish Nationalist Party (SNP) held just 6 Scottish seats (out of 59) in the British Parliament, which was still the highest number since 1979. Britain's Labor Party held the other 53 and had an effective lock on political representation in Scotland. The Nationalists ran an unsuccessful referendum on independence, losing narrowly. But they didn't stop there. Following this defeat, they went on to the General Election of 2015 to nearly annihilate the Labor Party in Scotland and achieve overwhelming dominance, winning 56 of the 59 seats to the

British Parliament. They managed to do this by making the Labor Party (the established left-wing party in the UK) look right-wing by comparison and out of touch with the desires and aspirations of Scottish voters. The loss of the referendum on independence set up a strategic win a short time later. The referendum had given the Scottish Nationalists a chance to change people's mindset and established the Nationalists as a party with a strong brand and set of messages.

While this example is from another country, its issues are different, and there is a longer back story and history specific to Scotland, it is worth telling as an example of the scope, scale, and speed of political change and how fast voter opinion and voting behavior can change.

Our situation isn't so different. The political narrative of Scottish independence versus an American Space Program at scale may seem very different at first rub, but both have an ability to tell a story and inspire a vision that can resonate with voters. Both have an ability to connect with fundamental aspirations and values and portray a different future. The Scottish Nationalists were dormant for a long period until they achieved a remarkable breakthrough, rewriting what everyone thought possible. The lesson here is that anything is possible, no matter how implausible it sounds at the start.

Public will is up for grabs. The future is always a jump ball.

American politics has a void in the center. There is a giant hole of reduced expectations that neither party is currently catering to effectively, leaving an opening for populism and extremism from either side of the political spectrum to exploit. The right offers a wall to keep immigrants out paired with trade barriers to supposedly protect American jobs. The left offers everything free, taxes on the rich, and (also) trade barriers. Neither side has a viable path to a more prosperous future.

We can offer a narrative story to both sides of the political spectrum (or anyone) that squares our current political dilemma.

The question is how to connect tangibly. We will need an action plan to drive change at scale and speed. That is the subject of the next chapter.

MARS 1,000,000

Elon Musk plans to establish a Mars Colony of one million over the next 20-25 years.[3]

Given Elon Musk is the founder and owner of SpaceX and is putting real engineers behind this effort with a target of bringing the cost of travel to Mars down to $200,000 for a trip, I think this is a remarkable and credible vision and it warrants serious consideration.

Of course, having just written a lengthy essay focused on a seemingly different vision that does not speak directly to Mars, the question that should immediately come to mind is to what extent the Mars Colonization vision is a competitor or compliment to a New Frontier Future for Near-Earth Space?

The first obvious point is that if SpaceX can reduce the travel cost to Mars to just $200k roundtrip, it not only makes travel to Mars feasible, it makes the economics of Near Earth Space even cheaper than anything I have imagined in this essay. Getting to Near Earth Space is, by definition, cheaper than going all the way to Mars. If SpaceX can really get the cost of travel to Mars in the range of $200k per person, then the economics of Near-Earth Space are a slam dunk. Thank you, SpaceX!

Here's the second thing. Musk and the folks at SpaceX reportedly talk about the tiny area of overlap between two circles: A big blue circle representing people that can pay for a ticket to Mars and a big yellow circle representing people that might want to go to Mars. One illustration shows a tiny overlapping space that represents the number of people that would be willing to cash out their homes and savings and actually make that move to Mars. Of course, as the price comes down and a true Mars colony gets established, both circles get bigger and the overlap does as well.

But there is another possibility to consider. If you want to find people with an adventuresome, can-do spirit that can quickly travel the learning curve of working in the space environment safely and effectively, you would probably look for people already on the frontier of near earth space. People that have spent a good period of time in the space environment will be trained and experienced and the leap to Mars will be a smaller step to contemplate. They will also probably have had a good opportunity to accumulate the savings needed to afford the ticket. It seems obvious that a vibrant society in Near Earth Space enables the Mars adventure and makes it a done deal. Near Earth is a steppingstone to Mars and the circle of people that can both afford it and the overlap with those that would want to go is likely to be a large portion of the total in Near Earth space.

My point is simply this: These visions are complementary and Musk's passion for Mars may enable a much bigger human presence in Near Earth Space if, indeed, he can break the cost curve in getting people launched into space.

At the end of the day, however, we are trying to solve two different problems. Musk is trying to make humanity a multi-planet species (guaranteeing our survival) and enable a new level of human adventure. This is a noble dream and aspiration – the very top of Maslow's Hierarchy when applied at the level of an entire civilization. I have confidence Musk will make this dream a reality for the benefit of us all. His vision is an important one.

I'm trying to solve a different problem, more low-brow by comparison. I want to solve the dilemmas of wage stagnation and a declining middle class while ensuring our children have decent jobs, incomes, and prospects well into the future even in a world of increasing globalization, automation, Artificial Intelligence, and rapid technology change. I'm working at the lower base tiers of Maslow's Hierarchy.

At the end of the day, I want to find a viable means for people in the middle class to build the kind of savings necessary for that ticket to Mars and make it something all Americans can both aspire to and that our jobs and incomes can pay for (without having to cash out the house and the life savings).

The vision of a vibrant economy in Near Earth Space at scale is one that I imagine helps resolves some of those challenges. And if I'm right, it also gets us Mars by default. These are very compatible visions.

To get to a vision of one million people on Mars, I think we need four million colonists in near earth space who have learned to live in space and have the dynamism, confidence, and spirt to settle Mars in large numbers. Those people will be different than we are today. They'll be bolder, more confident, possessed of unlimited can-do spirit. They'll be more like our forefathers than us. Hit the milestone of millions living in Near Earth Space and Mars is a slam dunk along with the rest of the Solar System.

Conclusion

With this section, I have argued that we are pursuing the wrong vision for America's space program. Space exploration is an inherently small-scale business that cannot achieve scale or connect with the public in a sustainable way and we have failed to rally funding or public will for the better part of two generations. It has not worked for the last 50 years and it will not work for the next 50. It is time to try something different.

I have offered an alternative vision of a New Frontier Future, which entails a focused, large-scale effort to reduce the cost of living and working in Near-Earth space by 99% or more. I have argued that such a program will require funding for NASA in the range of $200 billion per year and that it is a program and an aspiration that can fundamentally connect with bedrock American values including:

- It embodies the American Dream and narrative story of a better life for our children in a bigger and bolder future than current trends suggest today;
- It draws a direct line to pocketbook issues and concerns, namely economic growth, jobs, and wages and offer a viable path to creating a stronger economy for all Americans;

165

- It resonates with our national frontier narrative of westward expansion from the Louisiana Purchase to the Homestead Act, connects with the historical affinity Americans have always had for seizing the wide-open spaces, and projects a far more inclusive and fair vision of a New Frontier Future. It may help heal the deep wounds of our past frontier narrative;
- It goes beyond a small elite of astronauts and the wealthy to offer a vision in space that potentially every American can participate in;
- It passes the test of stewardship by being fiscally responsible and offer not just a pathway to payback but a return on the investment of public funds that is large enough in scale to help us resolve some of the long-term financial challenges our nation faces; and, finally,
- It passes muster as a top priority for public funding against a long list of a long list of urgent and contentious issues because it can help us gain the economic growth, jobs, and wages that we need to support all of those other urgent priorities.

How does a New Frontier Future do against the five reasons that constrain space exploration? I would content it overcomes them handily. Let's take each in turn.

- *It's too expensive.* Compared to space exploration, a New Frontier Future is much more so, yet it offers a better value proposition. It offers a chance of direct payback and potentially a return on investment.
- *Earthly priorities are more important.* Earthly priorities will always trump high-minded aspiration and the desire to explore and gain knowledge. In contrast, a New Frontier Future is aimed directly at critical earthly

expectations: jobs, wages, and economic growth.

- *There's no direct payback.* A New Frontier Future offers a means to collect revenue directly and traceably and to eventually pay back the entire investment of public money.
- *There's no blank check.* We are going to ask for far more funding than space exploration ever did. Yet with the possibility of payback and the potential to increase prosperity on Earth, it is possible that no check is really too small, a proposition voters may agree with.
- *It's an elite sport.* A New Frontier Future is about forging and bending steel at scale. It is not a game of the few exploring on the behalf of the many, but a game of the many working to make the frontier real for all.

A New Frontier Future as a governing strategic rationale meets and exceeds all of the critical constraints that have held back space exploration for a generation.

Achieving a New Frontier Future requires acting on three dimensions to establish:

- Strategy & Doctrine
- Economics & Ideology
- Public Will

I've attempted to both describe what these three programmatic dimensions are and how they inter-relate. Together and in synergy, they are the key components of a vision for achieving scale in space.

The next chapter proposes an action plan for how to make it happen.

It is time to get to specifics.

Chapter 6: Action Plan

Vision isn't enough. Aspirations don't pay the bills. Dreams that require public money never take flight if you can't mobilize the votes to fund them. That in a nutshell is where we are today and why we have been stuck in Low Earth Orbit for the better part of two generations.

And yet, the future is always up for grabs. Public will, to borrow a phrase, is a force that can be awakened. But if we want to change the course of what our government will fund and support, the place to start is with a pragmatic assessment of where we are today.

The simple truth is that today, that *active and engaged* community of private sector, public sector, academic, and individual space enthusiasts represent a relatively narrow segment of the general population and it is even smaller in the bigger scheme of political interest groups, lobbying power, and ability to win votes on legislation. It is a very small constituency in terms of the ability to motivate and mobilize voters to engage their government representatives. It has also largely been unsuccessful in capturing the public's imagination.

Despite the legacy of Apollo which effectively puts America's space program on par with Mom and Apple Pie, less than one in ten Americans is 'aware and committed' when it comes to following the space program. The very term 'space enthusiast' is even a bit geeky in the old-fashioned derogatory sense, not the newly chic Silicon Valley version associated with a pathway to riches and fame (SpaceX excepted).

Tell people you advocate a big move onto the space frontier (or are writing a book on the subject) and they are likely to look at you rather sadly as if you never quite grew up and are probably still a Trekkie or have a toy Lightsaber in your closet. (Just to be clear, neither is true on the author's account. At least not entirely.). This is not just a humorous point. It's a strategic one. We are starting from a point in terms of general public perception where Apollo is an historical event with little resonance beyond collective pride in our past and the public's perception of space is shaped more by fictional movies like *Star Trek* and *Star Wars*.

In pragmatic terms, if you compare the most prominent space advocacy organizations with their peers on the environmental side (comparisons are pre-Covid) you begin to see the scope of the problem.

Space Advocacy Organizations
- National Space Society (<10,000 members, $500k – $2M in revenue depending on year),
- Mars Society (40,000 members, ~$8M in revenue)
- Planetary Society (5,000 members, <$200K revenue)
- American Astronautical Society (1,400 members, <$800,000 in revenue)
- Space Frontier Foundation (unknown members, ~$200,000 in revenue)

Mainstream Environmental Advocacy Organizations
- Sierra Club (2.4m members, 600 staff, $98M budget),
- National Resources Defense Council (2.4m members, $129M revenue),
- Environmental Defense Fund (1.0+m members, 500+ employees, $120m budget).

What should be clear is that the environmental organizations are large, well-funded, and have significant staff and resources. They have mass support and can drive the public agenda, albeit not without significant opposition as discussed earlier. By contrast, the space advocacy organizations are mostly small, have limited funding, and lack significant resources or leverage. They are on the fringe and fighting for the future with water pistols not howitzers.

When it comes to space advocacy, we are not starting from a position of strength. Money, members, and staff are directly proportional to influence, impact, and votes. Space advocacy is not a power player.

If you want to change what is possible in public policy, then you need more than a small group of enthusiasts, you need to engage a very large percentage of American voters and convince them that the program you are promoting will create something for them that they will value and that it is worth the sacrifices and the trade-offs in an age where economies are recovering from a pandemic and politics are dangerously polarized. Not only that, but you need to maintain that commitment in large enough numbers to drive a paradigm shift in public policy and funding and to sustain it over a time span of decades.

Change of this nature rarely occurs or lasts because of a new book (or essay), testimony to Congress, a stirring speech calling to our better natures, a commission report promoting inspiring moments, or a President launching a new initiative. These are transitory events that still require, and continually fall short of, the votes necessary to fund them, no matter how laudable.

Something different is needed.

Real change is more likely to come as the result of a multi-decade, sustained effort by many individuals and organizations generally marching in the same direction to bend the course of the future. Think of the environmental movement or the rise of modern conservatism over the last several decades and you'll have a sense of the scope, scale, and duration of the effort and commitment required. Getting from here to there will require converting an insular industry and a relatively small demographic of geeky oddballs (no offense intended) into a mass movement.

To achieve such ends, you don't need policy recommendations – you need an action plan. Policy recommendations are what you do when you have the votes. An action plan is how you go about trying to get the votes. A valid action plan will need to be based on three components and three metrics designed to measure progress in building mass interest in a vastly bolder future in space.

The three program components are:

- Build a Baseline
- Bend the Culture
- Bring the Votes

The three metrics that will determine success are:

- Increase the percentage of Americans 'Aware and committed' to the space frontier from 9% to 75%.
- Increase the percentage of Americans that believe we are 'Not spending enough on space' from 22% to 75%.
- Increase the percentage of Americans willing to support a 10x increase in NASA's budget from 'unknown' to 75%.

We'll explore each of these program components and how to achieve the metrics above. Then we'll talk about how to pay for a big program in space.

Let's start with building a baseline.

Build a Baseline

Who cares about space? Why should they care? What will it cost? What do we get out of it?

Those questions are at the crux of the current dilemma. Right now, we can't really answer any of them convincingly. We have no systemic roadmap or comprehensive economic rationale in place to rally around or engage the public with. Nor do we really have a clue what the public is interested in or willing to support. My guess on all of this is not much better than yours.

To establish a baseline around which to build public support, we will need:

- Baseline Polling
- A Technology Roadmap

- An Economic Roadmap

We'll explore each in turn.

Baseline Polling

We need data.

I have suggested that the American public is willing to support a more aggressive program in space. But this is an untested hypothesis. It needs to be tested rigorously.

The foundation of an integrated program to transform what the public believes is possible starts by conducting public polling to establish a baseline understanding of where the public is today, what it might consider under various assumptions, and what the constraints are for engaging the public in making the space frontier a priority. We will need to design and implement a polling program that can be carried out over multiple years in which the results are shared publicly and transparently.

Of course, you might feel some skepticism at this point. I've thrown out a bunch of assumptions about what Americans are willing to fund, but I have no real data to back it up and, truthfully, my opinion is no better than yours. It's a fair point. So, I decided to put my hypothesis to the test.

A few years ago, I went out Survey Monkey and purchased a random, political sample survey of 210 people. I asked six core questions and nine background questions meant to gauge basic demographics and likely voter participation. I have listed the six space-related questions in Table 1.

Table 1: Space Frontier and Politics Survey, 2016 (Survey Monkey)		
Polling Question	All Agree*	Likely Voters Agree*
Question 1: As a voter, would you support a NASA-led 10-year, $100 billion effort to create a manufacturing facility in space housing 1,000 or more American workers IF all of the public funds invested could be recovered through fees and taxes on private sector companies using the facility?	45.2%	50.7%
Question 2: The technology to mine asteroids in space is available today, but private companies cannot yet invest at scale because a market for these resources has not yet been created. Would you support a NASA-led program to purchase asteroid material from the private sector at a cost of $50 billion dollars over 20 years IF the materials purchased were then owned by the American public and were valued at $100 billion on the open market (a taxpayer profit of $50 billion)?	41.0%	44.0%
Question 3: If an economically profitable American presence in space could also spark strong economic growth at home in America, create millions of high paying jobs, and pay back all of the public money invested plus a profit, would you support a government program led by NASA to build it?	67.6%	71.3%
Question 4: If it would cost $200 billion per year (5% of the federal government's budget) for 50 years to achieve an economically profitable presence in space with enough self-supporting economic activity to return all of the public money invested plus a profit, would you support a NASA-led program to invest that $200 billion per year to make it happen?	43.3%	45.3%
Question 5: Would you vote to invest $10 trillion in taxpayer funds over a period of 50 years to establish an economically profitable presence in space IF that investment would return $20 trillion in taxpayer revenue by the end of that same period of time?	41.9%	44.7%
Question 6: If a Congressional candidate in your district backed a bold government-led program to develop an economically profitable frontier in space that would generate millions of jobs in America and would pay back every public dollar spent along with a significant profit, would you consider voting for that candidate?	52.9%	57.3%

For each of the six questions I have shown the percentage of respondents that selected either 'Strongly Agree' or 'Somewhat Agree' for both 'All Responses' (n=210) as well as a subset of respondents that were identified as 'Likely Voters' (using a modified Perry-Gallup Likely Voter measure) (n=150). If you want to explore the details of how this survey was done and the responses received, Appendix A provides the detail along with a discussion of the survey methodology. Appendix B has the top-line questions and the survey responses by the numbers.

So, what did we find?

Here are some highlights:

- A very strong majority of Americans surveyed (>67%) say they support a more expansive program in space if it drives greater economic growth and more high-paying jobs at home;

- There appears to be a baseline of slightly more than 40% of voters that are willing to support more aggressive space-related programs that cost as much as $200 billion dollars in annual funding (10x current NASA funding) IF these programs eventually repay the funds spent;

- More than half of voters (52%) and 57% of Likely Voters indicate they are willing to support a Congressional candidate that proposes a bolder program in space that is linked to more jobs and higher economic growth at home;

- The baseline support for each question is surprisingly consistent across all three political affiliations – Republicans, Democrats, and Independents – with only modest variation among Independents;

- The response from Likely Voters was consistently more supportive than the general sample by a few percentage points. The marginal lift (a few points) is explained by the larger size (75%) of the likely voters within the sample group; and

- Men are more likely to support a larger effort in space than women, but there is a significant portion of women that are also supportive. The baseline of support among women is in the 30-40% range when it is a 'hard' question with actual spending numbers. On the softer questions of support in principle, women support the space frontier with number >65%.

So, what do these findings mean?

Conventional polling has shown that Americans are broadly supportive of NASA and space exploration, but only 22% say they believe we don't spend enough on space exploration. That quandary has been discussed and built into the assumptions and conclusions of multiple commissions and their reports across many years about what kind of space program is possible for America.

Yet, what the results above suggest is the possibility that we have been asking the wrong questions and drawing the wrong conclusions. Compared to urgent and morally compelling needs on Earth, space exploration is always a cost and it has failed and will continue to fail the test of public support for increased funding. By contrast when offered a far more ambitious set of proposals to spend much larger sums and sustain that spending over many years, BUT tie it directly back to Earthly needs for economic growth and better jobs, baseline support is nearly twice as high. And it inches higher still when you consider likely voters, which, truthfully, is the group that every politician is most concerned about.

Why these results?

When we explicitly link America's space program to the creation of a profitable economy in space that offers a direct payback and also creates high-paying jobs, it connects directly with priorities here on Earth. We are in the midst of a low-growth, winner-take-all economy in which high-paying jobs are increasingly hard to find except for a small number of the highly skilled or well connected. A frontier that offers a chance for high economic growth and high paying jobs for Americans at all socioeconomic levels both in space and here on Earth is a fundamentally different proposition than funding a program of space exploration that involves an elite few leaving footprints in the dust of other worlds.

There are some caveats. As surveys go, this is not a perfect sample or professionally crafted survey. These results do not prove my point. They are just a start. What we need to do is engage professionals to create a true baseline survey and follow it up with focus groups and research. We need to understand what these results really mean and how firm or soft they really are. At best, this survey offers a hint, a glimmer of a possibility, that Americans might just be game for betting big on a much bolder future than we have given them credit for.

Finally, the survey was run in 2016. While a lot has happened since then, I suspect a new run of the survey will find similar sentiments. Nevertheless, these assumptions will need to be tested again.

The first step in building a baseline sense of what Americans support is a bigger, more concerted effort at polling and public opinion research to build on this tentative first step and find out what Americans are really willing to consider when it comes to building out the space frontier and achieving scale in space.

Technology Roadmap

We are going to need a Technology Roadmap.

As noted earlier, a strategy to achieve a New Frontier Future will require a roadmap that articulates the specific technologies and applications that will allow for the dramatic cost reduction (on the order of 99%) needed against today's baseline cost structure in order to achieve a New Frontier Future in the near earth space environment along with a timeline and a plan for fielding them. It must articulate the cost, the value proposition, and the business case that each specific investment or technology will have on reducing the overall cost of achieving a New Frontier Future.

Today, NASA has a set of Technology Roadmaps that are focused on the technologies needed for space exploration. That means safely sending a small number of people on long journeys and protecting them from the hazards of space. These are roadmaps to support astronaut numbers in the single digits. This is the right roadmap for the budget today and reasonable assumptions about the budget tomorrow.

But I'm not interested in reasonable. I'm after extraordinary.

These roadmaps miss the opportunity to envision a bolder program at much bigger scale. We need to articulate a bigger dream. We need a 'shadow' roadmap to a much larger presence in space.

What we need is the visionary Technology Roadmap that begins to articulate how we are going to support 100,000 people and more in Near Earth Space, how we are going to transport 25,000 people a year beyond LEO at a price point that is less than one percent of what it costs today, and how to build very large structures in space with a rapidly falling cost curve. And those are starting point numbers for mid-century.

That alternative Technology Roadmap must detail out how we will bring the cost of traveling to and living in near earth space down by 99.9% or more, how we are going to supply resources and grow food in space instead of lifting it from Earth, and what technologies we will need to create in order to build large structures in space.

To create such a roadmap, we should incent a variety of actors in academia, the policy community, and the private sector to develop a set of technical roadmaps and pathways to achieving scale in space. This directly corresponds to the program I sketched out in the previous chapter. An incentive could come in the form of a competition (we seem to love competitions these days) or could come in the form of small grants or commissions to various teams to make their own roadmaps to show how the space frontier might evolve, the technologies needed, what the specific steps would be, etc.

Should the funding be earmarked, it could also come in the form of a series of study groups or commissions jointly funded by NASA and the private sector.

The Technology Roadmap should become a continually updated baseline that reflects new innovations and discoveries and becomes the project plan for the future.

Economic Roadmap

The most important component of building a baseline will be an Economic Roadmap.

An effort will be needed to engage economists and policy makers to model out the economic assumptions in the earlier chapter and analyze how a massive investment in the space frontier to achieve a New Frontier Future can lead to scenarios for economic growth that would pay back the initial investment and significantly boost the American economy over time.

An economic roadmap would attempt to better understand how the flow of funding will cascade throughout the American economy. It would consider the larger set of outcomes in terms of sustaining and building industries, creating high paying jobs at home, and fostering new technology and advanced manufacturing leadership to drive a more prosperous American economy. Assumptions for this modeling should focus on what a future presence at scale on the high frontier would look like economically and the implications for the tax base and federal revenue through to the end of the century as compared to current projections.

It is critical that these studies map out a pathway and the requirements for achieving significant payback over time. We are playing the game for the right side of the graph – the one in the previous section that shows a dramatic lift-off for a space-based economy and what it means for rapidly increasing tax revenue.

Imagine a federally funded program that breaks even or achieves a profit. If it can be achieved, it would create a breakthrough opportunity for a vastly expanded effort in space.

Now, dream bigger. Imagine this was also the key to sustaining not just our federal budget, but for achieving a more globally equitable economy worldwide as well. If the pay-off from the space frontier is really exponential growth, it may represent a massive funding surplus that can be deployed for all of humanity. An economic study would attempt to analyze and map this out with more specifics.

There are massive ideological battles playing out over the future of America's fiscal and economic future. For the record, I consider the contours of most of these debates potentially obsolete. The economic roadmap should show the scope and breadth of how a presence in space at scale would both use and return funds to the public coffers and to what extent it addresses or compounds the challenges we face more broadly in the coming decades.

Modeling out these economic assumptions and impacts is a crucial step and has implications both for engaging the public and the political community. If we cannot create an economic model that shows a positive net impact on the American taxpayer, then it will be very hard to achieve scale in space. For me, it would be a non-starter.

Summary

With these first three baseline steps, what we will have done is prepare the baseline foundation around which to build engagement with the American public, policy community, and political elite in the form of white papers, studies, and points of view which can be synthesized into political messages, marketing data, and demographic segments.

Before we initiate the second set of activities, we must be sure that the first group has delivered actionable and feasible results. If the polling, technology roadmap, and economic forecasts do not provide a solid foundation for believing that a massive break-out onto the space frontier makes technical and economic sense or that the public will support it, then we can stop right there.

But I don't think it will. I think these activities will give us the messages, detailed roadmaps, and resonant themes that the public is hungry for.

Now it's time to use them. It's time to bend the culture.

Bend the Culture

Bending the culture means teaching people to dream big about a bigger, bolder future in space that is tangible and within reach. It means mainstreaming enthusiasm about the space frontier and a bold American venture in space. So how do you reach a large number of people in a way that changes their expectations and hopes for the future they and their children will have?

Some would argue for a social media campaign or an online outreach program. They might point to testimony by such luminaries as Neil Tyson or the example of a film by Erik Wernquist called *Wanderers,* which shared a powerful vision of a future in which humans have spread throughout the solar system. Examples like these have inspired many thousands and achieved significant online attention. But neither created any sustainable movement or traction in actual funding for space activities and this highlights the scope of the challenge in connecting with the public.

These individual events lack traction because they are isolated notes in the louder cacophony of noise as the broader culture flows ever onwards and individuals and firms jostle for people's attention, the headlines flare over the latest crisis or curiosity of the day, and yesterday's news, video, and vision fades into the past under the onslaught of ever more input today. A few bright notes or personalities may get attention and rack up views or achieve a following, but few have a truly lasting impact. Numbers in the thousands or millions sounds impressive, but they are fleeting, ephemeral moments at best. The film *Wanderers* has had a few million hits. *Gangnam Style* by South Korean pop star, Psy, has had over 2.5 billion. Neither has changed the world. Fame and attention are remarkably transient in the digital world.

A better metaphor for what we need to achieve is the marketing campaign for *Star Wars: The Force Awakens*, its' sequels, or any other comparable big release film. You'll see the marketing everywhere. Whether you like the film or plann to sit it out, it will be inescapable. The messaging will come from every direction and in every media. There are toys and product placements. Press and media galore. If you have children, you could not escape seeing, hearing, and probably purchasing a Star Wars themed toy in the case of that movie. And even if you didn't, your children's friends probably did.

Of course, we are not talking about an iconic film with an established brand and a massive marketing budget tied to specific near-term revenue generation event (film release) with a strong profit incentive. But neither do we need the same velocity or expense.

What we do need is a campaign that is financially self-sustaining, able to reach tens of millions, and can convey a vision of the future over a time span of decades. We need to engage people across a variety of formats and forums, through media and in person. And we will need to attract a large number of entrepreneurs, organizations, and partners to participate.

You can probably come up with some good ideas yourself, but here is what I'm thinking:

Space Expo/Fair

An estimated 3.5 million people attended the Texas State Fair in Dallas in the fall of 2015. But it's not just Texans who love their State Fairs. Nearly 1.8 million people attended the Minnesota State Fair. One and a half million went to the San Diego State Fair. The Erie County Fair in Hamburg, NY, drew nearly 1.2 million and one million went to the Western Washington Fair in Puyallup. In all, nearly 24 million visited just the top 16 state fairs in the US and those are just the biggest on the list. Every state has a fair, most have more than one. Sure, many of these have been cancelled in 2020 and possibly 2021 because of the pandemic, but this too will pass. The State Fairs will come back.

We need to build events around the country focused on space that have the same reach and impact as state fairs. People love fairs, but would they go to a space-themed fair or expo? Consider the Smithsonian.

The Smithsonian Institution is a complex of museums in Washington, D.C. that are free to visit. In a sample year before the Covid pandemic and before significant remodeling impacted the Air & Space Museum (we'll use the year 2018), there were some 28.5 million visits (not unique visitors) that were recorded, e.g. someone went to one of the museums or the national zoo and they were counted when they entered. The most popular of the dozen museums with a total of 6.2 million visits was the Air & Space Museum. The next closest is the National Museum of Natural History with 4.8 million visits. All the rest of the museums in the Smithsonian complex – from art to history – get just a few million visits by comparison. In 2017, there were 30 million visits to the

Smithsonian and the Air & Space Museum had 7 million visits (the Natural History Museum was second with 6 million).

What this suggests is a strong interest in space. Given a choice, people vote with their feet and are most interested in Air and Space. This data point offers a hint of how popular the space frontier might be to the general public if we developed it further.

But here's where the data point falls short of where we need to go: Ninety percent or more of what the Air & Space Museum portrays and exhibits is about our past glories and accomplishments, not about our future possibilities and dreams. Hence the word 'museum.'

What we need is a large format show that reaches the public in a physical way and that flips the ratio of past vs. future. We need a show that is 95% about the future. It may start small, but ultimately we need an expo in each of our top 25 metropolitan regions and our top 20 state fairs that people can visit and enjoy once a year that shares a positive vision of what a big future in space looks like, that meets their aspirational desires for a more prosperous, bolder America, and provides a format for advocacy organizations to connect at scale and volume with the American public. It should include all of the traditional features of a fair such as obscenely high-calorie fried foods, adrenalin-fueled carnival rides, and concerts by B-list musicians that still have a following. These events should be fun for the majority of Americans and we should pander to the masses aggressively.

Now, there are established events that allow you to reach millions of people. They come in a variety of forms. From conferences (think Comic-Con) to science museum exhibits to large public events like those state fairs and even air shows.

If you want to begin reaching people immediately or test the waters, you simply need to become an exhibitor and rent space. The price varies with the brand and nature of the event. The upside is instant access to an audience as long as you have the money. The downside is that you will be one exhibitor among many and your message will be diluted as a result. You will fight for attention in a crowded space and the number of people you truly connect with will be smaller than the total number of participants.

Instead, I would argue for engaging the public directly in a series of specific branded events designed to increase public awareness and engagement with a vision of the space frontier. There are multiple formats possible. I might start with a variation on a traveling exhibit that runs sequentially in multiple locations in the US and seeks to hit the top 20-25 top metropolitan regions every 12-18 months. Think of a Comic-Con for adults, an event for a market that wants more than make believe.

If I created such an event, I would start small with a set of pilots and build from there. But the long-term vision would always be to grow into a big format expo, or fair, that lasts weeks rather than days. The goal is to engage 50-75 million Americans each year with a vision of what our future could look like. We should aim to build a dream that will inspire millions, fundamentally change expectations about the future, and drive a behavioral change in voting.

Designing a one-off show is probably easy. Creating a brand that is financially sustainable and can continually draw the right content (exhibitors) and engage the public effectively over a run of decades would be a significant challenge, but the potential pay-off would be very large. It would allow you to engage and build a list of those millions of American voters and consumers who share a common dream and interest in America's future in space.

Live Events

I would supplement the show/fair type events with an annual or bi-annual live broadcast show.

For the live broadcast event, I would attempt to include some of the most significant luminaries in the technology/space field to promote a vision of scale in space. When I think of luminaries, I don't think of astronauts, former aerospace executives or NASA alumni – although we would want to include them as well. Rather, the headliners I think of are people with names like Musk and Bezos. These tech entrepreneurs are themselves people who believe that it is possible to have a big future in space and they have each made investments in the rockets to get us there. Much larger government outlays and program expenditures in these areas are very much in their self-interest. In short, this is a cause they might support and there is a compelling reason for them to do so.

The American public, in turn, is fascinated with entrepreneurial success stories, especially in the technology space. Each of these extraordinarily successful people are objects of fascination and the American public will mostly listen to what they say as representing smart commercial sense. In other words, they have more name recognition and public credibility then any politician, government agency head, or even Hollywood movie star. These are the voices I would attempt to deploy in an integrated way to engage the American public.

Of course their time is valuable, so an optimal use of scarce time is to focus on a live TV event, which I think of as being on par with the Oscars but focused on our future in space in which some of our most admired technology titans share with the American public why they think a big future in space is possible and in everyone's interest. Think of it as the '3 Tenors' of the space frontier. I don't use the analogy lightly. It may be these people are competitive, temperamental prima donnas and it may be hard to get them to work together. Conversely, they might also enjoy the chance to share the stage and connect with the public. And like that original show featuring three extraordinary opera personalities, a live event just might create a bit of magic as well.

If we can produce a public broadcast event to share a vision of the space frontier, then there is the potential to convert many tens of millions of people to supporting a vision of a more aggressive move onto the high frontier. Pair this up with a series of shows or expos traveling around the country with enough scale and frequency to engage a significant share of mind and the combination has the potential to change public awareness of what is possible and to do so at scale and speed.

Merchandising

I'm not a big fan of consumer culture, but – like it or not – the things you buy, the toys you give your kids, the books you read to them, and the games you play with them weave a subtle fabric and context that can have a lasting impact for the rest of their lives. The 5-year-old you read a story to will be a voter in 13 years. The 10-year-old you inspire will be a college activist or entrepreneur in ten more. The 18-year-old that finds a dream today will be a political activist in ten and perhaps a Congressional candidate twenty years out.

What we buy for our kids is a starting point that can have a lasting long-term impact.

When I go to a Space Museum or Science Museum, I invariably pay close attention to what their store sells. I have yet to find an impressive line-up of products. When I surf Amazon, I see a lot of stuff with a space theme, but not the kind of products that I would like to see and would like to buy for my children when it comes to the space frontier.

An action plan to bend the culture, therefore, also has a section on encouraging and inspiring companies to create and market products that cater to a potentially large market. Proving that market exists will be easier if you are able to create the shows and fairs and live broadcast events or prove that they are coming. What company will say no, if you bring a plan to send a few million consumers their way?

What would I like to see by way of products in the marketplace? Below is a short, illustrative, but nowhere near exhaustive list of potential products. This is just a starting point, an initial brainstorm of what I think would make a difference:

- A 10-pack of little Gold Books on life in a space settlement for children ages 2-6.
- A board game on par with *Ticket to Ride* or *Power Grid*, but set in near-earth space and focused on

building production platforms, harvesting asteroids, and producing fuel, water, and food in space. For the 10+ age group.

- A video game set in near-earth space with a compelling mystery or problem(s) to solve, but that provides an accurate view of potential living conditions. I'm not a fan of the shooter games, so what I would purchase is something different if it were for my kids.
- An iPhone app on par with the vibrancy of *Zen Garden* that offers a tour of a future space settlement.
- A version of Minecraft set in outer space that allows people to design and build space colonies, lunar bases, and Mars settlements.
- Books that show with art and illustrations how to build space settlements, production platforms, and harvest asteroids – think of books from David Macaulay – and that illustrate various aspects of life in near earth space, Moon colonies, or cities on Mars.
- Models with cut-away views of a near earth settlement, NASA and SpaceX rockets, or a moon base, Mars colony, etc. Some of this already exists from established brands, but most focuses on the past (Apollo, Space Shuttle) and not the future.
- The full range of smaller products that fill in the gaps at various price points from pins and posters to T-shirts and art all of it illustrating what the future in near earth space could look like in 50 years.

That's just a partial list of what we need to commercialize. Where it exists today, we need to find ways to help market it to the general public as part of a broad, coherent campaign with consistent messaging and a long-term impact. We need Amazon, eBay, and YouTube channels dedicated to the merchandising and productizing of this vision. Where it doesn't exist, we need to encourage its creation.

Movies and Streaming

Film is powerful.

As a medium, film is a powerful channel to reach people at scale and connect with their imagination in a way that no political add or public speech or motivational media campaign can rival. The video streaming services like Netflix, Amazon Prime, Disney+, and Hulu have also dramatically expanded both the universe of content available to the public, while also creating an insatiable demand for more.

Not every film or series is a success. Not every motion picture connects with the public or is memorable or finds an audience. Not every new streaming series on Netflix or Amazon Prime goes viral. Most lose money or fail to gain traction. With all the talent in Hollywood constantly using their considerable experience to create products that Americans will buy, the truth is that they get it wrong more often than right. Sometimes stunningly so. Despite these risks, the upside of film is enormous.

If we want to bend the culture, then we need to enlist Hollywood as a content producer in the cause. We need to consider how to influence the creation of a new genre of films and streaming series set in near earth space fifty plus years in our future and focused not on exploration (sending a few astronauts), but on large scale colonies in space where people live and work.

There is already a demand for content about space. Over the last several years, we have seen new series inspired by Elon Musks' vision of a Mars colony driving new shows either about astronauts exploring Mars whether fictional such as *The Martian, The First, Away*, etc. to documentary and hybrid series like *Mars* (from National Geographic), the *Mars Generation, A Year in Space*, etc. All of this content helps prove that there is a market and an intense interest in space.

But we need to capture people's imagination with a depiction of the near future in a way that draws a direct line to how they vote today. Think Erik Wernquist's *Wanderers* on steroids, feature length, and with a story.

Our action plan for promoting a big future in space and bending the culture, should have room in it for encouraging and seeking to fund the creation of movies, both in IMAX and traditional format as well as multiple streaming services. Such films and series would be set 50+ years in our future in a period where we have achieved break-out in space. They would portray a future where we have tens of thousands of humans in space settlements using technologies and engineering that are not beyond reach and imagination. The rationale for such movies is to be able to show a visual, practical view of what the frontier could look like fifty years from now, to make it seem normal and achievable.

If Hollywood can make film after film about characters, situations, and dramas in the more mundane reality of our everyday lives here on Earth, then we are almost certainly capable of coming up with compelling story-lines set against the backdrop of humanity in space 50 years hence.

There are multiple benefits to creating film and streaming content.

First, as we have seen, entertainment is a medium that has extraordinary power to impact what the public believes is possible. As noted earlier by Roger Launius, the release of *Apollo 13* had a role in transforming public opinion on the question of human vs. robotic spaceflight. Public opinion shifted decisively to favoring human spaceflight immediately after the film.[1]

In fact, in an opinion-editorial in *The New York Times*, Jeffrey Zacks, a professor at Washington University of St. Louis, described how a growing body of research has shown that films have the power to reshape what people believe are 'facts' when it comes to historical events. He was commenting on films from 2014 that included 'Selma', 'The Imitation Game', and 'American Sniper' and how they portrayed historical events. The research finds that people who watch films are strongly susceptible to adopting the 'facts' portrayed in the films by the filmmaker as actual facts even when they know that they may contain historical inaccuracies.[2]

In his article, Zacks was commenting on the issue of films that misrepresent historical events. However, the same concepts apply, and in a more positive light, if we want to portray the potential of a positive future in space and if, indeed, we want to shape public opinion at scale and speed. Film is uniquely powerful. It trumps political stump speeches, commercial advertising, and social media. It has the potential to transform what the public believes is possible in a decisive way.

Both of these data points speak to the power of movies and the role of the popular culture in shaping opinion and the potential for redefining what the public thinks is possible. *The Martian*, a Matt Damon film about a Mars exploration mission gone awry, was a significant hit in the fall of 2015. If we were to measure the impact on public support for a future Mars exploration mission, it likely moved the needle in terms of what people think is possible.

In the case of our proposed films and series set 50 years in the future, the goal would be to convince people that this is a destiny that we can create and to show in a tangible way what it looks like.

Thus, a film or streaming series, if crafted well and distributed across many channels, can potentially be one of the most powerful tools for reaching the broader public that is available and capable of shaping their view of what is possible.

Second, the production of a film or series creates a set of assets in the form of sets, visuals, models, characters, etc. and these are outputs that can be harvested and used to reinforce other activities and engagement with the public. These IP assets include both the sets and the models as well as software, illustrations, and images all of which can be leveraged and licensed into follow-on products from video games to toys. Content production allows us to engage some extraordinarily talented people in creating a setting for the future and we can then use those assets to pitch to the public far above and beyond the first run of the movie itself.

In effect, films allow us to circulate content back into the parts of the action plan we have just discussed such as fairs and shows and merchandising. It allows us to take advantage of the Hollywood marketing machine to turbo charge a broader effort to bend the culture.

Third, a good film has a chance to pay for itself. What I am envisioning is not intended to be a blockbuster, but to be entertaining and interesting. It will focus on a global audience. If it achieves pay-back, then it has created enormous leverage for the broader goal.

On those grounds a significant investment in one or more full length feature films or a series of joint productions with streaming services like Netflix or Amazon Prime might be both relatively high risk and also a responsible investment with potential to create a significant reward in the cause of building public support. If a film or streaming series has the potential for commercial return on investment, the initial funding can both be seen as an investment and as a source of leverage to attract additional funding.

Our action plan should target inspiring the creation of content for future movies through financial support, hosting contests, etc. We should seek to raise seed funds for a select number of films.

If such a program were done in synergy with efforts to launch and run large format fairs/shows and a live broadcast event, we have the potential to offer Hollywood access to a large market of interested consumers.

Bending the Culture – Summary

At the end of the day the set of activities outlined in this section – an expo/fair, a live broadcast event, a merchandising strategy, and a film/streaming initiative – are about engaging and bending the public and political culture in a certain direction. Each is mutually reinforcing and each as outlined here is just a starting point.

Will we help to finance and support a single movie directly or build a program to influence the broader pop culture through incentives and contests and prizes ranging from soliciting and supporting the most interesting scripts, books, and multi-media products? The truth is the effort may be broader than a single film or streaming series on Netflix, Amazon Prime, or Disney+, but discussing the virtues of a film or streaming service are good examples to start with.

And how does a fair/expo fit in? A fair is a vehicle that can begin to collect 'customer' names for future products whether books or movies. It can also be a forum for identifying and signing up donors and volunteers for future political campaigns. If we produce a movie concurrent with running an expo/show that hits the top 20 or 25 metro areas around the U.S., then it is also possible to believe we have a vehicle for signing up moviegoers and promoting a fan base for such films.

A merchandising strategy allows us to reach people of all ages with products that portray a future that is possible. It begins to weave a narrative for an American Dream in space at scale.

Finally, that live event is a chance to tie it all together and drive it to a higher level, especially if it occurs annually or bi-annually.

The sets of activities outlined are a starting point in a dialogue to define an integrated set of initiatives that can be used to shape the popular culture. They are and can be mutually reinforcing and – in synergy – potentially very powerful.

Ultimately, however, the point of bending the popular culture, of instilling a vision of what is possible, is to be able to rally the votes and shape the political process to turn dream into reality. How to do that is the subject of the next section.

Bring the Votes

If we want to truly open a new frontier in space and if that venture will require massive public funding, then we need to figure out how to shift public opinion at scale and speed. We then need to use the inputs from our efforts to 'build a baseline' and 'bend the culture' to transform public will, what the public demands from their political representatives, and, most importantly, how they vote.

We will need to establish a political action plan, a campaign to raise funds, engage an army of volunteers, and secure millions of votes. We will need a fully staffed contingent of lobbyists to cultivate politicians and the policymakers that support them with ideas. We will need to make our presence and impact felt on the ground and become a part of every politician's electoral math to winning higher office – and impose a penalty if they do not.

All of this is doable. It is hard and will take time, but it can be done.

To make it real, we will need to work on the basic ecosystem, take a few risks, and win some elections.

Ecosystem

If you look at what both Environmentalism and Conservatism have achieved over the last generation, you begin to realize we are at the starting point of a similar effort that may take a generation to realize and will require a massive effort by multiple organizations that are generally aligned and allied, but also competitively positioning for attention. These other movements have strong ecosystems driving political support and mass mobilization and I see no other realistic path forward to achieve something similar without a comparable effort.

We are going to have to build an ecosystem that can drive mass attention and uptake and then deliver votes. That ecosystem at a minimum has the following constituent parts:

- Organizations
- Think Tanks
- Donors
- Lobbyists
- Candidates
- Volunteers/Activists
- Voter data

These are the basic building blocks to creating a larger scale movement. We'll take them in turn.

Space Advocacy Organizations

We saw earlier that the current organizations supporting space advocacy, no matter how laudable and pioneering, are tiny on the political playing field. We need to grow them by several magnitudes of order. We will need a larger ecosystem of larger organizations to have a true impact on space.

Organizations like the Planetary Society and the National Space Society need to go from a few tens of thousands of members to ones with a few million members. They will need enough revenue to employ a large staff focused on driving the political agenda. These entities – or ones like them – need to employ lobbyists to work the political machine.

Of course, there is plenty of room for more and new organizations to represent the future in space and it is unclear now if the same names will lead the way or be supplanted by others that are more innovative and effective. The market will decide in this respect.

Think Tanks

I have outlined a series of requirements for ideas and detailed analysis in this essay and this type of work is the purview of professional research organizations, or Think Tanks, in the Washington parlance. It is possible that existing organizations from the Brookings Institute to the American Enterprise Institute to Third Way may contribute to this cause. But these Think Tanks have a broader agenda and it may be that we need to create and endow new organizations whose sole focus will be on the space frontier and driving the policymaking and analysis necessary to be successful.

Think Tanks also have an important role as both a landing spot and training ground for a new generation of policymakers and politicians. With that role in mind, it is probably important to have at least a few independent, dedicated organizations.

Donors

All of this will take money and so the role of the political donor is critical. It is clear that the current generation of space advocacy organizations have largely failed to attract large donors or achieve mass interest. Yet this is a fundamental building block necessary to drive change. It takes money.

I think a compelling value proposition can be crafted to attract donors in large numbers. We are talking about bending the direction of the future and unleashing double-digits economic growth for a sustained run of 100 year or more. We are talking about opening up a new frontier and creating a vibrant society that is free and democratic and represents the best of humanity.

Donors love this kind of thing and the wealthy can do the math on the implications for everything they hold and own from stocks to property. We need to make a focused pitch with a resonant message and begin building up a large donor base to support both political action, advocacy organizations, and supporting research.

If the value proposition for the space frontier is truly viable (and that is yet to be proven), then I suspect donors will be very interested and can be attracted in large numbers.

Lobbyists

You need lobbyists to drive legislative change. Lobbying has become a dirty word in our political lexicon, but is inherent to the political process and we will need to have a cadre of our own. These people follow the money, so if you have donors and organizations with large budgets, then obtaining them should not be particularly difficult.

Candidates

We are going to need to identify, train, and support a cadre of politicians who are strong supporters of an enlarged space program, by which I mean 10x larger than today. Some of these will be Democrats, some Republicans, and some Independents and non-affiliated.

There are likely very few existing politicians willing to stake out a position for massive funding at this point given the competing interests, priorities, and party platforms today.

Our job is to find candidates and arm them with a political rationale, campaign material, staff, and professionals, and most important the language of the future so that they can successfully make a case for change to their constituency and win an election. We have to prepare their constituency for such a message and be able to fend off the inevitable counterattack.

When Newt Gingrich spoke of moon bases during a Presidential primary campaign some years ago, he was widely mocked. We need to prepare the public better and arm our candidates with better messaging on how to make the case for space. When opponents of the space frontier can be successfully portrayed as obstructionists of a more prosperous future in a way that voters understand and agree with, then we will have achieved success and the candidates will come to us. But this is a long way off.

Volunteers/Activists

Politics requires boots on the ground in the form of a committed army of volunteers and activists who believe in what you are doing and why and are willing to donate their precious time in return for a chance to play a part in something bigger and more noble than the everyday routine of daily life.

Our job will be to enlarge the number of people who are interested in space from a small fringe to a much larger demographic of people that are excited by the future and willing to devote time and energy to efforts to make it a reality. I don't think this is going to be hard. I think if you build it, the volunteers will come.

Voter Data

Finally, we need to translate all of the above into voters willing to commit to our cause and we are going to need the kind of voter data that existing parties currently have and routinely use to support their candidates.

To summarize, building out an ecosystem will take time and effort, but it is absolutely critical to convert ideas and aspirations into actual votes. If we are bending the culture and pointing people to these organizations, then we can begin to build them up and they in turn will begin to have a larger impact.

The Big Play

It is not enough to just have a strong ground game, a bigger and better ecosystem. Those fundamentals are important, but every successful team also needs a few big plays up its sleeve. To me a big play means creating a 501(c)4 entity and raising and spending upwards of $10m on a given election cycle to create a turning point in public perception of what is possible.

When I think about big plays in the context of American politics and the American political landscape, I start with three fundamental principles. They are these:

- There is no such thing as a 'safe seat'- just a lack of good alternatives.
- Americans are hungry for a positive vision of a prosperous future – and have largely been disappointed to date.
- The space frontier offers a prospect of a much more prosperous future.

When billions are being spent on election cycles, a target of $10 million must look small, mere table-stakes in the grand scheme of things, but I would argue it can be deployed strategically and can achieve an outsized influence, far more than such small numbers suggest.

So here is what I would propose to do with that money: Defeat precisely two Congressional incumbents. One Republican, One Democrat.

Narrowed down to two specific Congressional campaigns in an off Presidential cycle year where donor money is not as abundant and attention is not as focused, the impact of $4-$4.5

197

million in a single Congressional campaign has the potential to be strategic and decisive. It doesn't matter to me which two incumbents we attack as long as it is balanced between both parties.

Attacking two incumbents and funding a challenger that is willing to go big on America's future in space allows us to battle test political themes while simultaneously educating the public about what is possible in creative new ways. To me this is a valuable proving ground to find out what is possible. It's a test of maturity of our ecosystem, one with strategic outcomes.

Consider the strategic impact if we win. The odds are long and it is a best case scenario. But if you successfully knock off two incumbents, you have done so because something resonated with the public's perceptions and desires. This is unusual when it occurs, is fundamentally powerful, and it instantly rewrites the rules for every other candidate. Every other political office holder – at the national level that means the other 533 remaining Congressman and Senators – will suddenly have to take notice. Knocking off two incumbents (preferably ones in 'safe' seats) means all the rest have to immediately evaluate, shift, and adapt. Every candidate would need to rebalance the political calculations that they make to get re-elected or defend their supporting coalitions. In practice, this means if you successfully find a winning theme that can cause a politician to lose office, every other politician will immediately try to absorb that theme in order to fend off future rivals. So much the better if it can be a bi-partisan theme.

In other words, we only need to win twice to change the game for everyone.

Now, politics is a funny business. Incumbents are 'sticky' because they are good at what they do and have built a coalition that supports them consistently. Incumbents have also been thoroughly battle-tested for their durability, public persona, and ability to connect. Challengers often think they are smarter or more polished, but few have faced the level of public scrutiny involved or been put under as much pressure where every sentence is parsed for offense, injury, or incompetence. We routinely underestimate the skill it takes to be a credible political candidate. We may love or hate our elected representative (mostly the latter), but we have to respect and acknowledge that they have won elections because they are good at getting elected and the losers are less so. The conventional wisdom routinely underestimates how much skill or talent (and professional advice) it takes to win public office, especially at the national level. While some candidates are capable of trumping these ground rules with rancor and populism, it is unlikely that this will work for very many and unclear if it will be successful in the long run for those that do.

But that leads to a more fundamental point. Few also appreciate how volatile the electorate truly is, how fast it can gravitate to a new idea or public persona, and how quickly today's powerbroker and safe seat can lose an election. Just ask Eric Cantor in 2014. Ask the Labor Party of Scotland in 2015. Or ask Hillary Clinton about the rapid rise and remarkable victory of Donald Trump in 2016. You can also ask Donald Trump about 2020. Things change. No one is safe.

Picking a credible challenger and equipping them with the right supporting messages while staying within the ground rules of political campaign law will not be easy and will require the input of professionals. You need a candidate with the right balance of charisma and substance combined with extraordinary levels of energy and the ability to communicate and connect. It will also require a bit of luck along with a flavor of something new and fresh on the political landscape.

I would personally consider it a long shot to win both targeted races, and maybe even one. But it is possible. And the mere act of trying has the potential to change the political landscape in a fundamental way. As the SAS motto says, 'Who Dares, Wins.' We should dare.

If the campaign is successful, our notional $10M is just a starting point and the 501(c)4 nonprofit we have created immediately becomes a focal point for a longer term, larger effort to engage in the political process and seek to influence elections across the full breadth of the national landscape. Winning will supercharge everything. Winning always changes the game.

However, it is those first two elections that are the key and the challenge. I would contend that they are worth the investment. And, frankly, it would be fun to do battle for the future of America in space.

Bring the Votes – Summary

The true test of success will be if we can bring the votes and overcome the opposition to fund a large-scale program in space.

We will have to build the ecosystem and we will have to fight and win elections. We will have to play hardball in the halls of power against veteran professionals hired to protect every special interest under the sun.

But if we can build up an ecosystem and a mass movement and start to gain traction through electoral wins, if we can bring the votes to the polling stations, then we will establish momentum to build on and we will have begun to bend the future of America in space and on Earth.

Summary

Achieving a New Frontier Future requires an action plan to shape public will to and changing what Americans believe is possible when it comes to achieving scale in space. Changing both public perception and the political landscape will lay the foundation for rewriting the script of America's future in space and on Earth.

The action plan assumes we act on three dimensions. They are:

- Build a Baseline
- Bend the Culture
- Bring the Votes

Three metrics that will determine the success of this effort are:

- Increase the percentage of Americans 'Aware and committed' to the space frontier from 9% to 75%.
- Increase the percentage of Americans that believe we are 'Not spending enough on space' from 22% to 75%.
- Increase the percentage of Americans willing to support a 10x increase in NASA's budget from 'unknown' to 75%.

What I have pitched here is beyond what one person can do or even one organization within the current community focused on space advocacy. We will need to build out a much more robust ecosystem and engage in a concerted effort that will last decades. We will need to convince a majority of Americans that a sustainable and profitable frontier in space is feasible and keep them engaged for the better part of two generations.

The first step is to build a baseline. Establishing a valid baseline is critical. This is the fact-based foundational material of technology roadmap, economic roadmap, and public polling that enables engaging the public in a substantive way to bend the culture and bring the votes. It is the essential starting point.

But it is just a starting point.

We will then need to Bend the Culture. That means large-scale public events like state fairs that engage tens of millions annually. It means live broadcast events that bring together the most prominent voices in our society and economy to share a vision of a space-based future. It means stoking the commercial culture with products that reinforce the message and the dream. It means enlisting Hollywood to create the visual backdrop of what the future could look like. These are just a few of the points on my brainstorming whiteboard. Others may come up with a better plan or a better set of suggestions. The point is to shape what people believe is possible and expect their politicians to deliver on. We need to bend the culture to the point people see the space frontier as less science fiction and more cultural expectation.

Once we have achieved a critical mass in public perception, we must Bring the Votes. We must build up an ecosystem for political action. Then we must engage in the hard fight of defeating at least a few incumbents and supporting the politicians that back our cause. It is what every other interest group or mass movement does and if we want to win, then we must play the same game with greater ferocity and determination than everyone else. We must proactively dive into the muck of politics at its most banal and dirty and deliver results that change how budgets are allocated. And we will then have to sustain that pressure for the better part of two generations.

If we do all this, then we will have a shot at seizing a frontier for a greater and more prosperous American and human future. We will have earned the right as a civilization to expand outwards and to become a species with a destiny greater than one planet alone.

Chapter 7: Paying For It

I have proposed spending $200 billion dollars a year, or as much as $10 *trillion* dollars in total, over a duration of 50 years. That's a big number no matter how you count it, even within the vast scope of the Federal budget. That naturally lends itself to the question of how I propose to pay for a vastly expanded program in space when no one has been successful before. It is a daunting challenge.

Take everything one of the richest people in the world, Jeff Bezos, owns and has earned over his entire life and career, sell it, and put it in the pot and you have the budget I am proposing covered for just one year or less (depending on the stock price of Amazon). The scale of the funding needed is massive and my thesis from the start is that it will require public funding at scale to build out an economically self-sustaining frontier in space.

In a government with a budget approaching $6.0 trillion per year by 2025 and above $7 trillion from 2027 and $9 trillion from 2032. We are talking less than 3.5% of the total. Yet, our deficits each year are running over $1 trillion and are projected to increase to over $2 trillion by the end of the decade. Funding to develop the space frontier is going to have to compete against a long list of earthly priorities as well as the need to raise money to close the gaps we have in paying for what we already spend.[1]

If we have done our job right, we will have the votes to increase funding. But where will the funding come from, how do you make it sustainable over multiple generations when competing with earthly priorities that are morally compelling and deeply urgent, and in an environment where no one really likes to be taxed and the ones with the most money will fight back as much as they can?

Most suggestions for bigger programs inevitably come back to higher taxes on the rich and so it is worth considering what that means and what is possible. The *New York Times* once ran an article about the kind of funding higher taxes on the richest 10%, 1%, or even .1% could bring in. The numbers are interesting and probably have not changed that much since the original article.

The top fifth of taxpayers have an average income of $321,000. The top 1% have an average income of $2.1m and those at the very top, the much vaunted .1%, have an average income of nearly $9.5m – every year. Out of 171 million taxpayers, there are just 115,000 in that very top .1%, more than 1.13m in the top 1%, and just shy of 24 million in the top 20% of all taxpayers.

If we increased the tax burden on the top 1% (1.13 million households that currently pay about a third of their income in taxes) to 40%, it would bring in $157 billion in revenue in the first year. Bump it up to 45% and the tax revenue generated would be $276 billion.

If you limit that same tax increase (to 40%) to just the top .1% (the households making on average $9.4m), then you would bring in $55 billion in additional tax revenue. Increase it to 45% and the tax revenue increases to $109 billion.

As the article points out, if you also increase taxes on those in the 95th-99th tax bracket (the 4.4m households that make on average $405k and currently pay just over 25% of their income in taxes) to 30%, you increase tax revenue by $86 billion and increase it to 35% and the revenue increases to $176 billion.

Alternatively, if you change the tax code to eliminate lower rates on capital gains and dividends, you get $134 billion per year in additional tax revenue.[2]

It's clear we could tax the rich more, but it is unclear if that is a sustainable way to fund a program in space. After all the rich are like you and me in one sense – no one really likes to see their money disappear into the general fund to be spent by flunkies (politicians) and bureaucrats as if it were their own. Where the rich are less like you and me is that they can subvert the process over time to eliminate those taxes, leaving any grand vision adrift or starved for funding – a sure-fire way to kill any real chance to create something sustainable and growing.

The Rich have also acculturated every trick in the book to minimize their contribution and they have accumulated every accountant and expert for hire with a novel way to hide income from the tax man. We have a culture of tax avoidance where the well to do admire each other for their ability to keep it rather than have Uncle Sam take it and spend it on things they don't like, don't agree with, or don't get direct benefit out of. And let's just be honest. If you or I were rich, we might just do the same, because we will have worked so hard for it, earned it and, therefore, we will think we deserve it, too.

Finally, what's also true is that tapping and taxing the rich is the favored strategy for virtually every other policy proposal to expand or pay for government and will be in the future. But that doesn't mean these will be successful. The primary campaign of 2020 tested many messages about taxing the rich and the most aggressive versions were the ones that failed the worst.

For all of these reasons, I'm less enamored of taxing the rich in a standard way without a better rationale or explanation and a more effective and sustainable mechanism. The good news is that there is a potentially good case to be made and a sustainable, potentially even attractive way to tax the rich in a mutually beneficial way.

Value Proposition

Let's start with the value proposition.

First, I would argue that a viable plan to promote rapid economic growth in America will greatly benefit the rich and increase the value of everything they own today from stocks to property and this is very different from the standard case for increasing public spending or vague talk of investments in our future. It is very much in the interests of the rich to promote a more prosperous future for the simple reason that they will benefit more than everyone else. There may be many ways to do so, but if we have done our job right, then we have begun to acculturate among all Americans the idea that the space frontier will create a vast opportunity for economic growth and this message should also resonate with the rich as well.

Second, if we are successful in building out the space frontier, then it will naturally drive the creation of many new industries and companies that will offer fantastically lucrative new opportunities for profitable investment and have the potential to create outsized returns. Most of these new firms will have investors, shareholders, and executives that will come from the ranks of the wealthy today and tomorrow. After all, the Digital Economy will have its run, but there are only so many unicorns possible without a new frontier.

Last, if the macro impact of the space frontier is or has the potential to be as large as I have speculated and if it could generate large positive returns to the public purse, then there is the potential that the future fiscal environment could be much more positive than today's. Imagine if we weren't facing an age of austerity, bitter political division, and nascent class warfare against the elites and wealthy. Imagine if our future were better, not worse in every way. Imagine if we could create public revenue off a new frontier that would provide relief to our contentious politics and allow for a grand bargain of lower taxes (on everyone, including the rich) paired with greater services, healthcare, and pensions for all. That future looks much better than the one that is emerging now in which a winner-take-all society faces an angry electorate with a confiscatory instinct and mood that is going to grow more extreme with each passing year of low economic growth and higher inequality all of which is amplified by a polarized electorate and a debt-laden recovery from a global pandemic.

Donald Trump was just the start. A major political struggle is happening in a bitterly divided country. Things could get a lot worse – and probably will.

A vastly more prosperous future of rapid economic growth, extraordinary opportunities for investing and achieving outsize returns (think Google, Facebook, and Apple x 100), and just possibly a political environment where government achieves significant revenues without resorting to taxing the rich. That is the value proposition we are talking about and it is one that is much more positive for the wealthy than the current trends and outlook suggest.

How, then, do you get there today in a way that can achieve consistent funding and realize this potential given how contentious public funding always has been and will always be? How do we tax the rich in a sustainable way to gain not only their acquiescence, but the seemingly impossible outcome of actually enlisting their support in the cause of their own taxation? I have some ideas.

Tax/Equity Hybrid

Financial Repression is when governments force the financial sector (re: banks) to purchase public sector debt instead of alternative investments and hold interest rates below the rate of inflation, in effect, forcing the private sector to subsidize government. A more sustainable way to tax the rich – and one potentially more palatable to the rich as well – is a variation on this theme.

Unlike any other government activity which is always a cost, a national investment in the space frontier has the potential to pay for itself over time. Therefore, it should be possible to collect revenue directly from commercial and economic activity in space in various forms (income tax, VAT tax, corporate tax, etc.). Further, we can expect those revenues to grow over time, potentially to very large numbers. A rough sketch of what kind of revenue might be possible long-term was outlined earlier. If these cash flows are possible, it means we can treat this as an investment and change how we finance it.

One option, of course, is create bonds to finance the program. That is easy to do. There is a vast liquid market looking for safe assets like U.S. Government Treasury Bills. But that would increase the government's debt at a time when that debt looks enormous already. That idea will face significant opposition. It's also an old-fashioned way of funding the future and it is subject to the same contentious political process and challenges of sustainability that any other program faces.

Therefore, I don't like it.

I'll offer you an alternative proposal in the form of a set of principles to define a new approach to financing the space frontier for your consideration:

Principle 1:

Charter a Trust. Charter a public investment vehicle and separate it from NASA. I see this as a public corporation charted to disburse revenue for future space-based activities. The same entity would also be chartered to collect tax revenues from all commercial activities in space under US jurisdiction, which can be expected to grow significantly over time.

Principle 2:

Tax the Rich. Fund the space frontier with a dedicated tax on the top 1-5% in the form of an extra 5-10% surcharge tax to raise the targeted $200 billion/year in space frontier funding.

Principle 3:

Give them a Stake. Design the taxes received to be a form of modified hybrid equity by which I mean it should have some of the properties of a tax-free municipal bond and some of the properties of an equity investment. In effect, a Tax/Equity Hybrid is a coerced (taxed) investment that may pay sub-par returns over time compared to other alternatives, but whose intent is to return the investment principle with a modest rate of return to those taxed at some point in the distant future, likely 50 years out. Therefore, it is not a 'tax' in the traditional sense. It is a tax in that it is coerced and legislated. But it has aspects of a loan that has the potential to be repaid. And it has aspects of an equity that can lose all of its face value if the investment fails. As a tax, it does not add to the nation's debt, unlike a bond issuance.

Principle 4:

Sunset the Tax. Create rules to phase out the collection of taxes at the point that space-based revenue collection exceeds program funding requirements. In other words, at the point that the space frontier becomes self-sustaining from a public funding point, then the tax phases out. If we manage the development of the space frontier to drive costs down and revenue up, we might reach this point much faster than planned, but the expectation is that this tax will take 40-50 years to phase out.

Principle 5:

Design payback. Make payback subject to very stringent conditions. I would design a payback regime to provide a modest rate of return on the Tax/Equity accrued and contingent on the public getting a bigger share first. Thus the rich are not going to make substantial gains just off this funding mechanism. For that, they will have to invest, innovate, and create industries, companies, and products in space. But they *will* get paid back. Payback would begin to occur as revenue takes off and exceeds program funding requirements. I would design a mechanism that designates a specific and limited share of positive net revenue (say 20% of the total) for pay back. So the public purse gains the other 80% to help make things better for everyone, but as the space economy grows over time, the 20% is used to cash out the coerced tax/investment and close out people's shares. We may also sweeten the pot by making the repayment tax advantaged in some form to increase the effective return.

Principle 6:

Penalize failure. If the effort to win the space frontier fails and does not achieve positive net revenue or is abandoned, then the investment is declared bankrupt and everything previously collected in taxes from the rich is treated as taxation without any obligation for payback. This is the same risk that any equity investor faces if their favored stock or company should go bust. The investment disappears without a public debt or obligation if the effort is eventually abandoned for any reason. If we fail, the equity is gone and this was effectively a tax.

Principle 7:

Make it tradable. If this is an asset, then allow it to be traded via a mechanism like a blockchain so that people have some control or choice over their asset and whether to sell it or hold it. Not everyone rich today will be rich 20 years from now or even next year. Some will need to cash in the chips they have much sooner. The 'Rich' are not a monolithic block that is the same year over year. Some rise, some fall – at least on the margins. Creating a way to trade the 'asset' even if at a steep discount early on allows people that have some of these 'shares' a set of options on whether to sell or hold these bets on America's future. It provides other investors a chance to accrue them.

These seven principles set up a potentially unique dynamic. No one likes to have money taken from them and everyone would prefer to invest their money themselves and gain the highest possible return. But if this program collects taxes and converts them into a hybrid equity share that will eventually pay off, then it's basically a forced savings plan for the rich that achieves a significant public good and a number of positive outcomes for all, including the rich.

Our strategy should be to coerce, seduce, and then enlist the rich in support of the space frontier and future government investments needed to make it sustainable. The coerce part is easy to understand from the above. We tax them. They don't get to opt out. They won't like this at the start. No one does.

But then we seduce them. We treat them like shareholders. We flatter them, thank them, and kill them with kindness. We give them annual reports and an economic report card app that shows progress in reaching sustainability, how much they have contributed and will get paid back based on various assumptions, and a forecast of when the tax will phase out. This progress becomes an annual report card, a newsworthy event. It is something that shows progress, and if progress is rapid, it is a tool that helps build and maintain support, gives the country (and the rich) something to root for that is tangible and specific. In the process, we make them patriots instead of villains. We thank them profusely, flatter their sense of importance, and make them part of an elite club. It's fine if they know we are doing it to them and why. They're used to it. Let's play the game.

Let them argue over every other tax line item in the federal budget, but make sure they can see direct cause and effect of where their money is going when it comes to the space frontier and how soon they will get paid back. Do that and you create a unique and new dynamic with this particular type of funding: The rich potentially self-enlist in the cause.

Here's how and why: Over time, the longer this tax regime is in place, the bigger the accrual of paid-in taxes by the rich, then the more important and significant the asset becomes for the rich to support. As the potential repayment gets bigger AND if the rich want to get their money back, then they have to help make the space frontier a success. This dynamic is unique. My position is that after the first decade or two – the point where opposition traditionally becomes overwhelmingly stronger – the opposite will actually happen. The sustainability element begins to be driven by those paying the taxes. They begin to put their political weight behind the program in order to get their money back – even if it means continuing to pay taxes or lobbying for additional funding and taxes. Nor can they afford to cut off the funding for fear of losing their investment. No one wants to write off an investment when they can get their money back.

Not only that, but it achieves large scale private sector buy-in. If the rich are all in on the public investment and they know it and not only expect the frontier to succeed, but are determined to back it until it does, then they are also likely to begin backing private sector firms that have the potential to capitalize on the space frontier and its economic potential. We need those firms and their breakthrough products to innovate and bring down the cost curve. The rich will back them because of the scale and certainty of the public investment – and this, once again, will amplify their support for the public program and their own taxation.

The simple truth is that there are many, many more great companies, many more future Apples, Googles, and Facebooks that will come if we are able to achieve an economically sustainable breakout onto the space frontier. You have only to think about the fabled East India Company to realize what is possible. That is how the rich will make true fortunes with returns vastly in excess of anything we consider today. To invest in those firms, however, investors need a sense of certainty about the future direction. That is why getting the Rich to support the public investment is so fundamental. And the Rich, I would speculate, will get this fact faster than anyone.

That is how I would pay for this program. Make the rich shareholders and treat them like VIP owners. Thank them, flatter them (shamelessly), and make them partners in the biggest story the human race will ever fund. Market to them as heroes rather than villains in the political process. And give them a stake in the venture and a compelling reason (payback and the breeding of unicorns) to support it for the long-term.

There is another public funding mechanism to consider.

Monetary Policy: From Helicopter Drops to Rocket Launches

If you follow the global economy, you'll know we are not in a great place. Just a short time ago, the advanced economies were in the doldrums, growth was slow, and wages were stagnating. Then came the global pandemic, the swing to expansionary fiscal and monetary policies, and a resulting crisis of inflation. Economic damage has resulted. Like it or not, we are going to be living with the fallout and debt from this public health and global economic crisis for a generation even as we struggle with the backdrop of a low growth future, high inflation, and economic volatility.

Prior to 2022, Monetary policy, the tool chest that central banks use to stimulate the economy was close to empty with all but the most extreme options already spent. We were hovering near the zero boundary on interest rates and some countries were already experimenting with negative interest rates, a concept that would have been considered radical and extreme a decade ago. No one had a decent plan or path forward and the next tool in the chest was printing money and 'dropping it from helicopters' (metaphorically speaking) in the form of giveaways to stimulate spending.

The incoming Biden Administration launched several rounds of stimulus during their first year in office and the result on top of pandemic induced supply chain challenges was increasing inflation. Then, in early 2022, Russia invaded Ukraine and precipitated a global economic crisis in energy and supply chains in addition to upending the global security framework.

Today, in 2024, we are in a grim place to contemplate the future. We are exceedingly vulnerable to the next crisis, recession is on the horizon if the U.S. Federal Reserve isn't exquisitely careful with the interest rates it has increased to halt inflationary pressures, and if a downturn comes, we are then still hostage to a future of less prosperity and secular stagnation.

But there is another outcome of our current predicament: Ideas once considered extreme a decade ago are effectively now on the table and the door is wide open to consider additional tools. While all eyes are on the inflation crisis, we still have a growth problem and we need to solve it or the West as we know it will decline from the levels of prosperity that we have grown used to. The money, as one author has opined, will eventually run out.

In all of this, I am intrigued by the recent history of the Federal Reserve in expanding the monetary supply through Quantitative Easing in an attempt to stabilize the economy after the Great Recession, which could have easily been the Great Depression 2. The Fed's response to the Global Pandemic does, itself, not appear to have resulted in the inflation plaguing all if the Western economies. This was likely caused by massive fiscal stimulus in a disrupted, structurally tight economy.

Quantitative Easing (QE) is a monetary policy in which central banks, such as the Federal Reserve, buy financial assets (e.g. Mortgages, Loans, Bonds, etc.) from banks, which increases the price of those assets (through increased demand), lowers the yield (interest rate), and increases the overall money supply in the economy. As a strategy, it is meant to expand the economy and is usually done when standard monetary policy tools such as buying short-term government bonds to lower interest rates don't work because interest rates are at or nearly at zero already. The risk is that increasing the money supply may also result in higher inflation.[3]

Paul Krugman, a Nobel Prize winning economist and columnist, offers a critique of this program that is worth considering. Krugman argues that greatly expanding the Fed's holdings (printing money) by adding financial assets to the banks has helped make credit easier, but has largely increased bank's balance sheets without necessarily putting that money to work in the form of loans and increased economic activity in the 'real' economy. In other words, not enough money that is created is then loaned out to businesses to increase jobs and economic growth outside of the financial sector. This makes sense when you consider that a lot of economic analysis prior to the pandemic suggested that we have a demand problem – not enough consumers able and willing to spend – and that was limiting the willingness of companies to invest or take out those loans from the banks to drive more economic activity. We were caught in a trap of circular stagnation: Consumers weren't driving demand so businesses weren't investing and creating jobs, therefore consumers didn't have more jobs and higher income to support spending money and buying more goods and services.

In this context, Krugman suggested a better strategy would have been to buy 'stuff'.

However, the purchase of 'stuff' is what fiscal policy (federal budgeting) is intended to do and that is driven by Congress. During the Great Recession, a Republican-led Congress followed a contractionary fiscal policy in an attempt to achieve a balanced budget (classical economics would consider this unwise at a time of economic recession). Fiscal policy was contractionary while the Fed was expansive. Had the two worked in greater concert, there is a possibility we could have emerged faster and more vigorously from our Great Recession of 2008-2009.

Then, during the Covid Pandemic, Congress did the opposite, funding a bold economic rescue package that put money directly into people's hands but at a great cost. Congress did what it took to keep the economy going during an election year. Then, as noted above, it went further and continued stimulating the economy with nearly $4 trillion in additional spending. A massive wave of fiscal stimulus paired with monetary stimulus and global supply chain and energy market disruptions all combined to unleash inflation.

The debate over what caused inflation will go on for years after inflation is tamed (assuming it is managed successfully). But the key issue is the concept of purchasing more 'stuff' at scale on the space frontier and finding a mechanism for inflating a space-based economy that will likely operate at a higher cost basis compared to the American terrestrial economy.

Is there a role for expanding the monetary supply to inflate and grow that future space-based economy and, if so, how will that grow in the future? Can we do so in concert with the tax/equity repression approach suggested previously and can the combination work to dramatically increase growth of both a profitable space-based economy as well as our own domestic economy on Earth – without unleashing the inflation monster again?

I think this is possible and here is why.

Let's replay the context again. Inflation is top of mind now, but the cure for inflation is sometimes a recession. We will then return to the underlying issue of prolonged stagnation that has been haunting most of the advanced economies for the last few decades. After all of the stimulus and all of the debt, when the dust settles, we are still going to be stuck with a low growth economy with limited productivity gains and structural challenges to future growth even while balancing on the edge of a recession in demand. The Global Pandemic and Russia's invasion of Ukraine have caused economic turmoil, but they did not fundamentally change the underlying economic dynamic.

We need a viable pathway to future economic growth and dynamism. We need a structural solution to a lack of demand, innovation, and dynamism. A future economy in Near Earth Space may offer the best structural bet to inspire that growth and dynamism at large scale. We need a frontier.

A non-traditional program to inject liquidity into a future space-based economy would be the 'pull' to complement the 'push' of the fiscally driven tax/equity repression mechanism offered earlier. The Fed has the tools and the means to support the rapid build-out of a space-based economy if it simultaneously fosters a more dynamic economy at home as well, which is their mandate.

Is there a hybrid mechanism for creating a quantitative easing-like program that creates credit and expands the money supply in space and allows for innovation and economic growth? Can we use monetary policy to expand a space-based economy at the same time we are using fiscal policy (tax, spend) to build out an infrastructure in space and pay for imports from Earth? Can we do this in combination without creating an inflationary burst at home, once again?

Here's one possibility. As we begin to build out a space frontier, we will create cities and industries in space. To do so, we must fund them. We can charter space-based entities that are public (municipal/colony governments) and/or private (banks or investment funds based on the frontier and investing entirely in frontier ventures) entities that issue long-term bonds which the Fed can then purchase. (Effectively, this is space-based quantitative easing, what I think of as *Quantum Easing*.) These funds can be used to support and amplify economic activity in space by injecting funds that will be used to drive both municipal colony construction as well as business formation and innovation.

Once we have built up the capability to construct a space colony, you start by chartering a municipal government that will run that colony. You issue it a loan from a space-based entity (a bank or public trust). The loan will be big. The municipal authority uses the loan to build the colony. Once built, it leases out space for commercial activity and it owns, for a long time, all of the residential property from which it collects rent. These cash flows from commercial and residential activity go back to paying the original loan. This process is pretty standard. The only thing new is the location.

If we get to the point of building out large habitats in space, we are effectively positioning a smart, innovative, and entrepreneurial work force in space and presenting them with a huge number of opportunities to create new products and services. If we have also created a market-based economy for goods and services in which wages and prices find their natural balance point, then we can inject liquidity in the form of further loans that give people a chance to create those businesses and innovate within this market-based economy. We are talking Silicon Valley on steroids, a dramatically turbocharged space-based economy. Public funding and fiscal policy will get us the stuff. In space, there will be no shortage of opportunities for innovation and growth for many generations if we can create mechanisms to fund innovative private sector entrepreneurialism and we operate an economy that is market-based instead of centrally planned.

This is a rough idea at best, but some variant is almost certainly possible – because it has already been proven possible on Earth. If we have a fiscally driven program to spend $200 billion a year on the space frontier AND we have a monetary policy to inject $200-$300 billion in liquidity into that same space-based economy on an annual basis during

217

build-out, then in effect, we have the means to dramatically increase the level of economic activity in space and this has important implications for our economy at home as well. It will drive high productivity economic growth that cascades throughout our economy.

At the end of the day, the Federal Reserve's goals are to support a strong US economy. We need to strongly encourage the Fed to begin thinking creatively now about the best tools for growing the economy of a space frontier that has the potential to grow exponentially for a long period of time thereby deriving benefits for the American people and our domestic economy as well.

Private Sector Investment

Throughout this section on funding, the topic has been mobilizing public sector investment at scale through fiscal and monetary policy. But there is a third leg of funding that will also come into play if and when there is a level of certainty and belief that the public sector investment is sustainable and will be maintained for long enough to build a truly self-supporting economy in space: Private sector investment.

No other data point illustrates this point more than the example of a current aerospace company that shall remain nameless that returned $25 billion in cash to shareholders during a single 5-year period from 2010, but has not, to my knowledge, invested its own money in a reusable rocket such as the ones that SpaceX has been building for much less. Nor is SpaceX alone. Blue Origin is doing the same.

I would argue that companies like this are simply not yet seeing a crucial market signal. Elon Musk and Jeff Bezos are trying to create a market in space. They are the exceptions.

Most every other normal company in our economy looks for a market that exists in order to invest into it. They do not take on risk or make big bets on products and strategies that require markets that are beyond their control. There is no stampede to invest in products that companies and their leaders do not believe there is a current market for and for which incremental revenue can't be quickly obtained.

If, however, we have a massive public sector investment being implemented with enough certainty that it will be sustained for a long period of time and that is used to create a market-based economy in space with prospects for rapid growth for centuries, I believe that will drive investment decisions throughout our economy like dominoes. Once a fiscal and monetary policy are articulated and put into place, the private sector will mobilize vast sums to build the future instead of just making YouTube videos about it.

This turn to investment will have profound implications for domestic economic growth.

An active large-scale presence in space represents a platform for innovation and the creation of wealth. It represents an historic opportunity to invest in the future. Once we have an active frontier in space, we can complement public funding with private-led venture funding and corporate investment. The sums are potentially in the hundreds of billions per year.

Economic Conjugation – A Bonus for Humanity

I've suggested previously that it might be possible to 'conjugate' our domestic economy by creating a clone in space that operates at a higher level of prices and wages, a plural tense of our domestic economy, if you will. I think of it as an Economic Conjugate. Mobilizing public and private investment in the range of many hundreds of billions of dollars per year creates that conjugate and it has potentially huge implications for our Earth-based civilization.

Conceptually, I think of the space-based economy as operating at wage and price levels that are 10-20x those of our own domestic economy. A minimum wage in the most progressive cities and states today is or will soon be $15. In space, an equivalent minimum wage might be closer to $250 an hour. The interplay between these two economic tenses will need to be studied and understood better. The implications, however, are far reaching.

What if another 5-10% of our population could earn as much as all of the rest combined and these people don't come from the ranks of the wealthy, but from the ranks of the middle class? What if they are rotated every 5 years? That means a much larger percentage of the Middle Class would have access to a period of very high earnings. What if their taxes could mostly be used to help pay our Earthly bills (and potentially without argument and political divisiveness)?

Printing money should be inflationary, even hyper-inflationary, but our experience with Quantitative Easing prior to the pandemic was that it barely kept us out of a deflationary spiral. Core inflation only started growing when we unleashed a combination of monetary and fiscal stimulus with multiple global economic and energy shocks.

If we build a space-based economy, we are going to have to expand the money supply for that economy to operate. We are going to print money to 'inflate' a future space-based economy. Much of that money supply will stay within the space-based economy, but some of it will flow back in the form of taxes and savings. We will need to understand how that impacts our domestic money supply and whether it has an inflationary impact or has other side effects such as mispricing assets at home.

To some it will seem obvious that it must do so, but I believe the impact will be modest. What if the expectation is that costs are going to decrease over time, driven by innovation and scale, and that our space-based economy is going to grow exponentially over the decades? If that multi-thousand-dollar cup of coffee is going to decrease over time to 'just' $200 and perhaps less and the circulation of currency allows the space-based economy to operate effectively, then a conjugated economy without dramatic inflation might be possible.

Likewise, if the flow of revenue back to the domestic economy is in the form of public tax revenue and corporate and individual income, will it have an inflationary impact or can the negative outcomes be mitigated and controlled? Can we safely inflate a space-based economy using the US Dollar or do we need to create a separate currency?

For America, the positive outcomes of solving these problems and creating a conjugate are huge. Can we create a bonus in tax revenue that can help us address many of our Earthly problems? Want to finance a living wage for all? What if the answer is 'No problem?' Want to pay for the transition to a zero-emission economy without passing on any additional costs to business? Check. Want to reduce taxes on the wealthy? Done. Want to build out universal healthcare, early childhood education for all, and rebuild our crumbling infrastructure. Check, check, and check again. What if our politicians could make political promises and actually keep them? What if we can unlock a significant source of cash flow for our future in the back half of this century?

An economic conjugate of our own economy operating in space at higher levels of wages and prices has the potential to pay a sizable bonus back to our public coffers at home and to change our future on Earth if done at scale.

On the political front, what if the Left and Right could each achieve core objectives (more spending, less taxes) in an economically sustainable way? Would they just push further to the extreme or could they actually compromise and get along? Wouldn't it be interesting to find out?

Here's another possibility. If every economy on Earth is able to conjugate as well, if we can help them build their own economic clones in space, then we are talking about a self-sustaining financial jackpot that can help us resolve some of our largest problems on Earth. Want to finance a massive build-out of public infrastructure in developing countries? Check. Want to eliminate extreme poverty with a social safety net for all? Check. Want to get high quality healthcare for all of humanity fielded, deployed, and operating in every corner of the world. Done.

There are going to be challenges to work through. How do you couple the conjugate with the original without creating inflationary spirals? We'll need to figure it out. Is there a limit to inflating a conjugate in space with public finances before we create distortions in the domestic economy on Earth? I don't know. Let's put our best economists on the case to study it and figure out the guardrails and safety mechanisms.

The bigger point is that if America can pilot a full-fledged economic conjugate in space and figure out how to manage the linkages, then it is possible to conceive of deploying this model for all of humanity by the back half of the century. Where others see doom and gloom, I see the possibility of creating a fountain of prosperity from a space-based economy – precisely because the cost of living and working there will be much more expensive than in the abundance of Earth. Humanity can achieve a major bonus in prosperity if we seize the possibilities of the space frontier and harvest some of the benefits.

Want to jump the wall of Fermi's Paradox? This may be how you do it. You start by figuring how to finance the expansion onto the space frontier in a sustainable way that produces a significant return to our Earth-based economies.

Conclusion

For nearly two generations, our space program has been starved for funding and we have not returned to the moon nor gone further than Low Earth Orbit as a result.

Even if we see a return of astronauts into space in the mid-2020s, funding is the Catch-22 to the opening of a frontier in space. Until we have scale, costs are extraordinarily high and only a few national governments and the extremely wealthy can afford the trip. Only when we have scale and certainty on funding, will we be able to open up the space frontier and create a full-fledged economy in space.

I have proposed two strategies for public sector funding: Fiscal and monetary. A tax/equity hybrid vehicle could generate $200 billion per year in funding. And a variant on Quantitative Easing (Quantum Easing) by the Federal Reserve that could be used to inject liquidity and inflate an economy in space, potentially at similar levels of funding. We can argue about whether these strategies make sense and what the numbers look like.

But here's something to consider. Today, NASA has a funding level of $25 billion and we are a society that has consistently been unwilling to pay more for a program focused on space exploration. By contrast, a space program focused on a New Frontier Future and the creation of an economically self-sustaining presence in Near Earth Space that creates high-paying jobs and high-single digit economic growth at home has a viable pathway to sustained funding, both fiscal and monetary, in the range of $500 billion per year.

My proposed funding is 20-25x greater than NASA's current budget and is potentially more sustainable than current funding for space exploration precisely because it draws a direct connection, a direct strategic line, to a more prosperous economy with high-paying jobs and robust economic growth that will benefit all Americans and that are the top Earthly priorities for most Americans today.

Not only that, but my program has a shot at being supported by a majority of American voters in a way that space exploration does not. If the initial survey that I have run is any indication, we already have a majority of Americans that support the principal of a space-based economy that returns a profit to Earth and we have a near majority of voters (40-45%) that are supportive when specific numbers (even very large numbers) are put next to that question. If those numbers represent the baseline of public will before we have even articulated a true strategy for the space frontier, then we are starting from a very strong position.

The level of investment I am proposing – $500 billion annually when including monetary policies – may sound scary or big to many people that read this, but I would argue they are viable politically because they can drive significant and prolonged economic growth that results in good jobs and higher wages for a vast number of Americans. To move the needle of growth on an economy as large as the one we have today, simply requires thinking more boldly and at a greater scale than has been previously considered. Going big has big benefits and is potentially more politically and economically sustainable as a result.

Not only that, if we can truly create an economic clone of our domestic economy, one that operates at a much higher level of wages and prices, then we have the potential to finance many of our more politically divisive challenges here on Earth. We can do that not only for America, but if we can pilot the model and make it work, we can expand it for all of humanity. We can create a bonus for all of humankind if we dare to try.

Conclusion

This book advocates a large-scale future in space because that New Frontier may offer a vast payoff in public value for our economy and country as a whole and for your children individually and specifically. This is what it could mean:

- Minimum wage jobs in space that pay $250/hour or more, come with a 5-year contract, and end with $1M in personal savings.
- An economy in space that operates at a higher level of prices and wages (an **Economic Conjugate**) than our current economy on Earth, which RESULTS in:
- A massive public return on investment (**ROI**) on public money invested in space collected via taxes and fees on that space economy, which then DELIVERS:
- A **Trifecta Economy** on Earth of low taxes, high benefits, and no public debt, which then also DRIVES:
- A high growth economy that is more equal, creates prosperity for all, and FINANCES:
- The cost of a full transition to a carbon-free, net-zero economy, the elimination of all poverty, and the creation of modern institutions and services from higher education to healthcare that are accessible to everyone and the pride of all.

This is a pretty good future if you can get it. And for the record, I think we can get it. It will not happen overnight, but over the course of decades if we are bold enough to try.

Why haven't we achieved that future already?

Besotted with our past success in landing men on the Moon more than a generation ago, our public policy has focused on pursuing space exploration as the governing strategic vision for human spaceflight even though there is ample evidence to suggest that this is not what the public truly wants and aspires to nor what our political system is willing and able to fund.

There are five reasons why this is true:

- It's (too) Expensive
- Earthly Priorities > Space Exploration
- There's No (Direct) Payback
- There's no Blank Check
- It's An Elite Sport

Despite repeated Presidential initiatives, we have yet to return to the Moon or go onwards to Mars. The pending use of NASA's SLS (Space Launch System) rocket (first test flight completed in 2022) and the potential flight with astronauts around the Moon by 2025 may seem like a return to progress. But the bigger signal will be if Congress allocates more funding. That prognosis is grim. NASA is unlikely to be funded at significantly higher levels given competing national priorities, certainly not in amounts that will result in anything more than a few people in space at any one point in time. And that is even if every SLS launch over the coming years is a roaring success.

An underfunded NASA has become so acculturated it has become a Hollywood cliché, illustrated by films like *Interstellar* in which NASA has (literally) become an underground organization and we need help from an external 'alien' civilization to help humanity seize the space frontier. That cliché was rivalled by another film, *Gravity*, in which the space environment was portrayed as so dangerous and hostile that we should be exceedingly grateful to merely stand on the Earth's surface and feel the wet, muddy ground beneath our feet.

We are awash in Hollywood clichés channeling the popular zeitgeist showing a NASA with its wings clipped and an America without the strength, character, or optimism to seize the High Frontier. Either too dangerous to chance or beyond our abilities without external help, we seem to have lost confidence that we can achieve this frontier on our own or that our own public will support it. That is not the only contradiction. While NASA remains one of the most trusted and admired government agencies, the number of people that think it deserves significantly more funding is less than 20%.

Is it even possible to think big? If not in America, China certainly is. In 2021, China began a study to build a 'colony' ship a kilometer long. In reaction, our press cited American experts dismissing this idea as impractical because the cost of launching and maintaining the International Space Station, a much smaller structure, has been so expensive over the past several decades. Yet, as noted in the Introduction, the cost to launch into space has fallen dramatically, over 95%, since the ISS was launched, driven by innovations from Elon Musk's SpaceX. Our press could find no expert citing that dramatic change. While China has the *gravitas* to dream big, America is falling terribly short on any such vision

The truth is we can do more.

The untested thesis of this book is that there is a great hunger for the Frontier deeply embedded in our culture and in the aspirations of virtually all Americans. We are built of the stock that braved the voyage from far shores and ran the gauntlet to cross the border. We are the ones that dared to uproot our families in search of a better life and more opportunity. Whether Pilgrims, Pioneers, or Boat People, recently arrived or generations removed, legally here or not, we are an immigrant nation blended, bred, and optimized to go forth and seize new frontiers. *We are the ones that dared.* It is literally in our DNA.

A New Frontier Future offers a strategic doctrine paired with an action plan for achieving scale in space and is an attempt to offer a vision around which it is easier to rally and inspire greater public support than Space Exploration, despite its much greater expense. If we are going to play this game, we should play it big and we should play it to win.

How does a New Frontier Future do against the five constraints to space exploration? It demolishes them. Here's how and why:

- *It's too expensive.* Compared to the cost of space exploration, a New Frontier Future is much more so. Yet, it offers a better value proposition. It offers a chance of direct payback and potentially a return on investment.
- *Earthly priorities are more important.* Earthly priorities will always trump high-minded aspiration and the desire to explore and gain knowledge. In contrast, a New Frontier Future is aimed directly at critical earthly expectations: jobs, wages, and economic growth.
- *There's no direct payback.* A New Frontier Future offers a means to collect revenue directly and traceably and to eventually pay back the entire investment of public money.
- *There's no blank check.* We are going to ask for far more funding than space exploration ever did or will. Yet, with the possibility of payback and the potential to increase prosperity on Earth, it is possible that no check is really too small, a proposition voters may agree with.
- *It's an elite sport.* A New Frontier Future is about forging and bending steel at scale. It is not a game of the few exploring on the behalf of the many, but a game of the many working to make the frontier real for all.

A New Frontier Future as a governing strategic rationale meets and exceeds all of the critical constraints that have held back space exploration for nearly two generations.

Not only that, but an informal survey suggests the possibility that Americans are willing to bet big on our future when it comes to space. A poll using Survey Monkey found a strong majority of Americans (>65%) support a space program that results in an economically profitable space-based economy that creates stronger economic growth and high paying jobs here on Earth. When offered various options for programs that spend substantial sums ($200 billion/year) for extended periods of time (50 years), there is a strong baseline of support (40-45%) among respondents (and slightly higher among Likely Voters) for these programs as long as they offer the potential for jobs and payback. Last, two-thirds of voters are willing to consider a Congressional candidate that proposes a bolder American space program as long as the program also results in higher economic growth and better paying jobs at home. Support for a bolder program in space, surprisingly, may also be shared equally across the political spectrum among Democrats, Republicans, and Independents. When was the last time that happened?

These numbers are not perfect. The survey behind them is not a professional one. The questions are admittedly leading. The results need to be tested more rigorously. And yet these findings offer grounds for optimism that our public is interested in boldness. The truth could be that we are a people looking for a big, expansive dream in which 'normal' people get a shot at being in space paired with a viable proposal and narrative for a more prosperous future for all.

The great irony, of course, is that space exploration and related science, a program I have criticized as an overall *governing* vision, would be greatly expanded if we were to build a New Frontier Future. A vigorous and expansive human presence in space would be a shot in the arm for exploration and science, whether robotic or human. If there is a large sustainable presence in near earth space, then there is a low-cost base from which to explore deep space and a very high need to do so at far greater scale and frequency. There will be many more such missions within this context than are even remotely contemplated today. Simply put, building a New Frontier Future includes space exploration at greater scale and tempo by default.

It also includes a lot more science. Go big in space and we are going to need to understand much more about that environment and its impact on humans. We are going to need new forms of propulsion and new materials. We are going to have to develop a way to protect people from radiation without tons of materials for shielding, which is incredibly expensive. We are going to need an exponential increase in virtually every field of science and engineering to make living in space feasible and to travel down the cost curve to make it economically sustainable.

I've argued we have a good chance of selling a New Frontier Future to the public as a vision and I believe we can engage in the political process in a way to get the votes to reboot an American space program at scale.

As the enabling levers of lower launch costs and asteroid mining come into place, we can grow to dominate the frontier of Near-Earth space and build a permanent and self-sustaining human presence as a foundation from which to grow beyond Earth.

The frontier beckons.

We do not need a new rival nor do we need a new Sputnik moment, either rhetorically or in fact. We don't need to go hat in hand to the international community to find partners willing to pay for that which we are not willing to fund ourselves. What we need is a vision upon which to act and the will to go forth. We have been hugging the shallows of Low Earth Orbit for too long.

It is time to go beyond.

Getting to that large-scale future in space will not be easy. We are not flush with cash and we face a daunting list of challenges. The forecasts of our long-range fiscal situation are increasingly grim. Our national debt has grown enormously from multiple crises and it is likely to get worse. Economies across the globe have become unstable. Inflation has reached a 40-year high and the cure to this illness may cause yet another recessionary disease. The economic outlook is increasingly poor and the people that will suffer the most are those with the least means. Income inequality may yet worsen from historically high levels already.

In the face of this grim domestic news, military conflict has broken out in the heart of Europe and every region of the world is now more dangerous driven by Russia's war against Ukraine and China's increasing menace of Taiwan. Our future is going to require prioritizing more guns over butter. At the same time, we face a warming planet that is likely to impose significant costs in the future. These issues are occurring against the backdrop of a polarized and poisonous partisan political environment. We are a divided nation that seems unable to reach consensus on anything, choosing conflict, lies, conspiracy, and propaganda to feast on instead. The list of calls on our resources both now and in the future is long, urgent, and morally compelling and any grand new program will face the opposition of every vested interest.

Underlining this litany of challenges is a gaping hole in public confidence. Neither party has articulated a vision that inspires much confidence beyond the standard ideological rhetoric. Americans are not fooled. Survey after survey suggests a majority of Americans believe their children's generation will be less well off than ours today and faith in our governing institutions from Congress to both political parties has collapsed. This is an indictment of our current politics and a profound failure by our policy elites to articulate a governing vision for the future.

The surest sign of a failure in political vision is when outsiders rise as serious political candidates on all sides of the political spectrum and voters reject governing elites and experts and their supposed wisdom and competence. This is happening today in every advanced economy of the western world, not just America. And why not when all our politicians offer are obsolete ideologies and ineffective policies leading to jobless recoveries and stagnating wages or over-stimulative inflationary spirals? Why not when status quo politics can't solve basic problems from the cost of housing to public safety to quality education for all of our children?

The year 2016 will surely be seen as ground zero in the political earthquake that has shaken the West. From Brexit to the improbable rise and victory of Donald Trump in the US Presidential election, voters rejected the status quo of governing elites that had created more Have-Nots than Haves. But that trend did not start in 2016 and it certainly did not end with the polarized result, insurrection, and Big Lie of

2020. That battle is being rehashed in 2024 in countries all around the world from Europe to the United States.

But that may not be the worst of it. Against this backdrop, there is a growing debate over whether the golden age of American growth is over for good. Best articulated by Economist Robert Gordon, his thesis is that the big transformations – electricity, automobiles, airplanes, manufacturing, modern healthcare – have played out and the much-hyped technology innovations of the digital economy today are at best merely incremental improvements on current trends by comparison. Digitizing chatter and making money from advertising hardly compares with the creation of the flush toilet, the light bulb, the networked home, the Model T, antibiotics, or the airplane. Facebook is profitable. It's not profound even if you rename it Meta and make it fully immersive. Gordon suggests the possibility that the future will look more like the recent past: slow economic growth, increased inequality, stagnating wages, and a declining American middle class.

If that is our future, then it is a grim forecast.

In the face of such woeful tidings, this essay attempts a counterargument. It articulates a specific pathway to a high growth future, a future that can lift tens of millions of Americans into high wage jobs and reverse the trends of a declining middle class.

The century from 1870-1970 was an extraordinary one filled with a number of innovations that have already reached saturation and those specific innovations won't be duplicated at scale in the future.

We believe the biggest transformation in human history still lies ahead and is nearly within our grasp. It represents a second 'Special Century' for America. It entails the massive build out of the space frontier. It includes factor inputs of resources on an unlimited scale. It implies building cities in space and colonies on other worlds. It requires building a transportation system that spans the solar system. It means exploring innovations like variable gravity agriculture and zero-G manufacturing. And it creates a forcing function for a dramatic increase in total factor productivity. Labor and capital will be incredibly expensive when you have to lift them from the surface of the Earth or your drinking water comes from an asteroid. Therefore, every activity will inspire and require an effort at innovation.

These are the engines of future economic growth. This is profoundly more powerful and exciting than digitizing chatter and charging for advertising. This is much bigger than snapping, tweeting, or searching. This is forging and bending steel at scale in an environment of extraordinarily high cost and with no established, vested interests or competitors. It is a virgin frontier that beckons the hardy, the entrepreneurial, and the brave. Sound familiar? It should. That used to be us.

This future is possible and it can be ours again.

We face a low growth future only if we choose to live in a closed system.

My counter-thesis to the growth-is-over argument is that we are, instead and at long last, on the verge of a 100-year burst of sustained high single digit and possibly double-digit economic growth that will drive more jobs, higher wages, and a sustainable economic future for America and also all of humanity. The counterpoint to the thesis of secular stagnation is a strategy to create an **Economic Conjugate** in space that creates a minimum wage job that pays $250 per hour, $500,000 per year, and comes with a 5-year contract, a job available to tens of millions of American by the end of this century. It is built on a vision of creating a duplicate economy in space that returns a vast surplus of earnings to Earth within 50 years, effectively lifting all boats in all nations. There is a growth explosion at the far right of the economic model of a New Frontier Future that we can capture for the benefit of our children and all of humanity, if we but choose to try.

A better, more prosperous future is within our reach. It is a future that will be led by the society that can best harness the technology, the public will, and private sector innovation along with a sustainable means of financing the breakout. When the *Economist* magazine called the end of the Space Age at the retirement of the Space Shuttle in 2011, they

233

got it wrong. We merely finished the first chapter. Something bigger, bolder, and more extraordinary is beginning to ramp up. We have the potential to build an economically sustainable frontier in space.

We are a country that has made such big bets and gone to such great lengths in the past.

We are the country that made the Louisiana Purchase, bought Alaska from the Russians, and built the Panama Canal. We are the country that funded the Marshall Plan, inspired the United Nations, and legislated the Land Grant universities. We are the country that built the Interstate Highway system, created the Internet, and landed men on the moon.

We are still that country.

It's not too late to imagine a future in which we can do much more at home and abroad on the back of a dynamic and rapidly growing economy. It's not too late to imagine a future where our children do better and are more prosperous than we are today. It's not too late to build a new frontier and create a new destination for all of humanity. It's not too late to build a future we can be proud of, regardless of our politics. It is not too late to be bold, to build, and to make big bets again.

We don't have to live in a closed global economy forever characterized by win-lose competition, jealous of every job lost. We don't have to stand by watching our middle class stagnate and decline because too many jobs are being automated or globalized. We don't have to build walls, turn inward, and hunker down, pointing fingers of blame in every direction except our own.

We can do more and go further.

If you are looking for the soundbites for why we must go into space at scale and with boldness, if you are looking for the pitch lines to use with Americans of all walks in every situation, if you are looking for the talking points for explaining to someone in the unemployment line in the midst of a recession that has no job and is losing their home that spending $200 billion a year to conquer a new frontier is more important than their personal need right now at this moment, then here are those soundbites to explain what is possible and why we must try:

- We must be the generation that dared to expand our horizons instead of the generation that was too scared to try.
- We must be the generation that lived up to our legacy of American leadership and made the bold investments to move humanity beyond the confines of a single planet.
- We must be the generation that chose to build the new products and new industries of a new frontier where no one else can compete.
- We must go into space because we must escape the secular stagnation of our economy and the polarization of our politics.
- We must go into space because it means re-establishing the narrative of the American Dream on a frontier of limitless opportunity and exponential growth.
- We must go into space because it is the only way we can establish a bolder, more prosperous future for our children even if it requires sacrifices today to make that future real.
- We must go into space because it is this generation's responsibility not to squander the exceptional calling of America for the frontier, even as our forebears made the bold decisions of their eras to expand our nation's horizons.

These are the reasons we must go into space at scale and speed and for which we must make sacrifices today for a better more prosperous future tomorrow. The world needs an exceptional and prosperous America. We can be that beacon of opportunity and hope once again.

This can be your future. It is a future that will be earned one vote at a time. It starts with yours.

Some people are going to tell you that we are not ready for a big new vision for America in space. They will say we can't afford it. They will tell you that Congress will never approve it. They will say Americans will never vote for it. They will shake their head and tell you that it just can't be done.

Ignore them.

The naysayers are wrong. Why that is so can be summed up in just four words:

The world has changed.

In 2016, we witnessed a political earthquake rock the Western World from Brexit in the UK to the victory of Donald Trump in America. Ever since, Populism and protest have been locked in struggle against the status quo in America and Europe. It may not win every time, but the ugliness has exposed just how alienated, angry, and desperate our publics are. In the midst of economic pain, political elites have failed to deliver a believable narrative of future growth and prosperity that benefits the majority rather than a lucky few and electorates are seeking alternatives, no matter how extreme.

Political failure has opened the door to Populism.

But the Populists have a quandary. The charismatic people who have been most successful in capturing voter dissatisfaction with promises of a better future have no real agenda for achieving what they have promised. They can demonize and attack. But you can't just wave your hand and magically conjure economic growth. You can't get more jobs by building walls, putting up barriers, pulling back from competition, and starting trade wars. You can juice short-term results with massive tax cuts or debt, but eventually the bills will come due. The most likely outcome is the exact opposite of a prosperous future.

But neither can the established parties defeat Populism by making promises of more benefits and programs without a narrative to achieve economic prosperity through growth and by dumping the tax bill on people who don't feel they can afford it. Both sides need a believable path forward to growth and prosperity. Neither yet has one.

The U.S. election of 2020 amply illustrated the ideological stalemate. The election of 2024 is simply reinforcing and repeating the same argument.

Any vision that offers a narrative of a more prosperous future with better jobs and opportunities for all is one that now has a shot at serious consideration like no previous time in recent history.

The truth is we need the growth of a frontier that has the scope and size of the Louisiana Purchase, the Homestead Act, the Interstate Highway System, the Marshall Plan, and the Panama Canal all rolled into one. The space frontier is the only candidate that qualifies.

The time to go big and be bold is now. The vision of a prosperous America and West is not a luxury that we approach and argue for over time with incremental baby steps. It is an urgent necessity today and the future of the world as we know it now depends on our success.

It is time to stop talking about small-scale space exploration by the few and start talking about the extraordinary benefits to the many of a mass break-out into space on a frontier of limitless opportunity and exponential growth. It is time to build a New Frontier Future.

Now is the time to seize the frontier of space and the single best way to end this essay is with the quote from Carl Sagan that started it:

> The visions we offer our children shape the future.
> It *matters* what those visions are.
> Often they become self-fulfilling prophecies.
> Dreams are maps.
> Carl Sagan, *Pale Blue Dot*, 1994

Appendix A: Space Frontier & Politics Survey

More than 4-in-10 Americans Support Large-Scale Investment in a Space Frontier

Executive Summary

Despite widespread popular approval for NASA (77% favorability rating) and an expressed interest in sending American astronauts to Mars, no more than 22% of the American public has been polled as willing to pay more for space exploration. However, in a recent online survey using Survey Monkey, it was found that more than 40% of Americans were willing to spend very large sums to develop an economically profitable space frontier given two explicit caveats: If the program can be clearly linked to payback of all public money spent AND if it results in high-paying jobs being created in America.

Overview

Despite a high level of interest by the American public in sending American astronauts to explore other worlds, the American public has traditionally seen space exploration as a very low priority for funding compared to other earthly priorities. In one survey, it ranked 16th out of 18 choices offered as priorities. In the General Social Survey of 2012, the percentage of American willing to spend more on space exploration was just 22%.

There have been numerous attempts to explain the seeming disconnect between high levels of interest and enthusiasm for space exploration and the lack of willingness to fund it. These range from suggestions that Americans don't really understand how little of the federal budget is spent on NASA (.5%) to the premise that Americans might not be that enthusiastic for space exploration when confronted with real spending choices.

An alternative hypothesis was tested via online survey that past polling of support for America's space program has been asking the wrong questions and, therefore, deriving the wrong conclusions. Further, that when offered an option for an expanded program in space that costs much, much more, but offers the potential for a return on investment (payback), a significantly higher percentage of Americans would be supportive.

Methodology

The survey asked 15 questions and was comprised of three components.

The first was a set of three basic demographic questions (Age, Education level, and Registered voter status/party affiliation). These provided a foundational set of data points on which to measure the participants in the survey.

The second part was a modified Perry-Gallup (PG) questionnaire of likely voter participation based on six of the seven standard PG questions. The Perry-Gallup Likely Voter questions attempts to determine who are likely voters and identify those highly likely to vote in an election.

The six questions asked were:

- Have you ever voted either in person or by mail in your precinct or election district? (**Yes**, no, Don't know)
- How often would you say you vote — always, nearly always, part of the time, or seldom? (**Always**, **Nearly always**, part of the time, Seldom, Never, Don't know)
- How much thought have you given to the coming November election? (**Quite a lot**, **Some**, Little, None, Don't know)
- How likely are you to vote in the general election this November? (**Definitely will**, **Probably will**, Probably will not, Definitely will not)
- In the 2012 presidential election between Barack Obama and Mitt Romney, did things come up that

kept you from voting, or did you happen to vote? (**Yes**, no, Don't know)

- How would you rate your chances of voting in November's election for president on a scale of 1 to 10. If 1 represents someone who definitely will not vote and 10 represents someone who definitely will vote, where on this scale of 1 to 10 would you place yourself? (0-8, **9**, **10**)

Points were then scored based on one point for each question where the answer is one of those in bold with a total of six points possible. If a voter is not registered to vote (an earlier question), their total score is set to zero.

Because one question was discarded in the interest of cost (Do you know where in your neighborhood to go to vote), we used a point score of five or six to identify likely voters vs. the standard scoring of six or seven. This approach may introduce flaws or be less reliable, but we believe that it is directionally accurate as it still captures participants that are a) registered to vote, b) have voted in the past, c) have expressed interest in the election, and d) indicated they plan to vote in the election.

In the third section, six questions were asked about their potential support for an American space program that is distinctly different from a program focused on space exploration. Two questions were general principal/directional questions without specific numbers. The other four questions were 'hard ball' questions that asked participants to consider specific amounts of spending ranging from $50 billion to $10 trillion and with extended timelines ranging from 10 years to 50. All questions were phrased with terminology indicating the payback of public money was both feasible and a primary goal/rationale for funding and that earthly benefits included more economic growth and high-paying jobs.

The six questions are listed below in Table 1 along with the percentage of people that were either 'Strongly' or 'Somewhat' in agreement with the question. Two data points in the columns on the right are provided – the response from all respondents and that of a subset identified as Likely Voters.

Table 1: Space Frontier and Politics Survey, 2016 (Survey Monkey)		
Polling Question	All Agree*	Likely Voters Agree*
Question 1: As a voter, would you support a NASA-led 10-year, $100 billion effort to create a manufacturing facility in space housing 1,000 or more American workers IF all of the public funds invested could be recovered through fees and taxes on private sector companies using the facility?	45.2%	50.7%
Question 2: The technology to mine asteroids in space is available today, but private companies cannot yet invest at scale because a market for these resources has not yet been created. Would you support a NASA-led program to purchase asteroid material from the private sector at a cost of $50 billion dollars over 20 years IF the materials purchased were then owned by the American public and were valued at $100 billion on the open market (a taxpayer profit of $50 billion)?	41.0%	44.0%
Question 3: If an economically profitable American presence in space could also spark strong economic growth at home in America, create millions of high paying jobs, and pay back all of the public money invested plus a profit, would you support a government program led by NASA to build it?	67.6%	71.3%
Question 4: If it would cost $200 billion per year (5% of the federal government's budget) for 50 years to achieve an economically profitable presence in space with enough self-supporting economic activity to return all of the public money invested plus a profit, would you support a NASA-led program to invest that $200 billion per year to make it happen?	43.3%	45.3%
Question 5: Would you vote to invest $10 trillion in taxpayer funds over a period of 50 years to establish an economically profitable presence in space IF that investment would return $20 trillion in taxpayer revenue by the end of that same period of time?	41.9%	44.7%
Question 6: If a Congressional candidate in your district backed a bold government-led program to develop an economically profitable frontier in space that would generate millions of jobs in America and would pay back every public dollar spent along with a significant profit, would you consider voting for that candidate?	52.9%	57.3%

The online survey tool was Survey Monkey. Concerns about the validity of online polling have some merit, however, Survey Monkey has reportedly been able to overcome many of these concerns by leveraging a very large audience (reportedly 3 million or more) in order to achieve a sampling profile that is more accurate and representative. Survey Monkey has been widely credited with correctly identifying many recent political surprises (ex. The 2015 Scottish election) that other traditional professional polling organizations have missed. A recent article by the Los Angeles Times describes how and why Survey Monkey may be a viable tool for polling and the results achieved relatively representative of the general American population.

The survey sample size was 210. This is small relative to standard professional polling surveys that more typically have sample sizes ranging from 1,500 to 2,500 in order to achieve a representative view of the American public. We found the data to have a good distribution between Republican, Democrat, and Independent populations and generally well distributed between different age groups (slightly skewed older) and education levels (relatively even distribution). Scoring based on the Perry-Gallup index suggests a relatively high percentage ~75% of likely voters and this may be due to choosing a 'political' template from Survey Monkey which it then may have matched to participants in political surveys that are more likely to be engaged. This is not necessarily a bad thing, however. Likely voters are a more indicative group when looking at potential support for future policies and Likely Voters are what politicians are most interested in.

Overall, we recommend this survey and its results be considered as a directional point of view at best vs. a perfectly representative sample of what the American public is thinking. It is our hope that further research is undertaken along similar lines.

Results

Polling data over multiple decades has found a relatively small percentage of Americans are willing to spend more than currently budgeted on space exploration. It has been reported that the highest percentage of the American public that believes we are not spending enough on space exploration is 22%. The conventional wisdom, therefore, is that Americans are not willing to pay for a bolder American space program.

Yet when we asked different questions, very different results were achieved.

In our own survey, we used multiple questions to determine the willingness of Americans to consider an alternative to space exploration as the governing theme of America's space program. A common characteristic of all the questions is the premise that a) that large sums invested in creating a space-based economy will create economic growth and high-paying jobs for Americans at home on Earth, and b) that a profitable space-based economy will eventually pay back all public funds invested. These questions explicitly link a bolder program in space directly to earthly priorities (economic growth, jobs, etc.) and offers a direct payback to the taxpayer.

The first question tested whether Americans would support the creation of a manufacturing facility in space housing upwards of a thousand workers if it cost $100 billion over 10 years to construct, but with a strong conditional statement that all funds were paid back over time by user fees from private companies using the facility. Just over 45% of all respondents agreed (strongly or somewhat) that they would support such a program and the number increased to over 50% when likely voters were considered. Among likely voters, support was higher among Democrat voters (60%) than either Republicans (41.7%) or Independents (51.0%). Men who are likely voters were more supportive (63%) than women (39.0%). Likely voters with a college education (64.1%) and post-graduate education (49.1%) were more supportive than likely voters with less than a high school education (33.3%) or some college (44.4%).

Question 1: As a voter, would you support a NASA-led 10-year, $100 billion effort to create a manufacturing facility in space housing 1,000 or more American workers IF all of the public funds invested could be recovered through fees and taxes on private sector companies using the facility?

	All Respondents (n=210)			Likely Voters (n=150)		
	Agree	Neutral	Disagree	Agree	Neutral	Disagree
Republican	42.9%	23.2%	34.0%	41.7%	22.9%	35.4%
Democrat	54.4%	22.8%	22.8%	60.0%	18.0%	22.0%
Independent	45.2%	30.3%	24.9%	51.0%	29.4%	19.6%
All	45.2%	26.2%	28.6%	50.7%	23.3%	26.0%
Male	55.1%	25.5%	19.4%	63.0%	21.9%	15.1%
Female	36.6%	26.8%	36.6%	39.0%	24.7%	36.4%
High School	19.0%	38.1%	42.9%	33.3%	44.4%	22.2%
Some College	41.3%	31.7%	27.0%	44.4%	31.1%	24.4%
College Grad	54.2%	13.6%	32.2%	64.1%	5.1%	30.8%
Post-Grad	47.8%	28.4%	22.4%	49.1%	26.3%	24.6%

In a second question, when participants were asked if they would support a program led by NASA to purchase asteroid material from the private sector at a cost of $50 billion over 20 years that would then have a value that was nearly twice what it cost, or $100 billion, 41.0% of all respondents agreed (Strongly or Somewhat) that they would support such a program. Among likely voters, the percentage was 44.0% that Agreed (Strongly or Somewhat). Once again, men were more likely (50.0%) to support the idea of a government program to promote asteroid mining that cost $50 billion than women (33.0%). Both men and women that were Likely Voters were 2-3 percentage points more supportive than all respondents.

Question 2: The technology to mine asteroids in space is available today, but private companies cannot yet invest at scale because a market for these resources has not yet been created. Would you support a NASA-led program to purchase asteroid material from the private sector at a cost of $50 billion dollars over 20 years IF the materials purchased were then owned by the American public and were valued at $100 billion on the open market (a taxpayer profit of $50 billion)?

	All Respondents (n=210)			Likely Voters (n=150)		
	Agree	Neutral	Disagree	Agree	Neutral	Disagree
Republican	41.1%	19.6%	39.2%	39.6%	18.8%	41.7%
Democrat	40.4%	28.1%	31.6%	44.0%	26.0%	30.0%
Independent	43.8%	30.1%	26.0%	49.0%	31.4%	19.6%
All	41.0%	27.6%	31.4%	44.0%	25.3%	30.6%
Male	50.0%	25.5%	24.5%	52.1%	26.0%	21.9%
Female	33.0%	29.5%	37.5%	36.4%	24.7%	39.0%
High School	38.1%	28.6%	33.3%	44.4%	33.3%	22.2%
Some College	34.9%	36.5%	28.6%	35.6%	35.6%	28.9%
College Grad	42.4%	22.0%	35.6%	48.7%	15.4%	35.9%
Post-Grad	46.3%	23.9%	29.9%	47.4%	22.0%	29.8%

The third question was a general principles question without a specified cost. The question tested the general level of support for the premise of an economically profitable American presence in space that created economic growth and high paying jobs at home in America AND repaid all of the public funds invested. Among all respondents, the level of support was quite high at 67.6% and among those identified as Likely Voters, the response rate was higher still at 71.3%.

Once again, men (73.5%) were more likely to be supportive than women (62.5%) and the percentages for both increased among Likely Voters with men at 75.3% and women at 67.5%.

Among the respondents with some college education, a four-year degree, and / or post-graduate education, the level of support was the highest, ranging from 67% to 79%. The rate among respondents with a high school or less level of education, the rates was much lower (38%), however, the sample size was very small and not necessarily statistically valid.

Question 3: If an economically profitable American presence in space could also spark strong economic growth at home in America, create millions of high paying jobs, and pay back all of the public money invested plus a profit, would you support a government program led by NASA to build it?

	All Respondents (n=210)			Likely Voters (n=150)		
	Agree	Neutral	Disagree	Agree	Neutral	Disagree
Republican	67.8%	8.9%	23.2%	68.8%	10.4%	20.8%
Democrat	70.2%	17.5%	12.3%	74.0%	16.0%	10.0%
Independent	69.9%	13.7%	16.4%	72.5%	13.7%	13.7%
All	67.6%	14.8%	17.6%	71.3%	13.3%	15.3%
Male	73.5%	10.2%	16.5%	75.3%	12.3%	12.3%
Female	62.5%	18.8%	18.8%	67.5%	14.3%	18.2%
High School	38.1%	28.6%	33.3%	33.3%	33.3%	33.3%
Some College	68.3%	12.7%	19.1%	71.1%	11.1%	17.8%
College Grad	67.8%	17.0%	15.3%	69.2%	15.8%	15.4%
Post-Grad	76.1%	10.5%	13.4%	79.0%	10.5%	10.5%

The fourth and fifth question tested support for large-scale expenditures over extended periods of time. Question four asked if the respondent would support a space program that cost $200 billion per year for 50 years if the funding was eventually paid back in full with a profit. Question five proposed the same question in a different way, asking if respondents would support a 50-year program that cost $10 trillion dollars if that program would eventually return $20 trillion in revenue (a $10 trillion profit).

For question four, more than 43% of respondents supported the long-term program lasting 50 years with expenditures of $200 billion per year that repaid the entire investment over time. Among Likely Voters, the number increased to 45.3%. Men were more supportive (53.1%) compared to women (34.8%) among all respondents and slightly more so among Likely Voters (men at 56.2%, women at 35.1%).

With question five, the same total was raised in a different way. Respondents were asked if they would support a NASA-led program that spent $10 trillion dollars over 50 years (the same amount as question four), but then resulted in revenues of $20 trillion by the end of the same period.

Question 4: If it would cost $200 billion per year (5% of the federal government's budget) for 50 years to achieve an economically profitable presence in space with enough self-supporting economic activity to return all of the public money invested plus a profit, would you support a NASA-led program to invest that $200 billion per year to make it happen?

	All Respondents (n=210)			Likely Voters (n=150)		
	Agree	Neutral	Disagree	Agree	Neutral	Disagree
Republican	44.6%	19.6%	35.7%	43.8%	22.9%	33.3%
Democrat	45.6%	22.8%	31.6%	48.0%	20.0%	32.0%
Independent	42.0%	31.5%	27.4%	45.1%	31.4%	23.5%
All	43.3%	26.2%	30.5%	45.3%	25.3%	29.3%
Male	53.1%	21.4%	25.5%	56.2%	21.9%	21.9%
Female	34.8%	30.4%	34.8%	35.1%	28.6%	36.4%
High School	33.3%	28.6%	38.1%	33.3%	33.3%	33.3%
Some College	46.0%	30.2%	23.8%	48.9%	28.9%	22.2%
College Grad	45.8%	18.6%	35.6%	51.1%	12.8%	35.9%
Post-Grad	41.8%	28.4%	29.9%	40.4%	29.8%	29.8%

Roughly similar numbers were found with this question as well. Nearly 42% of all respondents agreed with the idea of a large-scale, long duration program that created a net profit for taxpayers. Among Likely voters, the total increased to 44.7%.

Men (at 53.1%) were more supportive than women (at 32.1%). Among Likely Voters, support by men increased to 58.9% and among women declined slightly.

Question 5: Would you vote to invest $10 trillion in taxpayer funds over a period of 50 years to establish an economically profitable presence in space IF that investment would return $20 trillion in taxpayer revenue by the end of that same period of time?					
	All Respondents (n=210)			Likely Voters (n=150)		
	Agree	Neutral	Disagree	Agree	Neutral	Disagree
Republican	44.6%	25.0%	30.4%	43.8%	29.2%	27.1%
Democrat	45.6%	28.1%	26.3%	48.0%	24.0%	28.0%
Independent	39.7%	24.7%	35.6%	43.1%	29.4%	27.5%
All	41.9%	26.2%	31.9%	44.7%	27.3%	28.0%
Male	53.1%	23.5%	23.5%	58.9%	24.7%	16.4%
Female	32.1%	28.6%	39.3%	31.2%	29.9%	39.0%
High School	28.6%	28.6%	42.9%	33.3%	22.2%	44.4%
Some College	46.0%	25.4%	28.6%	48.9%	26.7%	24.4%
College Grad	40.7%	23.7%	35.6%	46.2%	23.1%	30.8%
Post-Grad	43.3%	28.4%	28.4%	42.1%	31.6%	26.3%

For both questions, the percentage of Republicans and Democrats that were in agreement (strongly or somewhat) was virtually identical (44.6% for Republicans, 45.6 for Democrats). However, among Likely Voters, the percentage of Democrats increased to 48.0%, whereas, the percentage of Republicans that were in agreement decreased slightly to 43.8%.

The final question asked respondents whether they would support a Congressional candidate in their district that proposed a program to create an economically profitable frontier in space that created jobs at home and repaid all of the money invested along with a profit.

Among all respondents, a majority of 52.9% agreed. For Republicans, the number was 57.1% and for Democrats it was 61.4%. Independents were slightly less willing to support at 47.9% of respondents. Among likely voters, the overall percentage increased to 57.3%. For Likely Voters, Democrats increased to 66.0% whereas Republicans decreased slightly to 56.3%. Independents increased to 51.0%.

	All Respondents (n=210)			Likely Voters (n=150)		
	Agree	Neutral	Disagree	Agree	Neutral	Disagree
Republican	57.1%	16.1%	26.8%	56.3%	18.8%	25.0%
Democrat	61.4%	22.8%	15.8%	66.0%	20.0%	14.0%
Independent	47.9%	37.0%	15.1%	51.0%	37.3%	11.8%
All	52.9%	26.7%	20.5%	57.3%	25.3%	17.3%
Male	59.2%	23.5%	17.3%	64.4%	23.3%	12.3%
Female	47.3%	29.5%	23.2%	50.6%	27.3%	22.1%
High School	28.6%	33.3%	38.1%	44.4%	22.2%	33.3%
Some College	55.6%	22.2%	22.2%	57.8%	24.4%	17.8%
College Grad	50.8%	30.5%	18.6%	59.0%	25.6%	15.4%
Post-Grad	59.7%	25.4%	14.9%	57.9%	26.3%	15.8%

Among Likely Voters, 64.4% of men agreed they would consider voting for a candidate that supported a much more expansive space program, but 50.6% of women also agreed, a slight majority. Among Likely voters, those with some college, college graduates, and post-graduates that agreed they would consider supporting a Congressional candidate ranged from 57-59%.

Discussion

The survey results need to be taken with some degree of caution. The sample size is small (210), the surveyed group skews slightly higher in age, and the likely voter mix is greater than the general population. The wording of the questions might be too complex or hard to follow. And it's hard to know what respondents really thought about these questions without running some focus groups and conducting a more robust poll with a larger sample size and conducted by a professional polling firm using rigorous standards.

Those caveats aside, the results open up a new line of potential dialogue. Many in the space community have grown resigned to the prospect of limited public support, tightly constricted public funding for space exploration, and competition over which mission gets funded. However, there is a possibility that the space community may have been asking the wrong questions and drawing the wrong conclusions. What this poll suggests is the possibility that Americans are willing to think big and spend sums well beyond anything currently considered if there is an earthly pay-off to an expansive effort to build an economically profitable frontier in space at scale.

These findings are new and to my knowledge have not been specifically articulated or captured in any previous surveys or polling to date, although there have been hints in the Technology surveys done by Pew Charitable Trust that suggest Americans are expecting a bigger future in space 50 years out.

To put these findings in counterpoint and to highlight how impactful they potentially are, it is useful to consider an alternative point of view in the form of an essay in Scientific American from August, 2015, titled, *"The Inexcusable Jingoism of American Spaceflight Rhetoric"* by Dr. Linda Ball, a science communications researcher. In her essay, Dr. Ball suggests that discussion of the space frontier is overly nationalistic (America only), exploitive in focus, and something only appealing to a limited demographic (white males).

It is not wildly surprising to find a science communication researcher advocating a view that is more in favor of scientific exploration than development of a space frontier. The science community has traditionally seen human spaceflight as a competitor for scarce funding. (See Appendix C for the author's response to *Scientific American*.)

What is unusual is to suggest that interest in a space frontier is limited to white males based on anecdotal observations and past polling. By contrast, the objective data from these survey findings suggest this assertion is wildly off-base. It is best captured by the response rate to Question #3, "If an economically profitable American presence in space could also spark strong economic growth at home in America, create millions of high-paying jobs, and pay back all of the public money invested plus a profit, would you support a government program led by NASA to build it?"

This question effectively encompasses the very definition of what a space frontier means and some of its key defining attributes. What was the response?

Men were overwhelming supportive with 73.5% of all respondents and 75.3% of Likely Voters either agreeing 'Strongly' or 'Somewhat' with this question. But here's the kicker. Women were, too. Women were also overwhelmingly supportive, 62.5% of all women respondents and 67.5% of women that were Likely Voters, also agreed with this question. These are very strong majorities.

As noted, these survey findings need to be explored more robustly, but when you tee up the question to ask if people support a space frontier that achieves outcomes that are economically positive for people here on Earth, there is overwhelming support and it is, with minor variations, uniformly strong regardless of political affiliations and gender. Based on educational background, it has the least support only among those with a high school education or less.

The numbers drop for all groups when you get to questions that get specific on funding with specific amounts for specific durations. The number for women softens to numbers in the range of 30-35%, which is a strong core to build on, but much less than the two-thirds majority supportive of a space frontier in general. However, it is possible that support by women could be improved significantly. It may be that women's support is softer because they are factoring the risk that funding for the space frontier could crowd out or come at the expense of other core programs (e.g. education, healthcare, college, etc.). If this concern can be answered, then it is possible that support by women for more expansive efforts on the space frontier could increase significantly.

The fundamental point is that characterization of the space frontier as something that is primarily of interest only to white males appears extraordinarily incorrect. A very strong majority of women support a space frontier in concept and more than a third are supportive when you get to specific funding for specific programs which imply tougher choices.

It is possible that policymakers in general have been assuming that enthusiasm for the space frontier is a fringe interest group or something only white males are interested in. This isn't entirely wrong. Many men do like to see big rockets go whooshing up into space. I'm a man. We love that stuff.

But if you begin to analyze the interest in the space frontier from a perspective of jobs, economic growth, and payback of public funding over time, then a much broader level of support begins to come into view. If you draw a direct and credible link to practical and pragmatic issues (vs. rockets going whoosh into space) that have the potential to help us resolve some of our more intractable issues on Earth, then support is much greater and this is probably true both at home in America as well as abroad among our likely international partners in any such great endeavor.

What's very interesting is that the baseline numbers found in this poll exist even before any systematic campaign to share a vision of the space frontier with the American public that is directly linked to Earthly concerns such as jobs, economic growth, and the prosperity of future generations. If a sustained campaign to communicate that vision is started, it is possible that these numbers will rise significantly.

Conclusion

The numbers captured in this survey using Survey Monkey suggest the possibility that the American public is willing to consider a vastly larger commitment to an expansive effort in space as long as that program contributes to resolving earthly concerns for economic growth, high-paying jobs, and public funding payback. Space exploration does not offer that bargain or compact. Creating a self-sustaining and economically prosperous frontier in space does if it can be done at scale and it promises to have a positive, material impact on our economy at home.

A top priority for space advocacy organizations and enthusiasts is to fund a more professional and thorough research effort to validate whether these numbers hold true under greater scrutiny.

Appendix B: Top-line Survey Questions

Space Frontier & Politics Survey, conducted 2016
  N=210

Q1: What is your age?

<18	3	1.43%
18-24	20	9.52%
25-29	18	8.57%
30-39	37	17.62%
40-49	34	16.19%
50-64	62	29.52%
65+	36	17.14%

Q2: What is the highest level of education you have completed?

High school or less	21	10.0%
Some college	63	30.0%
College graduate	59	28.1%
Post-graduate (> 4 years of college)	67	31.9%

Q3: Are you registered to vote in your state as a Republican, Democrat, Independent / no party preference, Other party, or not registered to vote?

Republican	56	26.67%
Democrat	57	27.14%
Independent	73	34.76%
Other party	3	1.43%
Not registered	21	10.00%

Q4: Have you ever voted either in person or by mail in your precinct or election district?

Yes	170	80.95%
No	34	16.19%
Don't know	6	2.86%

Q5: How often would you say you vote — always, nearly always, part of the time, or seldom?

Always vote	84	40.00%
Nearly always vote	64	30.48%
Vote part of the time	27	12.86%
Seldom vote	12	5.71%
Never vote	18	8.57%
Don't know	5	2.38%

Q6: How much thought have you given to the coming November election?

Quite a lot	125	59.52%
Some	50	23.81%
Only a little	18	8.57%
None	15	7.14%
Don't know	2	0.95%

Q7: How likely are you to vote in the general election this November?

Definitely will vote	160	76.19%
Probably will vote	26	12.38%
Probably will not vote	6	2.86%
Definitely will not vote	18	8.57%

Q8: In the 2012 presidential election between Barack Obama and Mitt Romney, did things come up that kept you from voting, or did you happen to vote?

Yes, voted	161	76.67%
No, did not vote	43	20.48%
Don't know	6	2.86%

Q9: How would you rate your chances of voting in November's election for president on a scale of 1 to 10. If 1 represents someone who definitely will not vote and 10 represents someone who definitely will vote, where on this scale of 1 to 10 would you place yourself?

1-Definitely will NOT vote	17	8.10%
2	4	1.90%
3	0	0.00%
4	3	1.43%
5	5	2.38%
6	3	1.43%
7	4	1.90%
8	4	1.90%
9	16	7.62%
10-Definitely WILL vote	153	72.86%
Don't know	1	0.48%

Q10: As a voter, would you support a NASA-led 10-year, $100 billion effort to create a manufacturing facility in space housing 1,000 or more American workers IF all of the public funds invested could be recovered through fees and taxes on private sector companies using the facility?

Strongly agree	30	14.29%
Somewhat agree	65	30.95%
Neutral	55	26.19%
Somewhat disagree	27	12.86%
Strongly disagree	33	15.71%

Q11: The technology to mine asteroids in space is available today, but private companies cannot yet invest at scale because a market for these resources has not yet been created. Would you support a NASA-led program to purchase asteroid material from the private sector at a cost of $50 billion dollars over 20 years IF the materials purchased were then owned by the American public and were valued at $100 billion on the open market (a taxpayer profit of $50 billion)?

Strongly agree	30	14.29%
Somewhat agree	56	26.67%
Neutral	58	27.62%
Somewhat disagree	30	14.29%
Strongly disagree	36	17.14%

Q12: If an economically profitable American presence in space could also spark strong economic growth at home in America, create millions of high paying jobs, and pay back all of the public money invested plus a profit, would you support a government program led by NASA to build it?

Strongly agree	59	28.10%
Somewhat agree	83	39.52%
Neutral	31	14.76%
Somewhat disagree	15	7.14%
Strongly disagree	22	10.48%

Q13: If it would cost $200 billion per year (5% of the federal government's budget) for 50 years to achieve an economically profitable presence in space with enough self-supporting economic activity to return all of the public money invested plus a profit, would you support a NASA-led program to invest that $200 billion per year to make it happen?

Strongly agree	26	12.38%
Somewhat agree	65	30.95%
Neutral	55	26.19%
Somewhat disagree	23	10.95%
Strongly disagree	41	19.52%

Q14: Would you vote to invest $10 trillion in taxpayer funds over a period of 50 years to establish an economically profitable presence in space IF that investment would return $20 trillion in taxpayer revenue by the end of that same period of time?

Strongly agree	30	14.29%
Somewhat agree	58	27.62%
Neutral	55	26.19%
Somewhat disagree	31	14.76%
Strongly disagree	36	17.14%

Q15: If a Congressional candidate in your district backed a bold government-led program to develop an economically profitable frontier in space that would generate millions of jobs in America and would pay back every public dollar spent along with a significant profit, would you consider voting for that candidate?

Strongly agree	34	16.19%
Somewhat agree	77	36.67%
Neutral	56	26.67%
Somewhat disagree	18	8.57%
Strongly disagree	25	11.90%

Appendix C: Exploring Economic Conjugation

One idea introduced in the *New Frontier Playbook* that seems conceptually interesting and potentially new is the idea that an 'economic conjugate' can be created in Near Earth Space and that said conjugate represents a parallel economy operating at a higher (plural) tense of prices and wages to its domestic Earth-bound twin. The brief discussion earlier in this essay suggests that at scale several positive outcomes may be possible from creating such a conjugate. This appendix attempts to explore a few more questions related to economic conjugation and to at least sketch its boundaries, shape, and potential ramifications for future analysis.

I will confess at the start that I am layperson when it comes to economics. There are limits to how far I can take this exploration. Deeper analysis must be the provenance of trained economists rather than an amateur's musing about what may be possible. That said, it is my hope that the discussion below provides a starting point for more thorough analysis and thinking in the near future.

Context

The premise of an economic conjugate is based on a simple realization. Earth, our home world, is a lush oasis of abundance and this reality underlies everything about our contemporary economies. We often take for granted this bounty and its implications. We get it intellectually, but we don't really feel it or realize its importance in a bedrock economic sense. Here is what I mean.

Water literally falls from our skies and flows in streams and rivers past our homes, our farms, and our towns, virtually free for the taking. Water is the essence of life on Earth and we are blessed with this gift of Nature's abundance. Water is an essential building block of life and you also need it for almost everything we do. You need it as drinking water for survival, to grow the food we eat, to manufacture almost every type of product we use, and it goes into every material (from wood to cement) we use to construct just about everything we build. Water is an underlying, fundamental input to almost every economic activity. The extraordinary truth is that everything we drink and eat is modest in cost in all but the most extreme cases of shortage, extravagance, or mismanagement because they are grown, raised, or made based on the foundation of an input (water) that is essentially or nearly free for the taking as a gift of nature.

You could say the same about air. It exists all around us and we breathe it without thinking. No matter how rich or poor a person is, no matter where they live, no matter their station or circumstances, the air they breathe at the place they are standing in that moment of time is free for the taking in all but the most extreme micro-climates or situations. We are at least that equal. (Although *where* you are standing determines what you breathe and the where is certainly not always equal.)

Space will be different. When you have to squeeze every drop of water you drink from a carbonaceous asteroid ferried from millions of miles away or harvested from Lunar regolith and transported to point of use, every drink you take and every bite you eat will cost exponentially more. This fact is inescapable.

The air a person in space breathes will also have to be manufactured and transported. This comes at a cost. Currently, that cost is extraordinarily high, but even if we break out into Near Earth Space at scale and produce that air 'locally' from local materials (e.g. in situ), the cost of every breath taken will never be free. It will be inherently and forever more expensive than what we breathe for free today in the atmosphere of our home world.

Given the realities of extraordinary expense built into the foundation of every good and service in space, the question becomes: Can we create a self-sustaining economy in space in the face of such extraordinary cost? Counterintuitively, are there potentially very big advantages to doing so? I think the answer is yes to both questions, but it will take a concerted effort by economists to truly answer these questions satisfactorily *because this is new*. There is no parallel in human history on Earth in which water is as scarce and expensive and that operates at large scale. Civilizations and settlements have always grown up around free sources of water that can support life, grow crops, and nurture a community and economy and they have withered away when those sources dry up, disappear, or become overly expensive.

With that as a context, what are the defining topics and boundaries to use to sketch out what we mean by a conjugated economy and how will it relate to its domestic singular tense on Earth? Here are some categories to explore:

- Market Economy
- Cost of Living
- Wages
- Property Rights
- Printing Money
- Leakage & Inflation
- Inequality
- Baumol's Disease.
- Transition

We'll take each in turn:

1) Market Economy

In space, everything from a glass of water to a loaf of bread to the air you breathe will have to be manufactured at very high cost. There will be no freebies. As a result, these higher costs will cascade throughout the space economy requiring wages to be higher in comparable measure. In turn, that will drive the cost of any services delivered by people, no matter how basic, to extraordinarily high levels (in Earth terms). Getting a haircut in space by anything other than a robot or a friend will seem frighteningly expensive from afar.

Some will argue that this makes no sense and that we can simply pay good wages at Earth rates (with a risk bonus) and supply basic goods to the workforce centrally. I think of this as the Astronaut Model. In the Astronaut Model, we pay our astronauts an Earth-based wage and we supply everything they eat, drink, consume, or use free of charge. The astronaut effectively banks their salary (or continues paying the bills at home). This works because their visits are short, transitory, and in small numbers and all goods, services, and mission materials are produced on Earth and budgeted and covered centrally.

This model works fine in small numbers. However, it quickly collapses at scale because it is neither politically or economically sustainable.

Here's why: Someone has to pay the difference.

If an astronaut is paid $100,000 in wages, benefits and bonuses, but the actual cost of sustaining that astronaut in space is $5,000,000 per year, then someone has to pay the difference. Even if we collapse that cost dramatically over the course of a generation to $500,000 per year, the gap between cost and what an astronaut earns has to be covered by someone. None but the most far-sighted and deep-pocketed private sector actors will sign up for losing money like this in the short-term, much less at scale (without a compelling cost/benefit/risk rationale). That leaves space the provenance of the public sector and implies the taxpayer has to cover this cost by default. However, taxpayers facing competing priorities and austere budgets won't fund the Astronaut model at scale when you reach tens or hundreds of thousands of people in space and hundreds of billions of dollars in annual expenses.

The Astronaut Model is a path to nowhere.

Because a subsidized model at Earth prices won't work in space at anything like scale, it is likely that we will want to create a market economy that allows goods and services in near Earth space to be bought and sold at their true cost and those costs will have to be borne by the residents of that space-based economy.

Ultimately, if workers have to pay their costs of living in space, the taxpayer does not bear this burden directly. In addition, a market economy has the virtue of creating incentives for dramatic innovation and productivity gains in a way that the astronaut model does not. If prices reflect costs, then these are signals for innovation and entrepreneurship. If we have these signals paired with ownership and entrepreneurialism, then there is the potential to create a powerful dynamic to inspire competition and drive costs lower. This is what a market economy is all about.

Therefore, a fundamental conclusion is that the first characteristic of a future space-based economy is that it must be built based on or at some point transitioned to a market economy where prices and wages reflect actual costs and this is the most likely way to create a self-sustaining economic presence in space at scale. I think of this market economy as an economic conjugate because it will inevitably be at a plural tense to its domestic Earth-bound twin in relation to prices and wages. The cost of water, everything you grow and eat, the air you breathe, and the goods that are consumed will all come at costs that are a step-jump higher, likely exponentially so. That is the next point.

2) Cost of Living

The cost of living in space is going to be enormously higher than it is on Earth. We all get that intuitively, but just how expensive it will be, and how different that is from past and current experience, bears some consideration.

First, think about the cost of living between cities in the United States. The median income and cost of living in our most expensive cities is 'just' 1-2x greater than that of living in the smaller towns of our less prosperous states and counties. Remarkably, the gap between living in Manhattan and living in Plano, Texas or Yakima, Washington is not that great at a median income and cost of living level. The basics of life are more expensive in Manhattan, but not exponentially so.

To see this in more detail, try using a cost of living calculator like that provided by bankrate.com (http://www.bankrate.com/calculators/savings/moving-cost-of-living-calculator.aspx) and running a comparison assuming you are moving from Yakima, WA, to Manhattan, New York. What it tells you is that if you have a salary of $50,000 in Yakima today, you would need to make $118,000, or 136% more than what you made in Yakima to live at the same level and consume the same amount in Manhattan. That is higher for sure, but not exponentially (10x) so.

Bankrate's cost of living calculator offers some surprising insights. The cost of housing is what appears to be driving the bulk of the cost differential. An average home price in Yakima is $295k, but in Manhattan it is nearly $1.5 million. You can rent an apartment for less than $700 in Yakima, but the comparable rent in Manhattan would set you back nearly $4,000.

But what the calculator also shows is that most food items are very close in cost. A hamburger in Yakima is $4.19, but $4.09 in Manhattan. Bananas are the same price. Peaches in Yakima are $2.58, but $2.82 in Manhattan. In fact, most food items are slightly more expensive in Manhattan as you would expect, but not dramatically so. Lettuce is $1.32 in Yakima, $1.70 in Manhattan. Orange juice is $3.64 and $4.14 respectively.

As you would expect, most goods and services are also more expensive in Manhattan than they are in Yakima and the range is 50-100% greater. A haircut is $11 in Yakima, but nearly $23 in Manhattan. You can take your dog to the vet for $41 in Yakima, but it will cost you nearly $100 in Manhattan.

In general, cost of living seems to be explained by the high cost of housing and property and how that cascades back down through all goods and services.

On a recent trip to Manhattan from Portland, I tested this assumption using water as an example. In Portland, Oregon, a 1 liter/20-oz bottle of water at 7-11 costs just $1.69 plus a plastic bottle deposit, but one brand is 2 for $2. In Manhattan, a local 7-11 sells the same bottled water for $2.29 or two for $3. The difference between the two is probably not the inherent cost of the water or the supply chain behind it, but the higher cost of renting property in Manhattan vs. Portland.

While housing (and property) is dramatically more expensive between high and low cost locations in America, basic goods like food and water are not dramatically so. Most of the variation in cost of living can be explained by the higher property cost and how that flows back into wages, rents, and prices, although there may, of course, be other factors at work. What is surprising is how modest a variance there is outside of housing.

Now consider the cost of living in space.

We know that water in space will not be free, nor will air. Everything will have to be manufactured. We can assume that the cost of living in space will be amplified not just by a much higher cost of housing (reflecting the cost to build), but also by the dramatically higher cost of the food chain and the inputs necessary to support it.

At best, a bottle of water in space will still cost hundreds of dollars in the future (it's tens of thousands now). And that is after an efficient supply chain has been put in place and costs have been squeezed out. Hundreds of dollars is probably the best case scenario for many generations.

While the gap between living in a low cost location in America like Yakima, WA, and a high cost location like Manhattan is roughly 1.3x, the gap between Manhattan and any future settlement in space will be far, far greater. It will likely be 10-20x higher at a minimum and possibly 100x greater in practice.

If prices reflect actual cost, then a bottle of water may run $350 and a cup of coffee may cost $500. A bowl of noodles may come with a price of $2,000. The apartment (or bunk) a worker sleeps in will come with a rent that may make even Earthly tycoons blush (or salivate).

These costs then drive what a future worker in space will need to be paid in order to cover their cost of living. It implies a dramatically higher wage in space than anything ever considered or contemplated on Earth. It also offers a compelling business case why companies like Starbucks may want to have a store or two in every future space settlement. The margin on a cup of coffee on Earth and space might be the same. The marginal dollars earned for each cup will certainly not be the same.

3) Wages

In a market economy in space, workers will have to pay for their food, housing, and any other items all at very high prices (compared to Earth). Thus, another defining characteristic (highlighted earlier in brief) is that these workers' wages will have to reflect the true costs of the goods and services they must purchase. The implication is simple: Those wages will be extraordinarily high in comparison to Earth.

Today there is a movement to increase the minimum wage in some higher cost locations to $15 per hour, a movement that is considered politically contentious.

By contrast, it is possible that a minimum wage in space (in constant dollars) will need to be at a level that is closer to $250/hour or higher at today's rates. A minimum wage salary may be $500k per year or greater.

Imagine that.

Now, that minimum wage worker will have bills to pay, too. Living costs will be proportional (food, entertainment, rent), but savings, taxes, and every other cost will be much higher in absolute terms as well. Proportionally speaking, the space-based minimum wage worker may pay taxes like the wealthiest 5% on Earth. They may also save money at the same rate. The implications for this are merely interesting if it is a few thousand people. But it's profoundly exciting if it grows to tens of millions by the back half of the century.

While I've postulated that a minimum wage will likely be $250/hour, that may actually undershoot the minimum salary needed to cover the basic costs of living in space for a very long time.

Transitioning to a market economy in space from the astronaut model will not happen instantly, but will by necessity be a phased activity and so wages early on may be Earth-comparable before costs are fully understood and a base wage can be set. But the act of purchasing goods and services creates economic activity and increases the velocity of economic growth. It allows economic activity to be monetized, growth to accelerate, jobs to be created, and innovation to happen, so there are compelling reasons why a market economy with market prices and wages will be created in space. Those prices and wages will almost certainly be very high compared to Earth-based measures.

4) Property rights are tricky

I've long thought the two biggest risks to a large-scale human presence in space are meteorites and property rights (assuming radiation is a manageable risk).

The first risk is obvious. If a structure with people gets hits, people could die. But if studies are to be believed, this risk is extremely small. By comparison, property rights sounds trivial by comparison, but it is potentially more challenging and critical to get right.

Once the transition to wages and costs relative to the space environment has occurred, it enables an outpouring of economic innovation. High prices for goods and services create an incentive for innovation if we can enable entrepreneurs with opportunity, incentives, and ownership rights. Otherwise, we are just engaged in factor inputs and the velocity of economic activity and opportunity is curtailed and we are stuck with a centrally planned economy with all of its inefficiencies and distortions.

We have to have property rights and the possibility of ownership in a space-based economy to create a market economy. This is without question. But there is a risk to be managed. We have to avoid a first-mover, winner-take-all advantage.

If you assume that for many generations what it means to be a worker in space is someone who will be there for the duration of 5-7 years on a contract, but someone not settling forever or raising a family in space, then the first mover challenges become clearer.

The first waves of colonists (contractors) have an outsized advantage over subsequent ones if they are allowed to own property such as housing stock and retain this ownership after they return to Earth. They effectively gain outsized rents for life. It's a great deal if you get there first. But subsequent waves of colonists will not have the same opportunity or advantage. There is only so much housing stock that can be built into each colony. If everyone else becomes a renter and has to pay an outsized share of their wages in rent, then the first mover advantage is not fair, nor is it productive, innovative, or growth enabling. Allowing the first settlers to own physical property is therefore very problematic.

If a population in space is not settling permanently, but on time-based contracts, and will be replaced by subsequent workers on similar contracts, then land and property in space settlements may need to be restricted and owned by a central authority. Innovation and entrepreneurialism may be more productively focused on creating businesses, processes, and ideas rather than on owning physical property.

Let's take an example.

A large space settlement is built late in the 21st century and the first wave of workers arrives from Earth and are granted the right to purchase their living quarters. These people stay only 5-7 years, but they get to buy and own their apartment unit and retain it after they leave and return to Earth. While in the colony they pay a proportional share of their wages in mortgage cost. When they return, they still own the apartment. The next wave arrives. These people cannot then purchase their own housing. They have to rent from those that own. The original first settler that opted to buy gets to earn a rent at conjugated pricing for life and that may be high enough for them to never have to work again. It's a great deal for the first mover, but subsequent settlers are denied this opportunity to acquire equity and ownership. It's also a terrible deal for our domestic economy because it removes any incentive for a potentially very productive worker with cutting edge skills to engage in work instead of living off their economic rent in space. The owner still spends in the domestic economy and that is an economic benefit, but my guess is that it is smaller than if they held a job or created a business.

The same thing applies to the owner of the first coffee shop in space. Imagine you are the first person to set up a café in a space settlement. After your contract finishes do you get to own that café in space even if you return to Earth? We would say yes without hesitation on Earth and there would be no question. But given the massive public investment required to create any structure for settlement in space, when is it fair to allow individuals to gain ownership and how do you manage that in the context of defined contracts of 5-7 years?

Property rights for physical assets built at extraordinary expense via public funding feel problematic and I don't have an answer other than to suggest that we may want to minimize first settler winner-take-all economics. Yet as we move to a market based economy in space, we also want to do all we can to incent innovation and entrepreneurship which includes ownership of private property. Finding the right balance between these competing two principles will be a central political and economic challenge for the transition to scale in space.

A possible balancing solution is to own physical property and structures centrally and encourage private ownership of knowledge and intellectual property, from brands to processes.

5) Printing Money

A suitable monetary policy will be needed to inject liquidity for growth into the space economy. If recent experiments with Quantitative Easing have been about injecting liquidity into the US banking system, effectively printing money and adding to the central bank's balance sheet by purchasing bank assets, in the future, a space-based economy may need something more akin to Quantum Expansion – an order of magnitude greater and decades in duration – to inject liquidity into its economy and support rapid economic growth and scale and it will need to be driven by space-based entities.

Here's why. As the space economy grows and additional workers begin living and working in space, we will need a means to inject capital into this fast growing, yet nascent economy. The relatively small numbers of initial settlers belies the fact that they will be working in an environment of exponentially higher wages and prices as discussed earlier. This will require quantitative easing directed into a small space to provide economic liquidity. As a means of promoting economic growth it is also likely to be far more effective than purchasing government debt or financial assets. The injection of liquidity, e.g. printing money (digitally or in kind) creates and drives economic activity in an enclosed community/economy that accelerates the velocity of growth through the purchase of goods and services.

On Earth in a domestic economy characterized by low growth, printing money threatens to unleash inflation. However, in space, the economy will be growing at a rapid rate and the horizons are unlimited. Injecting liquidity to promote economic activity and circulation will not necessarily drive inflation because it can be done in increments mapped to physical factor inputs (people, resources, etc.).

Let's say you are building a space settlement to house 50,000 people and adding one of these structures every 6-12 months as your production base in space grows. As those next 50,000 people arrive to take up residence and begin work, you have to expand the monetary supply (digitally speaking) to provide funds for those workers to be paid a salary and to use it for the basic economic activity of living in a new city.

As the number of settlements grows and the population of workers grows, you have to continually expand the digital money supply to support the economic activity they are engaged in.

Can we use printing money/Quantum Expansion to drive economic growth directly in a sustainable way?

Here's one scenario: What if new space settlements are chartered by a central space authority as a governing entity and issued a credit line for its construction? The central authority guarantees the loan and the loan is issued by one or more space-based banks. The newly chartered settlement entity contracts for its construction from existing settlements. The construction cost is paid out to workers and firms for materials and labor to construct the new settlement. Once the settlement is constructed and populated with workers, the chartered entity (space settlement) still owns its physical housing and space. It charges rent to its workers and uses that income to pay back the original chartered loan. As long as the chartered space colony keeps its workers actively engaged in economic activity and work earning a salary and paying rent, it has the income to pay off its loans.

In this way, it seems plausible that once the infrastructure and supply chains are put in place to construct settlements in space, it can expand rapidly and be self-sustaining while growing a space-based economy. Finance seems less an issue than technology and politics. For a central space authority working with locally chartered banks to guarantee loans is straightforward. The fact that banks will then effectively create money by issuing loans is also straightforward. That is what they do today.

Once a basic political and financial infrastructure is created, it will have the ability to rapidly scale up a space-based economy in a sustainable way. That broader space economy will grow because it can continually charter new settlements that drive growth within the ecosystem of existing settlements.

Printing money at scale to support a space-based economy's rapid growth and build out is potentially a sustainable and attractive way to support the economic growth of the home world, Earth-based economy as well because some portion of taxed income from economic activity in space will return to the sponsoring Earth-based government for that settlement. Those taxes may be small at first, but several decades downstream, their combined impact may be quite significant.

6) Leakage & Inflation

If we inject liquidity into a space-based economy and it flows in large amounts back to the Earth-based domestic economy in large enough volume, will it then drive inflation and create negative outcomes such as asset bubbles? This risk is real, but I believe it is modest and controllable for a very long time.

Some flow from the plural to singular tense is desirable and welcome. At the government level, it will come in the form of tax revenue back to the central government which will support programs or pay down debt. It seems plausible that as the space-based economy grows ever larger, this flow creates a perpetual (at least for a century or more) fountain of funding that may well eliminate our national debt and drive a very different economy on Earth, one where poverty is no more, the environment is clean and increasingly pristine, and political polarization is focused on how to spend the bounty, not how to screw over the other side. (Okay, that last one may be an aspirational stretch goal.)

Companies will also benefit from contracts to provide goods and services to the nascent and eventually more sizeable space economy. There will be many benefits to both firms and workers from these contracts, but they will start small and come with significant competition. They should not be managed like typical cost-plus contracts today, but should be managed to continually push the envelope on innovation and cost. Over time, much of this activity will expand on the frontier itself as first simple and then more complex supply chains develop in space. Earth will need to move up the value chain to stay ahead.

At the personal level, it will come in the form of repatriated savings and earnings. People working in space will be able to save a portion of their salary. It may be a similar portion (15%-20%) as Earth-based workers, but in absolute dollars it is likely to be 100x higher. Those savings may be used while workers are still in space (repatriated earnings to support a family), but I suspect most space workers will save the bulk of their income for the future.

For a generation, these combined flows will be large enough to invigorate segments of our economy and a portion of the population, but not necessarily large enough to cause significant inflationary risk more broadly because it will take 40-50 years before a presence in space reaches a number in the millions. We do want it to get that big eventually. But even when it does, the aggregate flows at the person level will be distributed among people that are geographically disbursed when they return to Earth. In other words, not everyone is going to return to a single location like Silicon Valley and so the economic benefit will be widely shared and the risk of asset bubbles at least for physical goods and property will be widely disbursed and harder to accumulate.

Will it cause bubbles in stock prices? If more money is chasing fewer assets, that may be a very real risk. But if a space frontier drives new firm creation in the space-based economy, it may soak up excess funds as well.

On the public side, it will also take time for the aggregate tax flows to grow significantly and we can choose to direct the use of this funding in a way that minimizes and distributes the risk carefully between debt reduction and domestic spending.

Within the private sector, as the size of the space economy increases, an increasingly large portion of goods and their associated supply chains will move into space to be as competitive on cost as possible.

If a future space-based economy becomes so big that it is many times larger than its domestic Earth-bound twin, then we will almost certainly have created serious challenges and distortions as a result. But we will have also had a century of economic growth and plenty of time to prepare. As a problem, this qualifies under the category of 'nice to have' and we can only hope future generations are so lucky as to be faced with the challenge of having to manage it.

The risk of inflation on Earth is not the only risk that a future economy will face. There is also a risk of deflation occurring in the space economy over time as innovation and efficiency lower costs, potentially dramatically. This will take time to materialize, but will impact wages and contracts for workers and will also need to be explored and its disruptive potential, if any, managed.

7) Inequality Vanquished

A future space-based economy will likely be very egalitarian and equal in terms of wages and earnings for a very long time and if it scales, it may well help resolve some of our challenges with inequality at home on Earth. The caveat to this is that the solution will take a long time to have a meaningful impact. But given some authors have recently suggested that the only way more egalitarian societies arise is through war, plague, and economic collapse, I think the possibility of an alternative pathway is worth exploring.

Let's look at this idea in more detail.

First, wages will be relatively equal for the first number of decades as scale builds on the space frontier. The gap between executives and workers in a space colony or settlement should be very narrow as a matter of practicality, economics, and culture.

In practical terms, let's start with a look at the wage requirements and cost of living for both a minimum wage worker and an executive or manager in space.

The minimum wage worker will, of course, be happy to make what looks like a huge wage by Earth standards based on their skill set. It will be 20-30x higher than what they would earn on Earth in a similar role. This minimum wage will be a basic requirement for a worker to live in space and pay their bills.

But will such a wage suffice for more senior administrators and managers? The answer is yes, because in Earth terms, it will also look like a handsome sum as well.

According to the US Bureau of Labor Statistics, the median annual salary of chief executives in the United States is $175,110. Only the highest 10 percent make more than $187,200. Top executives such as general or operations managers make a median of $97,730 annually, although the top 10 percent also make more than $187,200. (https://www.bls.gov/ooh/management/top-executives.htm#tab-5)

The median is misleading. That covers a wide range of firm sizes and a large population of over 300 thousand CEOs and several million other top executives and managers. The top 10 percent of this large cohort is the group making between $187k and $300k. But those multi-millionaire CEOs we hear so much about are a very tiny minority that are at the very top of the distribution and they are leading the very largest multinational corporations, financial firms, and technology companies. They are not the norm even for CEOs.

What that means is that a salary of $500-$750k (or 1-1.5x the potential minimum wage in space) would be far higher than what most executives would make on Earth in the vast majority of positions. It is very likely that a wage modestly higher than minimum wage in space would, therefore, also meet the needs of a senior executive with the skills to manage a full-sized space settlement or direct its operations and population.

The wage in dollar terms should be decent enough, but what about the demands these executives make for ever higher salaries in America? Will a similar culture translate to the space frontier? I think not. Here's why.

Culturally, the drivers pushing up executive pay won't be the same in space. First, luxury goods and accommodations will be in short supply or non-existent. Nor will the culture of future space societies provide elites with the ability to withdraw into enclaves or live in elite communities. The physical space will be too limited, too visible, and too transparent. Workers, administrators, and entrepreneurs will have to live in very close proximity in what is essentially a very risky and dangerous environment on the frontier of space. They will need to rely on each other.

For all these reasons, the space community is likely to foster and sustain a culture of restraint that could be self-reinforcing over time. Higher status will be likely conveyed more by communal activity (making wine in a group, for instance) than by conspicuous consumption (showing off a new Maserati to strangers). I see very limited room for conspicuous consumption, winner-take-all dynamics, and selfish behavior. I see lots of room for the culture to restrain such behavior.

If we create a true market economy, then at some point there will be new trends that start to drive greater inequality, but the cultural and practical dimensions may provide a long-term restraint on wage growth among the elite for a very long time.

Life in space will be very special in this sense. The most menial worker will likely make almost the same as the most senior executive on site. They will rub shoulders in the same space. Eat in the same dining halls. Play sports on the same teams. One person may have a job that does not require managing people. The other may have responsibility for the entire facility and all its people resting on their shoulders, but they will both exist in a relatively egalitarian social circle – at least while they live in space. Culturally and socially, we as a nation need this experience at scale for the benefit of all Americans and our increasingly polarized and isolated culture at home on Earth.

With that as background, here is a recap of why it is unlikely that we will see income inequality on the space frontier between minimum wage workers and the executives and managers that will run operations in these future space settlements and colonies. The reasons are:

- Not a Superstar Job. Income inequality in our domestic U.S. economy is primarily driven by winner-take-all economics in which a small bench of superstars earns out-sized rewards because their skills are in high demand and these superstars can demand out-size rewards whether in athletics, technology, or finance. The senior positions in a space colony will be more akin to factory and operations managers on Earth. People that can run a large base or operation of hundreds or thousands. We have a deep bench of people with this skill set and it is not inherently a role that only a small number of people can do.

- Demand Inversion. Superstars are in high demand in our economy when Boards, Investors, or Owners believe they can create an outsize return and they are nearly unique. This drives a bidding war for perceived Superstars. By contrast, jobs, even senior ones, on the space frontier will be in demand by candidates who want the prestige and experience of operating on the very cutting edge of our economy and who want to be a part of an historical human adventure. A salary that is very high in Earth terms, but relatively equal and modest in space terms will be perfectly adequate to attract a large pool of talent for these jobs.
- No luxury spending. For many generations there will be no luxury goods or conspicuous consumption opportunities on the space frontier. This will drive restraint as well. The minimum wage worker and the senior administrator will likely eat, live, and play in the same space and rub shoulders on a daily basis.
- Shared culture. Workers on the space frontier will live and work in a very high-risk environment and will rely on each other for survival. This will be a very communal environment and the distance between these people will by necessity need to be very close and this will drive restraint and equality.

For all of these reasons, I believe the space frontier may trend towards high levels of equality for a very long period.

What is more intriguing is to consider the potential impact on Earth-based income inequality over time and with greater scale on the space frontier.

If the space economy is a transitory experience for most workers and it comes with very high wages for a period of 5-7 years and results in new and advanced skills and exposure to an entrepreneurial and socially cohesive community experience, consider what the circulation of these workers back to Earth by the millions would mean for equality here in America.

A minimum wage of $250/hour means that a space worker is effectively in the top 10% or even 5% of society for the period of time that they are working in space. They accumulate savings, skills, and can-do attitude. When they return to Earth, they would likely have skills to do good jobs, but they will have accumulated enough savings to buy their own property and invest in anything from education to a business. Even the lowest worker in space will return as a member of the upper middle class at home on Earth. Culturally, they will return from this experience with a can-do attitude, strong group cohesion, and not afraid to socialize across bubbles. I believe they are the key to rebuilding our democracy.

If we can create a circulatory mechanism where large numbers of people get their space experience (and the financial benefits), and return to Earth, we may be able to drive down inequality at scale and rebuild our middle class over time. And we might just save our democracy. (And it wouldn't require war, pestilence, or economic collapse to achieve these outcomes!)

8) Baumol's Disease

In the 1960s, William Baumol and William Bowen postulated the idea that the cost of human wages and therefore all services requiring labor would always increase over time. Labor never gets cheaper as cost of living increases. Therefore, personal services provided by the public or private sector such as education, healthcare, etc. are all doomed to increase over time even as many other costs (manufactured goods) decrease at sometimes dramatic rates because these goods benefit from automation and innovation in a way that personal services do not. The term Baumol's Disease was coined to describe this phenomenon of ever increasing prices for personal services.

In space, this concept may get turned on its head for a period of several centuries. It may be possible to have decreasing labor cost for an extended period of time on the space frontier and I think of this as a Baumol Inversion. This may last a century or more although the steepest declines will be early on in the first half century.

In space, innovation and scale efficiencies will drive costs down very, very fast putting downward pressure on costs for an extended period of time lasting most of the century before the floor is reached and costs begin to grow again. Recall that today an Astronaut may cost millions of dollars per day to support at the International Space Station and even when we get to early scale (thousands), the cost to support each worker in space may still be millions of dollars annually.

But this will change.

Future space settlers will still cost a lot to transport to and from space and their cost of living in space will be very high. But that cost curve will begin to decline dramatically over time as engineering innovation, business acumen, and scale economies and supply chains give us more cost effective ways to get into space and back as well as harvest and utilize resources in space.

The cost of transport is one example. It costs $70 million and change to fly an astronaut to the ISS. Elon Musk, however, is postulating that he can get a person to Mars for just $200k in the not too distant future. Transportation is just one input into the cost of supporting a worker in space, but we will likely see these rapid cost declines occur across the spectrum.

These expected cost efficiencies imply that human labor cost will decline over time until we have hit a floor at which innovations are no longer reducing cost significantly. At some point, the Inversion must eventually plateau for a period before the Disease finally reasserts itself again.

The application of Baumol's theory to the space frontier and the phenomenon of increasing labor cost for personal services is interesting and warrants explanation and further study.

9) Transition

As highlighted earlier, transitioning from the Astronaut Model of a centrally planned and supported economy at Earth prices to a market economy reflecting locally relevant wages and prices will be tricky and will require advance planning.

Here is the issue. Initially supporting a small population in space will be extraordinarily expensive, in the millions of dollars per year per person. If we are on a path to scale and are able to address the engineering and innovation challenges, those costs will begin to decline on a per person basis very rapidly. Elon Musk's promise to reduce the cost of going to Mars from billions of dollars per person to $200k per person is an example of how dramatically costs may drop.

In a very tactical sense, then, how do you write a contract for a worker coming for five years when costs are in a phase of rapid deflation? When do you transition to market contracts with local wages? If you do it too soon while the cost curve is at its steepest and fastest, then how do you adjust a worker's contract in real-time as costs decline? Or do you give a worker that arrives today a set contract for five years at the same wages when a worker that arrives next year will have a contract that pays less? How do you manage a deflationary environment in the most economically efficient way and when that deflation is highly desirable to promote growth and scale?

In the more strategic sense, the questions raised earlier on property rights, income inequality, and the shift to a market economy are all important to study and create a transition plan to address. But these are just a start. There are others as well.

For instance, how do you create a labor market if everyone is brought in on a 5-7 year contract for a specific job, the housing market is tiny and at full capacity, and everyone with a job has a place to live? If you allow entrepreneurialism and innovation in principle, how do you enable it in practice? How do you allow someone on a 5-year contract to create a business when they are filling a specific job already? If they quite their job, someone else has to fill that role and will need a slot for housing. Yet to unleash innovation, we have to be able to free up a pool of labor both to be entrepreneurs as well as to be employees and those people will need a place to live.

Do you allow businesses to fail, a key concept in market economies? If you do, how do you manage periods of unemployment, which is also a feature of market economies? Do you provide support, even temporary, or do you put the onus on individuals to sort out their situation or return to Earth?

And then, of course, there is the really big question of when and how do you allow for families? That is one of the biggest transitions, but my model assumes that initially the space frontier is more akin to an Antarctic research station or an oil rig in the North Sea. These are not exactly family friendly work environments. The transition to families seems to be assumed as easy and obvious to proponents of large scale space settlement. While it may be true in concept, the details are critical and the timing challenging. To support families, you will need medical services for pregnancy, childcare, pediatrics, schools staffed with teachers, sports and after school activities. And that's just a start. You will need to modify the terms of employment for women with children and you will need to allocate physical facilities as well as staff. The economic costs of supporting families are enormous on the space frontier and so this challenge will also be enormous. Yet you cannot have a self-sustaining economy in space without, eventually, a self-sustaining civilization and society that is built on a population that is raising families.

These questions and the associated timing drive consideration for how to plan and manage the transition to a market economy. They have barely been explored and will require much more consideration and analysis. As yet, I don't have good answers for any of them.

Conclusion

Economic conjugation is something I backed into in stages while writing the main essay, *New Frontier Playbook*, and it has captivated my interest even as it remains nascent in development. Somewhere between exploring the purchasing power parity comparison between Los Angeles and Dhaka and the realization that the basic building blocks of life in space (water, air) will have to be manufactured at great cost and will never be as cheap as they are on Earth, came the idea of economic conjugation.

It is an idea that feels a bit like alchemy. The idea that we can create a self-sustaining economy in space at a price and wage level that is 10x or even 100x that of our Earth-based equivalent and that such an economy could also provide significant revenues back to Earth sounds a lot like conjuring gold from lead. Alchemy is in bad repute these days. We use it as a slander to disparage people that are doing something fundamentally wrong or deluded whether contemporary bankers or the metallurgists and chemists of the Middle Ages.

But what if it is possible? What if we can effectively spin up a conjugate in Near-Earth Space and the mechanics are relatively easy conceptually and financially to envision? What if the economic and political benefits to our Earth-bound economy are potentially enormous and highly relevant to our stage of technological development?

If these things are possible, then it lends new urgency to solving the engineering and political challenges that are holding us back. The best I can do with this brief appendix is explore some of the questions that arise in my own mind. I cannot answer any of them definitively. That is for trained economists to engage in greater detail with more academic firepower. Hopefully this brief overview will provide some food for thought and additional exploration for those with the training and skills to take this concept to the next level.

(But please feel free to call me should you need any help.)

Appendix D: Unions in Space

A final concept, perhaps only briefly mentioned throughout this work, is worth introducing and exploring in this appendix to the Playbook. It starts with a simple premise: The frontier of space will not be won by astronauts, engineers, or tech workers. It will be built and settled largely by machinists, iron workers, and farmers.

This premise sounds simple, but it is earth-shaking in its political, social, and cultural implications.

If machinists, iron workers, and farmers are the people that are the key to our success in space, then hiring and moving them into space in large numbers will reinvent and reinvigorate what unions stand for, how they operate, the skills their members develop, and the value of their members' labor both in space and when they return back on Earth. Space is going to be very good for unions if we plan ahead.

Unions have been on the decline for two generations as globalization, outsourcing, and technology have changed the demand picture for union labor in America and across the Western world. These global trends were complemented by the simple fact that America (and to a lesser extent other advanced industrial economies) began cutting back on building infrastructure and new physical plant and equipment relative to higher levels of investment during the post-World War II period. This resulted in a slow wasting away of capability and talent in the physical trades and a migration from rural and formerly industrial towns to urban areas where knowledge jobs were growing the most, the most in demand, and the most highly valued. These trends resulted in workers in the skilled trades being systemically undervalued and underutilized given the availability of lower cost alternatives in other geographies.

In our view of a large-scale future in space, all of these trends will be completely reversed on the space frontier. To build large structures in space needed to settle and maintain a population, the most important workers are not software engineers or tech workers. Those people will be employed largely on Earth. This is likely a shock to many of them. They are not going to be the future in space. But it is an inescapable conclusion. There is simply no need for software engineers in space.

The people that matter the most and that will be the most in demand and the most highly valued are the people that can actually build physical structures in dangerous environments (like space) and can then grow and sustain a population through the production of physical goods and agricultural food supplies. Software can be beamed up. A colony has to be built from literally nothing by actual workers in the physical place where it is meant to exist. A loaf of bread has to be grown, baked, and served as much as possible on-site because otherwise it will cost a fortune to bring it from Earth.

There will be no elongated supply chains that are populated with endless middlemen each taking their cut as they coordinate the flow of goods between low-cost labor in one country and high paying consumers in a destination market. This model will not exist in space. The supply chain will be very short, no more than one or two degrees of separation. Whether it is a pair of trousers or an apple, every end consumer in space is going to know who made what they are buying and that person or persons will likely be their neighbors.

If you want to live on the frontier of space in this future, you will have to make it, bake it, or build it. So: Learn to weld. Become a machinist. Or learn how to be a high-yield, high-tech farmer. Learn to bake or cook for large numbers (cafeteria food not Michelin stars). The inversion in how we value people in our current economy will be a complete mirror image on the space frontier and it is going to be a shock for many who see themselves as the bright stars of that future just as much as it will be a revelation for those who are currently undervalued by our economy at home.

IAM 2M+

I believe this means the long decline of unions will reverse. One of the unions I will be watching is the International Association of Machines and Aerospace Workers (IAM). This union has been on the decline for two generations. Its membership was once 650,000 as recently as 2006, but even this was down significantly from 925,000 in 1973. Today, the number of dues paying members (not retired, but actively working) is reportedly less than 350,000. The IAM includes people in the machinist trades and aerospace workers of all forms. If a large-scale future in space comes to fruition, then it is not hard to imagine an IAM in 2050 with one million members and two million or more members by 2075. The future could be bright for the IAM.

Caveats do apply. If we do not build a market economy in space, but operate based on Earthly pay scales and wage tiers (the Astronaut Economy, as I have called it), then it will be harder to diverge from Earth-based biases and power structures when it comes to wages, communities, and social cohesion. If we cede the future to corporations to do as they wish, then we can expect a very different outcome based on very different rules and values. This could be better, worse, or the same. Many different economic models are possible.

The skills that a future space worker learns in space may also potentially make them highly valued on Earth as well.

Every product, process, and stage in building and sustaining a presence in space will require developing and deploying the most advanced and innovative solutions possible. A space colony is going to be a laboratory and factory for innovation. Its workers are going to be on the cutting edge of the most advanced technologies and methods for building anything and everything in the most efficient, resource optimized way possible. The high cost of living on the frontier paired with very scarce resources will require that these communities be incredibly innovative.

That means the workers who build and innovate in space will return with skills and knowledge that can also help build and update productive capacity on Earth as well. Every business and factory that creates a product or builds a structure will want to innovate and invest in the most efficient production processes possible. To do so, they will need the talent that knows how to do it. A tour in space should generate high demand for people coming home from a tour in space. This will, in turn, translate into high wage opportunities once home on Earth.

Conclusion

For now, this essay seeks merely to introduce the concept that unions may potentially play an important role on the space frontier and that the type of people that will be most valued in space - farmers, welders, and machinists - are some of the trades that have been the least valued in the last two generations on Earth. This turnabout seems fair and intriguing to consider not only for what it means for the people that will work in space, but also for their future when they come home to Earth.

Notes

Chapter 1
1. NRC, Pathways to Exploration, section 3.1.1-2, page 108-110
2. : ___, "The End of the Space Age, June 30, 2011, http://www.economist.com/node/18897425

Chapter 2

1. Lanier, Jaron, Who Owns the Future?, Simon & Schuster, 2013, p. 366
2. Gibney, Bruce, What Happened to the Future?, Founder's Fund, 2011, http://www.foundersfund.com/the-future/#/introduction
3. Pontin, Jason, 'Why we can't solve big problems,' MIT Technology Review, Nov/Dec 2012
4. Wolfe, Tom, "One Giant Leap to Nowhere," *The New York Times*, July 18, 2009
5. DeGrasse Tyson, Neil, Space Chronicals: Facing the Ultimate Frontier, W.W. Norton &I Company, New York, 2012, p. 253
6. https://www.cnn.com/2020/11/02/tech/nasa-jim-bridenstine-report-card-scn/index.html
7. (http://www.people-press.org/files/legacy-questionnaires/51.pdf) (http://www.people-press.org/1999/10/24/optimism-reigns-technology-plays-key-role/)
8. (http://www.people-press.org/files/legacy-pdf/625.pdf)
9. http://www.pewinternet.org/files/2014/04/US-Views-of-Technology-and-the-Future.pdf)
10. Pew Research, Majority of Americans Believe It Is essential That the U.S. remain a Global Leader in Space, June 6, 2018, https://www.pewresearch.org/science/2018/06/06/majority-of-americans-believe-it-is-essential-that-the-u-s-remain-a-global-leader-in-space/
11. Fowler, Wallace, "Anniversary Shows us that NASA and Space Exploration are Worth Their Costs, July 21, 2014, http://www.utexas.edu/know/2014/07/21/anniversary-shows-us-that-nasa-and-space-exploration-are-worth-their-costs/

12. Lafleur, Claude, "Cost of US Piloted Programs", March 8, 2010, http://www.thespacereview.com/article/1579/1
13. http://science.ksc.nasa.gov/pao/faq/faqanswers.htm
14. NATURE: http://www.nature.com/nature/journal/v472/n7341/full/472038d.html
15. Source: 2.7.5, Pathways to Exploration
16. http://www.thespacereview.com/article/2567/1
17. NRC report, page 1-7
18. Source: Augustine report, p. 21-22
19. ___, The 2020 Long-Term Budget Outlook, Congressional Budget Office, September 21, 2020, https://www.cbo.gov/publication/56516
20. ___, NRC, 2014, Section 3.1.3.1, page 112
21. Launius, Roger D., "Public opinion polls and perceptions of US human spaceflight," Space Policy 19, 2003, Elsevier, p. 166-168 http://www.academia.edu/179045/_Public_Opinion_Polls_and_Perceptions_of_US_Human_Spaceflight_
22. Madrigal, Alexis, "Moondoggle: The Forgotten Opposition to the Apollo Program," The Atlantic, September 12, 2012, http://www.theatlantic.com/technology/archive/2012/09/moondoggle-the-forgotten-opposition-to-the-apollo-program/262254/
23. ___, NRC, 2014, Section 3.1.2, pages 110-111
24. ___, IPSOS, https://www.ipsos.com/sites/default/files/ct/news/documents/2019-07/cspan-space-program-topline-2019-07-10.pdf
25. ___, "Majority of Americans Believe It Is Essential That the U.S. Remain a Global Leader in Space," June 6, 2018, https://www.pewresearch.org/science/2018/06/06/majority-of-americans-believe-it-is-essential-that-the-u-s-remain-a-global-leader-in-space/)
26. Backus, Fred, "Moon landing is still a source of pride – CBS News poll", July 15, 2019, https://www.cbsnews.com/news/moon-landing-is-still-a-source-of-pride-cbs-news-poll/
27. Strauss, Mark and Kennedy, Brian, "Space tourism? Majority of Americans say they wouldn't be interested," Pew Research Center, June 7, 2018, https://www.pewresearch.org/fact-tank/2018/06/07/space-tourism-majority-of-americans-say-they-wouldnt-be-interested/)

Chapter 3:

1. *Wikipedia: http://en.wikipedia.org/wiki/Criticism_of_the_Spa ce_Shuttle_program*
2. ___, SpaceX, Starlink Mission – SpaceS's 100th Successful Flight, October 24, 2020, https://www.spacex.com/updates/starlink-mission-10-24-2020/index.html
3. https://www.spacex.com/media/Capabilities&Services.pdf
4. SCR00CHY, "How much does it cost to launch a reused Falcon 9? Elon Musk explains why reusability is worth it", ElonX.com, September 20, 2020, https://www.elonx.net/how-much-does-it-cost-to-launch-a-reused-falcon-9-elon-musk-explains-why-reusability-is-worth-it/
5. https://spacenews.com/spacex-planning-major-increase-in-florida-launch-activity/#:~:text=By%202023%2C%20the%20company%20projects,%2C%20all%20from%20LC%2D39A
6. Berger, Eric, "Sadly none of the big rockets we hoped to see fly in 2020 actually will," arstechnica.com, July 13, 2020, https://arstechnica.com/science/2020/07/sadly-none-of-the-big-rockets-we-hoped-to-see-fly-in-2020-actually-will/
7. *Strickland, John, "Revising SLS/Orion launch costs", Space.com, July 15, 2013, http://www.thespacereview.com/article/2330/1*
8. _____, "NASA's Management of Space Launch System Program Costs and Contracts", NASA, Office of Inspector General, March 10, 2020, Report No. IG-20-012, https://oig.nasa.gov/docs/IG-20-012.pdf
9. https://www.sciencemag.org/news/2020/05/spacex-now-dominates-rocket-flight-bringing-big-benefits-and-risks-nasa
10. *Asterank (www.asterank.com)*
11. ___, "A flying turkey", The Economist, August 27-September 2nd, 2022, p. 66
12. Abrahamian, Atossa Araxia, "How the asteroid-mining bubble burst: A short history of the space industry's failed (for now) gold rush," MIT Technology Review, June 26, 2019, https://www.technologyreview.com/2019/06/26/134510/asteroid-mining-bubble-burst-history/

Chapter 4:

1. ___, Asteroid Retrieval Feasibility Study, Keck Institute for Space Studies, California Institute of Technology, Jet

Propulsion Laboratory, April 2, 2012, https://kiss.caltech.edu/final_reports/Asteroid_final_report.pdf

2. ___, Basics of Space Flight, NASA, *http://www2.jpl.nasa.gov/basics/bsf7-1.php*

3. ___, United Nations Treaties and Principles on Outer Space, https://www.unoosa.org/pdf/publications/STSPACE11E.pdf

4. https://www.gpo.gov/fdsys/pkg/BILLS-114hr2262enr/pdf/BILLS-114hr2262enr.pdf

5. ___, Artemis Accords home page, NASA, https://www.nasa.gov/specials/artemis-accords/index.html

6. ___, Artemis Accords text, NASA, https://www.nasa.gov/specials/artemis-accords/img/Artemis-Accords-signed-13Oct2020.pdf

Chapter 5:

1. ___, "Majority of Americans Believe It Is Essential That the U.S. remain a Global Leader in Space," Pew Research Center, June 6, 2018, https://www.pewresearch.org/science/2018/06/06/majority-of-americans-believe-it-is-essential-that-the-u-s-remain-a-global-leader-in-space/

2. Launius, Roger, "Public opinion polls and perceptions of US human spaceflight", Elseveir, 2003, page 8, URL

3. http://waitbutwhy.com/2015/08/how-and-why-spacex-will-colonize-mars.html/5#phase3

Chapter 6

1. Launius, Roger, "Public opinion polls and perceptions of US human spaceflight", Elseveir, 2003, page 8, UR

2. Zacks, Jeffrey M., "Why Movie 'Facts' Prevail', February 15, 2015, The New York Times, https://www.nytimes.com/2015/02/15/opinion/sunday/why-movie-facts-prevail.html

Chapter 7

1. ___, "The Budget and Economic Outlook: 2022 to 2032", Congressional Budget Office, May,

2022. https://www.cbo.gov/publication/58147#_idTextAnchor105

2. Cohen, Patricia, "What Could Raising Taxes on the 1% do? Surprising Amounts," October 16, 2015, New York Times, http://www.nytimes.com/2015/10/17/business/putting-numbers-to-a-tax-increase-for-the-rich.html?_r=0

3. ____, https://en.wikipedia.org/wiki/Quantitative_easing

About the Author

Scott Phillips is an author of both fiction and nonfiction.

His novels include 'The Prague Deception,' 'The Climate Fixer,' and 'Phantom Beach.'

His nonfiction explores issues in political economics, geopolitics, and technology.

Phillips is a former Peace Corps volunteer (RPCV Sierra Leone, West Africa). He lives in Portland, Oregon with his family.

He maintains a free email list on Patreon for readers that would like updates or sneak previews on current projects. You can sign up (free) at: patreon.com/scottphillipsPDX.

Printed in Great Britain
by Amazon

44143189R00165